SUEZ AND PANAMA

SUEZ AND PANAMA

BY ANDRÉ SIEGFRIED

TRANSLATED FROM THE FRENCH BY
H. H. AND DORIS HEMMING

HARCOURT, BRACE AND COMPANY *hb* NEW YORK

46485
386.42
S571S

CONTENTS

PART ONE

THE SUEZ CANAL

5

CONTENTS

PART TWO

THE PANAMA CANAL

MAPS

GRAPHS

SUEZ CANAL

PANAMA CANAL

SAULT-SAINTE-MARIE AND KIEL CANALS

PREFACE

Possibly it will be said that this book lacks unity. Suez and Panama have this in common, that both are canals joining oceans. At first glance I admit that that was the only resemblance that I could find. But our impression changes when we take a broad view of the network of maritime routes that link up the various continents. It then becomes apparent that these interoceanic canals have been the essential instruments of world unity. This unity was the magnificent achievement of the nineteenth century, which the twentieth century at first continued, but now seems bent on replacing by ideas of autarchy and economic subdivisions.

Though diversity may be the weakness of our book, it is also responsible for its wealth. We shall examine the two canals from many and varied points of view in an attempt to ascertain just what each implies. In this study we shall touch on geography and history, politics and finance, administration and hygiene, commerce, public works and maritime activity. Here we shall discover a veritable 'Arabian Nights' with harem intrigues and chancellories, bank scandals and Latin American revolutions, not to mention the more prosaic general meetings of shareholders, reports to boards of directors, parliamentary resolutions and diplomatic treaties. Before our eyes we shall see slowly evolving on the screen, or simply flitting silently across the background, pharaohs, Persian and Greek kings, Roman emperors, conquering Arabs, conquistadors, kings of Spain, Bonaparte himself with his generals and intellectuals, Egyptian viceroys, English aristocrats, American presidents, exploring-financiers and financial-explorers, geographers, parliamentary lobbyists, engineers (they were truly heroic!), and above all and dominating them all we shall meet the legendary figure of Ferdinand de Lesseps, whom we must rank alongside Vasco da Gama, Magellan, and other great discoverers of the highways of the world.

To tell the truth, it is astonishing how much has to be done before one can start digging an interoceanic canal. In the last analysis engineering is, I think, hardly a third of the difficulty. Engineers in the end always solve the problems which are set before them, and they nearly always succeed — provided of course the financiers do not order them to do this and that, and jealous politicians do not start crying scandal. It was above all by faith that de Lesseps succeeded with his first canal, and it was under the triple curse of finance, yellow fever, and political and financial intrigue, that he failed with the second. The Americans later succeeded thanks to modern technical methods which their predecessors did not possess, and, still more important, because of the bottomless purse provided by their Government.

The interoceanic canals are encouraging in so far as they prove that everything is possible provided that men, by their quarrels, do not forbid its accomplishment. For, to quote La Bruyère, 'Most men spend half their lives in making the other half miserable'.

WORLD TRAVEL ROUTES

I

THE face of the world is lined and furrowed by great commercial highways along which the trade of mankind is concentrated. The state of these routes, whether they are living, abandoned, or revived after having been deserted, is an indication of the constant changes that take place in the relationship of the continents. Similarly the interoceanic canals enable us to measure the world's arterial circulation at certain decisive points. Mons. Paul Morand very aptly considers the statistics of the Suez and Panama Canals to be the temperature charts of the planet. So in studying these canals we are feeling the pulse of the world and measuring its rhythm.

The layout of the world's economic highways is not the result of chance. Throughout history certain routes have been so persistent that they seem to be etched into the structure of the globe. On the other hand, with the evolution of economic life, the factors determining the success or decline of a trade route become more and more complex. Though geography remains supreme, other independent factors must also be considered, such as the development of the route itself, the conditions under which it can be utilized, the danger of political obstacles, the shifting of the world's centre of gravity and the technical progress made by the different methods of transport. We can thus work out a whole theory of transport in which the land, the sea, and the air will each have its own particular policies.

II

Suez, Panama, Cape of Good Hope and Magellan — here we have four routes, all essentially maritime and yet all dissimilar. These highways are complicated and diverse, and require a large amount of organization. At times their course is rigidly defined by narrow straits, by capes to be rounded, and by fixed points with which contact must be made. Again, they may depend on navigational problems, and then questions of equipment become all important — the maintenance of artificial canals or the many services which have to be paid for. The existence of such routes involves far more than merely drawing across the chart the line along which ships are to sail.

The countries which use these routes are chiefly those which are not self-supporting — trading countries that live on their imports and exports, possess colonies and maintain navies, all of which are essential to their survival. Take England for example. If her sea routes were blocked, her industries would close down for lack of raw materials, her warehouses would empty, and very quickly her population would die of famine. To others world trade may be a banal expression, but for her the words are charged with vital significance. A stoppage in Britain's trade circulation would be the equivalent of an embolism in the human blood stream. England, therefore, is ready in certain circumstances to go to war for a strait. It is not a question of power and prestige, but of her very existence.

The first two essentials of an ocean route are security and regularity of traffic. Let us not overlook private security either, by which I mean the assurance that travellers will not be at the mercy of pirates. This fear is happily out of date, but, be under no illusion, it would reappear soon enough if the British fleet ceased to exist! Further, there can be no commercial security if we are exposed to vexatious tolls and dues, or to arbitrary measures capable of paralysing trade. Those who use a canal regularly are bound to be concerned about the way in which it is administered. Political security is even more necessary, for strikes, revolutions, civil wars, indeed any form of disorder along the world's highways, produce conditions that are unhealthy for trade. And then of course there is the menace of aggressive powers. In other words what we need is a *substratum* of organized international civilization, such as existed throughout the nineteenth century.

Even if the nineteenth-century conditions still existed, however, the great maritime powers could not afford to dispense with their transport policies. The first article in their programme must be the control of the seas — the 'liberty' of the seas being only a euphemism — for otherwise their communications would be at the mercy of any powerful adversary. Such control requires a system of bases and naval stations so located that every section of the route can be supervised. The intelligence, persistence and attention to detail with which England has built up such a network is common knowledge. It is not merely a question of naval and military force. There must be coaling stations (now become oil stations), although as the result of recent technical achievements, navigation depends less on them than it did before. There must also be submarine cables and wireless stations.

Over and above considerations of equipment comes the vital question of international politics, for it is of first importance that possible adversaries lying in wait along the route should not be able to cut the communications, particularly when the course traverses narrow seas or inter-oceanic canals.

It is essential that an enemy should not be allowed to obtain a foothold anywhere along an important thoroughfare or in its immediate neighbourhood. The situation in the Mediterranean during the Great War, and again since the Abyssinian expedition, is a striking illustration of this kind of danger. The conditions under which a Mediterranean war would be fought call to mind Jules Verne's novel, *Mathias Sandorff*, with all its intrigues, its ambushes and its deeds of violence. The maintenance of her route to India has thus become a problem for England that is as intricate and as heavy with complications as any detective story.

III

The conditions surrounding an overland road are quite different. The policy of pre-war Germany in south-eastern Europe, without touching on the present situation, gives the idea exactly. We must not picture this land route merely as a highway, a railroad, or an *autostrade*. It is more like a dynamic current, indicating a line of expansion, penetration and conquest, along which trade will flow, and migration and armed invasions take place.

In the past there have been radical changes in the forms of transport, corresponding to the various ages and levels of civilization. Porters gave way to pack animals, followed up by draught animals, caravans to cross the deserts, railroads, oil pipe-lines, and now motor cars which are bringing to the fore once more old highway problems that had seemed to have vanished.

Even more than in the case of sea traffic, the delineation

of a land route depends on geographical considerations. Certain itineraries constantly reappear — their course is imposed by the existence of easily traversed zones as well as by points that cannot be avoided, such as mountain passes, valleys, wells, bridges and defiles. The obstacles themselves and the effort needed to overcome them all help to stabilize the road, and to hedge it in along a definite track. This question of dominating or even utilizing such a highway brings up the whole theory of overland routes. We shall find that, after making a few reservations and alterations, we are arriving at conclusions very similar to what we have just been analysing for the sea routes.

Before a highway can be dominated or even utilized, there must also be a policy, and, after making a few reservations and alterations, this question of policy will bring us back to the conclusions that we have just reached. Security is the first essential, and it is even more important on land than by sea. By security we do not mean merely matters which can be left to the local police, but problems connected with government and sovereignty. It is simply not good enough if all traffic has to be convoyed, for in the long run that will not work. The solution to the problem must be sought farther off and higher up, in fact by the establishment of a sort of *Pax Romana*, which will prevent the outbreak of disorder before it occurs.

Let us suppose that this result has been obtained, either by direct action or by the creation of a puppet state. Then it will be up to those who use the highway to see to it that the equipment is well maintained, that the administration is efficient, and that transit can be carried on smoothly. Preferential tariffs will naturally be obtained where possible, but at any rate discrimination will not be tolerated.

To obtain these results one has to establish political

influence over the countries to be traversed, or, still better, be in a position to control their administration and make them accept a corps of experts. Finally, one must get a foothold in the maritime terminus at the far end of the land route in order to be able to launch out still farther. The temptation to establish a political protectorate is greater with these overland highways than it is with maritime routes. That is why the German expansion in south-eastern Europe towards Constantinople and Baghdad is so dangerous and so difficult to limit.

I V

The aeroplane, during the last twenty years and particularly during the last five years, has been in the process of working out all these same problems in the sky. Here the factors seem to be simpler, for one need only control the points of departure and arrival, and any indispensable landing grounds in between. The air belongs to everyone, always of course with the reservation that one may not fly over the territory of a sovereign state without permission.

Owing to the constant increase in the power of aeroplane engines, intermediate landing grounds are becoming less and less vital. Thus the problem reduces itself simply to the departure and arrival stations. Still, the intermediate space is less homogeneous than one is apt to believe, for it so happens that although it is naturally desirable to fly in a straight line it is not always possible to do so. Meteorological considerations such as visibility and storms often make it inadvisable. Instead of following the arc of a great circle, one may prefer to take a longer route with less risk of fog and storm. Thus in winter Central Europe is avoided in favour of the sunnier Mediterranean.

Ground conditions may also suggest certain detours in order to make use of particularly well-equipped aerodromes, competent meteorological services and wireless that functions regularly.

The relative importance of the ground services increases as the pilot's initiative in selecting his route is restricted. He now receives his instructions by radio from the ground. An astonishingly complicated technical organization has grown up, requiring a conscientious administration quite beyond the capabilities of primitive peoples, but absolutely indispensable for a regular air service.

The aeroplane may have been liberated from the earth by sheer technique, but the air route organization has once more linked it as closely as ever to the ground. We cannot dispense with physical geography, nor even disinterest ourselves from political geography, for the State is apt to intervene, and often for reasons which appear devoid of common sense, it will impose conditions which practically forbid flying.

So one is tempted to choose the route that is safest politically, flying over friendly lands and seas, and carefully avoiding those that are liable to be difficult or even hostile. The air is not as free as one imagines. No doubt the birds know this when they determine the course of their migrations, which often are curiously similar to the tracks of the aviators. As the users of the main skyways cannot ignore any of these difficulties, there may be room for imperialism even in the heavens.

v

The route to India and the Far East via the Suez, and the one through the Panama and across the Pacific, are at present the two most important maritime highways in the world. The effective values are by no means stable, however, owing to the revolution that has taken place in the speed of sea-going vessels. A review of these two interoceanic canals involves studying the competing routes. It also brings to the fore economic problems concerning the equilibrium between the various groups of humanity. In spite of their immense differences, the routes by sea, land and air have this in common: their tracks must conform to the nature of things, and must obey laws that are more imperious than man, in his conceit, often imagines. The war of 1939 may completely upset the network of international communications, but it cannot permanently alter any of the underlying conditions which govern the existence of this network. So we have in these facts and tendencies a fine series of problems for our minds to grapple with.

PART ONE

THE SUEZ CANAL

CHAPTER I

THE GEOGRAPHY OF THE ISTHMUS OF SUEZ

I

OF all the world's highways, the route to India via the Isthmus of Suez is probably the most important to mankind, for it unites the two continents that for so long constituted the entire civilized world. Yet despite its long history it acquired its full importance only with the construction of the canal in its modern form. Its final completion in 1869 coincided with the advent of steam navigation, and with the magnificent expansion of Europe, which was being transformed by the industrial revolution. From that time on the old continent has continued to increase the rhythm of its economic activity, almost to the point of over-industrialization. This it could not have done, however, had it not been able to obtain supplies of raw materials from distant countries and also capture new markets. As the prosperity of modern Europe largely rests on this international trade, the Suez Canal, to use a hackneyed phrase, is its main artery.

Since the beginning of the twentieth century a new zone, which is practically independent of Europe, has been constituted, thanks to the United States and the Panama Canal, yet the importance of the Suez Canal has in no way diminished. Should the latter be obstructed, or its efficiency be impaired by maladministration, the material level of European civilization would feel the effect at once. There is an element of necessity in the existence of this great highway which leads towards Asia by way of the Mediterranean. We can neglect it temporarily, even for a few centuries, but we must revert to it in the end. Geography clearly tells us why.

II

The continent of Africa is compact and closed, having neither peninsulas nor a narrow waist line. It forms a massive and monotonous unit of great geological antiquity. Its isolation, however, is more apparent than real, and possibly has not always existed. In spite of the Red Sea, Arabia is only the continuation of the Desert of Sahara, for the same geological formation stretches from the Atlas Mountains to the Persian Gulf. We find identical characteristics along the entire length of this immense belt, for the ground is neither sedimentary nor subjected to folding. Except for a narrow fringe bordering the Mediterranean, we have the same desert climate everywhere, even throughout Egypt. The heavens never give more than ten inches of rainfall in a year, and all the water there may be in the delta is due solely to the Nile.

Nothing in this geographical description so far conveys the idea of a road, a passage, or a ditch. Yet it is precisely here that we find the longest and most extensive furrows on the globe. All the way from the Zambezi River to Syria there are gigantic cracks or fissures, like a series of enormous earthworks running north and south. The most southerly fissure has been filled in by the African lakes; the next one has been inundated from the Indian Ocean and so forms the Red Sea. At the north end this ditch forks, one branch continuing in the narrow Gulf of Suez and the depression across the isthmus. The other stretches up through the

Dead Sea and the Jordan Valley, past Baalbek and the Oronto River, to die out at the foot of the Ammanus Mountains near Alexandretta where this immense geological phenomenon terminates.

This construction naturally directs all traffic north and south, whether it be by the Cape-to-Cairo route up the Nile, or the passage to India via the Suez and the Red Sea. If, on the contrary, we try to go from east to west, we meet with continuous obstacles. Through the mountains of Lebanon and Anti-Lebanon there are only two passes leading towards Mesopotamia and the Persian Gulf. The first is at Homs, and the other is the road from Acre and Haifa, towards Damascus and the desert.

This cross-roads at Suez where two continents meet is so important that any power that is ambitious for world domination must of necessity have a foothold here. If I could tell who will control it a century from now, I should not need to ask who was master of the world.

Renan was not far wrong when, in welcoming Ferdinand de Lesseps to the Academy in April 1885, he reminded him of the classic saying, 'I come not to bring peace but a sword'.

'This saying must frequently have crossed your mind,' he said. 'Now that you have cut through it, the isthmus has become a defile, that is to say a battlefield. The Bosporus by itself has been enough to keep the whole civilized world embarrassed up to the present, but now you have created a second and much more serious embarrassment. Not merely does the canal connect two inland seas, but it serves as a communicating passage to all the oceans of the globe. In case of a maritime war it will be of supreme importance, and everyone will be striving at top speed to occupy it. You have thus marked out a great battlefield for the future.'

III

According to an old legend reported by Herodotus, the Egyptian priests believed that at one time the Red Sea and the Mediterranean were connected. Numerous scientific observations, such as the mixed marine fauna at Kabret south of the Little Bitter Lake, and sea shells from Suez on the Moqattam Hills at Cairo, certainly confirm the existence at an early period of a gulf and a salt water strait over all of what is now the delta and the isthmus.

The process by which it was transformed must have started when the most easterly or Pelusian branch of the Nile began to fill in the strait with its sediment. At the same time a rising of the earth's crust brought the Mediterranean Sea floor to the surface, and also steadily dried up the extreme easterly channel of the Nile which to-day is quite dry.

The formation of the isthmus must have remained long incomplete, for during the time of the Ancient Egyptians the Red Sea penetrated as far as the present Bitter Lakes by way of a gulf thirty miles long. This gulf was ill defined, being traversed by shallows and liable to tidal invasions. In the end a sand bar grew up and cut off the Bitter Lakes. Yet, even in 1860, Linant Bey observed that at spring tides the sea penetrated some ten miles inland.

Although on the Mediterranean side the isthmus is absolutely flat, it is flanked by the Massif of Sinai on the south-east, and on the south-west side by three other massifs. These are the Gebel Geneffa to the south-west of the Bitter Lakes, and Gebel Uwebid and Gebel Ataqa whose high cliffs loom up against the setting sun at Suez.

When during the construction of the canal they cut through the ridge at Shalûf, they encountered hard limestones which caused considerable difficulty; it evidently indicated a prolongation of the Geneffa hills. This ridge twenty or thirty feet high was but a feeble obstacle, however, in comparison with the rocks and landslides of the Culebra Cut at Panama! Even though the future may have belied him, there is something to be said for Philip II, who vetoed the proposal for a canal at Panama because 'God had manifested his will by creating a continuous isthmus'.

At Suez the case is exactly the opposite. The entire configuration of the ground, with its low levels and marine penetrations, and still more the signs of previous inundations, seemed like an invitation from Nature. At any rate she did not oppose the slightest obstacle to man's initiative.

Geographically there is a certain solemnity about the site of the town of Suez. The desert colours of Sinai and Ataqa make a striking contrast with the deep blue of the sea, which stretches away to the south as if leading to some strange unknown world. It is an inter-continental frontier without a doubt, and as such it grips the imagination. One has left Europe behind, and the mysterious East is beckoning.

CHAPTER II

THE POSITION OF EGYPT IN RELATION TO THE ISTHMUS OF SUEZ

I

IF the desert had stretched away without interruption to the west of the Isthmus of Suez, the political aspect of the route to India would have been much simpler. But instead an important State is situated close to the route, so although Egypt might possibly ignore the canal, the canal can never ignore Egypt.

After all, what does Egypt amount to? In truth it is just an oasis in the desert, an oasis which, without the Nile, would revert to desert once more. The country lives along the river and is totally dependent on it. The ancients appreciated this, indeed Herodotus referred to Egypt as a gift made by the Nile. The habitable territory corresponds exactly to the river valley and its delta, but goes no further, as it is closely hedged in by two deserts. On a map of Egypt the Delta looks like a flower in bloom balanced at the end of the thin and interminably long stalk of the upper valley.

The size of the Nile is well known, for it is one of the longest rivers in the world, being about 4000 miles from its source to the sea. It draws its waters from two separate tropical regions. The Blue Nile rises in the high table-lands of Abyssinia, while the White Nile comes from the great African lakes. These two branches unite at Khartum, where the Sahara section begins, 2000 miles from the river's source and about the same distance from its mouth. It is only at Wady Halfa on the Sudan Egyptian frontier that it reaches political Egypt. The second cataract, which is still more than 600 miles from the Mediterranean, marks the beginning of the cultivated valley, but it is below Aswan and the first cataract that strictly speaking Egypt may be said to begin. This is 500 miles inland. The delta commences at Cairo, 100 miles from the sea, or perhaps it would be more accurate to say that it begins at the delta dam thirteen miles below the capital city.

Just as the valley is interminably long, so it is extremely narrow, stretching like a thin green ribbon through the desert, which frowns down upon it from high rocky cliffs. The average width is from three to six miles, though here and there it may attain as much as sixteen, while at some points the cultivated area may be only a few yards on each side of the river.

Thus the whole of upper Egypt is a line without breadth in comparison with the vast empty spaces around it. The delta on the other hand is an equilateral triangle, with each side about 150 miles long. It reminds me of one of the great European plains like Lombardy, except that it is traversed by innumerable waterways and canals. Although the area of Egypt is about 400,000 square miles, scarcely more than 12,000 square miles of this vast territory can be used — an area about the size of Belgium. Geographically it is one of the most curiously constituted countries in the world.

As we have said, the climate is the same as on the desert, since it never rains. About one and a half inches fall in the year at Cairo, and practically none at all in the Upper Valley. And yet, although it receives no rain after passing Khartum, the Nile is still able to provide inexhaustible quantities of water, thus compensating for the total absence of humidity in the air, and making regular crops quite possible. This is what Herodotus meant when he described the country as a gift from the river. As a result people settled at a very early date, and as their livelihood was based on systematic harvests an organized and stable society was created. Thus Egypt civilized, organic and rooted to the soil, forms a striking contrast with the unorganized nomadic tribes of the desert.

The Ancients, knowing nothing of Equatorial Africa and its tropical rains, believed that the Nile was of divine origin, but for us its famous sources no longer hold any mystery. From the point of departure where the moisture of the Indian Ocean falls in the form of spring rains on the Abyssinian plateaux, we can easily follow its flood through its various stages. The waters arrive at Khartum at the end of April, are in Egypt at the end of May, and at Cairo towards the middle of June. The flood attains its maximum in September, and falls away rapidly after the beginning of November.

In studying the Nile we must distinguish between the water used for irrigation and the silt or Nile-mud which fertilizes and renews the soil. In this highly civilized land the flood water has always been remarkably skilfully handled, and yet modern methods are quite different from those of the past.

Irrigation previously was carried out by flooding: The water was allowed to cover the low lands, which were divided for this purpose into basins fed by canals. The silt settled, and fertilizer was never needed. This method, however, was inconvenient, as it kept the land out of action so long as it was covered by water. Nowadays irrigation goes on throughout the year, the water being held back in great storage reservoirs, such as for example the one at Aswan. Then by means of regulating dams, it is directed over the whole of the flat area of the delta through thousands of irrigation ditches. It is no longer necessary to inundate the plain, and the advantage of the new system is that the soil is always available and it will yield several harvests a year.

But Nature makes us pay for every concession. As the silt is no longer deposited, and as the water is perpetually evaporating away, the fields which have been inundated too long finally become salty and lose their fecundity. Also the permanent humidity of the climate becomes almost un-bearable. Egypt seems to be dotted with a hundred thousand puddles, when viewed from an aeroplane high up in the sky. The Aswan dam, which was constructed between 1898 and 1912, permitted this new form of irrigation. It was Mehemet Ali's idea, for he wished to develop cotton growing in order to increase his country's export trade. So Egypt in-voked the Nile once more, this time to procure a form of international promotion.

As a result of this vast programme of public works, the artificial character of the delta has been steadily accentuated. The seven branches of the Nile have now been reduced to two, while the number of the canals has been multiplied *ad infinitum*. The outlets have been closed by dams which cut off the river from the sea at periods of low water, when the river is actually below the level of the sea. The role of the river is now entirely agricultural, for it is made to assist in the exploitation of the soil rather than to serve as a means of communication, without transhipment, with the outside world. In any event the shore is being constantly silted up by a current coming from the west and bearing a great deal of sand. Thus for the most part it is a closed coast, and badly adapted to maritime activities.

The towns in the delta are merely local distributing centres, and are equipped for river traffic only. The coun-try's two great ports, on the other hand, are situated outside the delta. Alexandria, built on the rocky promontory of Pharos, lies to the west, and consequently is protected from the alluvial current. It is Mediterranean rather than Egyptian, but Port Said, at the eastern extremity of the delta, is a creation of the canal and is extremely cosmopolitan.

The Nile, and its accompanying humidity which constitutes its most valuable attribute, is thus solely responsible for the life of Egypt. The level of its waters tell us all we need to know. So true is this that in ancient times the Nilometre became a symbolic instrument, and even determined the level of taxation.

II

To paint a true portrait of Egypt, with its personality and many attractions, we must emphasize this geographic environment. In its maritime aspect it is Mediterranean, but it is African in its deserts, and Asiatic in its delta.

The climate, the atmosphere, and the colourful social life of Alexandria are incontestably Mediterranean, and to a lesser extent the same applies to Port Said. Here we have the same sea as at Naples or Marseilles, Athens or Beirut. The street life is the same though slightly more varied; fundamentally the customs are the same, a bit more Levantine it is true but to French eyes not very different. Yet how thin is this sham Western veneer! Two miles away, a few minutes in a taxi, and Asia begins at the Mahmoud Canal, which is the true brother of the Hindu canals.

It is in the desert, and in the Upper Valley which is influenced by the desert, that Egypt becomes African. At Cairo the genuine desert begins without warning a few steps away from the great cosmopolitan hotels. Then emptiness reigns, a vast territory populated by perhaps 40,000 nomads, thinly scattered over an area twice as big as France. However, to Frenchmen accustomed to Morocco and Algeria, there is nothing new in this.

The delta, however, gives the impression of being something quite distinct and unknown. What astonished me was the density of the population. It is almost impossible for a European to form any idea of it. In the inhabited districts the average density is over 1000 people per square mile in the open country, and nearly double this at more than one point. Such figures disclose a brand of humanity that is entirely different from ours, and proves that this section of Egypt is comparable only to the great stifling reservoirs of human beings that exist in tropical Asia. No need for statistics at this point, for it is enough for us to walk about and see for ourselves. People seem to spring from the ground. If something goes wrong with your motor car, you are quickly surrounded by a couple of hundred people. The problems that arise from such intense overcrowding are foreign to the Western mind; but anyone who has witnessed the compression of humanity in the Ganges Valley will understand.

This Egypt, which we can qualify in turn as Mediterranean, African, and Asiatic, is subjected to various influences. As a Mediterranean country she is attracted to the West and indeed forms part of it. In the educated classes many people are Western by race. That, however, is not the only, nor even the principal slant, for although the upper classes in the Eastern Mediterranean may be European, the bazaars are oriental. They turn towards the interior, which after all provides them with their livelihood. Beirut, Port Said and Alexandria may be influenced by the West, but Aleppo, Damascus, the Mohammedan parts of Jerusa-

lem, Suez and Cairo look towards Africa and Asia. The real
frontier of the East lies somewhere between these two types
of city with their windows facing different worlds. The
cleavage is too clean cut to leave any doubt, for it is here
that the Westerner turns his back on his natural environment
and enters the unknown. In *The Road to India* the author,
E. N. Forster, expressed the emotion that any European
feels when he crosses the dividing line.

He said that it is in the Mediterranean that humanity
finds its norm, and that when mankind leaves this exquisite
lake, whether it be past the Pillars of Hercules or through
the Bosporus, it approaches the world of the unknown
and the monstrous. It is however by the southern route
through Suez that one gets to the most foreign region of all.

The best way to appreciate the geography of Egypt is to
fly over it in an aeroplane. Its essential features and the
exact limits and contrasts between the various regions then
emerge with surprising clarity. For example when one
travels as I did by air from Jerusalem, one first crosses a
corner of the Mediterranean. Then one sees a low coast
from which a long spit of sand fringes an immense lagoon.
This is our first contact with Egypt. A complicated design
of sand and water etches an astonishing arabesque on this
mirror, which reminded me of the grooved motifs one finds
in oriental decorations. There is an extraordinary sense of
unreality about it all, whether it is the rosy tint of both land
and water, or because seen from above this amphibious
landscape seems to belong to the prehistoric ages of the
world. After crossing the lagoon the aeroplane heads for
the interior, and here sand reigns supreme. This district is
desert, one hundred per cent desert, with nothing but sand
dunes as far as the horizon. A few tiny oases can be seen
dotted here and there, and also black rectangles which look

like Bedouins' tents. But there are no signs of established human dwellings.

The monotony of this background makes it difficult to estimate distances, but in the west there soon appears a long thin line like a blue cord stretched across the sand; this is the Suez Canal. Away to the north it is lost in the haze, but in the south we can perceive where it opens out into Lake Timsâh. Farther off we can distinguish the Bitter Lakes. On the canal a few stray ships at long intervals appear stationary. The whole countryside is hard and congealed. Towards the west the horizon is barred by a heavy mist. That this is the delta is evident from a distance, because its humid atmosphere is in such complete contrast to the dryness of the desert air. A canal starts from Lake Timsâh and goes off to the west; it is the famous fresh water canal without which life could not exist on the Isthmus. It is straight, narrow, and bordered on each side by a green band of irrigated land which obviously is fertile. Beyond this strip, however, the desert again is in complete control.

As we approach it, the haze on the horizon becomes less opaque. A few minutes' more flying and the delta is lying beneath us illuminated by the rays of the setting sun, for already it is after four o'clock in the afternoon. I never believed that a map could give such a perfect impression of a country — for in reality it was simply the map with all its bright colours that I saw enrolled beneath me. The beige colouring of the desert, almost the shade of sandalwood, made a strong contrast with the delta, whose boundaries look as if they had been traced out clearly with a pencil. (I once heard a story of two children in Cairo who decided to go for a walk, keeping one foot on the desert and the other always on the delta!)

Then the colours change without transition from light to

dark. The whole vast irrigated zone is a sombre green, with
the Nile shining up through it like a silver mirror. One
realizes in an instant that Egypt is nothing more than a
gigantic oasis, which would cease to exist if irrigation
ceased.

We then fly quickly on towards the south-west in the
glory of the setting sun, with the citadel of Cairo rising up
before us. Beyond it is the Nile, and the Pyramids, and
after that the desert once more. Actually we land right out
in the Sahara at the aerodrome of Heliopolis. Then, without
warning and rather like stage scenery, an enormous modern
suburb arises, conceived and constructed on European lines.
Yet we know we are not in Europe on account of the swarming crowds, and the donkeys and camels that get mixed up
with the automobiles.

Let us now trace the fundamental structure underlying
this lesson in geography. There is a lack of continuity between Egypt and the canal, for they follow different axes,
with the desert lying between. In the delta the Nile flows
in two sinuous streams a long way apart, whereas the canals
are numberless and rectilinear. Civilized and artificial
Nature has supplanted Nature in the raw. Nevertheless the
desert is always present. It hems in the valley and the
delta; it presses against them both and stifles them by its
immensity.

III

It is not sufficient to take a bird's-eye view of Egypt as we
have done; we must also study its position on the map of the
world. This discloses it to be not merely a land of astonishing richness, but also an international cross-roads. Though
this dual character was fully understood in ancient times, it

has been greatly accentuated since the opening of the Suez Canal, and in fact governs Egypt's entire future.

One could quite well picture an Egypt living on itself without foreign relationships, and depending solely on the Nile. With its superabundant agricultural resources, its people will never die of hunger — maize, barley, rice, beans, onions, clover, sugar-cane, nothing seems to be lacking! Autarchy would be its natural economic policy, and after all such has been the traditional inclination of the fellah. He has always been exclusively concerned with the soil which he cultivates, and has remained indifferent to invasions and changes of regime. He has always survived unchanged in this 'Egypt eternal'.

Egypt can never lead an isolated existence, however, owing to certain aspects of its geographic position. The Nile has its source far outside the political frontiers, and in the management of the flood water some agreement must be reached to determine the relative importance of Egyptian and foreign needs. Under such conditions we must consider the whole course of the river as a unit, from its source right down to the sea. The delta therefore cannot disinterest itself politically from the Upper Valley of the Nile, nor from the Sudan, nor yet even from Abyssinia. Such preoccupations date back into remote antiquity. Nor can Egypt ever forget that she is on the old route of invasion. From the east she has seen the Persians arrive, the Greeks, the Arabs, the Turks, and in 1915 the Germano-Turkish Army. From the west she has met the Romans, the French, the English, and at times, has even felt the Italian menace.

The nineteenth century further increased this interdependence when Egypt became a cross-ways between two important world routes. One of these, the route to India by the Suez Canal, was then being revived and the other, that from Cape-to-Cairo by the great African lakes, was being discovered. It is true that, although the canal cuts through territory that is politically Egyptian, yet it leads a life of its own on a separate axis. Its international traffic crosses the isthmus like a surgical stitch, having no relationship with the economy of Egypt as such.

Yet it would never be possible to control an interoceanic canal in this part of the world without bringing Egypt into the discussions. Is its unique geographical position really an asset? Not far from another interoceanic canal, the Republic of Columbia may well ask the same question!

Along the Cape-to-Cairo road which has recently been utilized by aviation, the great names of Gordon, Kitchener and Cecil Rhodes are there to remind us of a world power that is accustomed to dominate, and which will scarcely disinterest itself from such imperial communications. Any country that happens to lie across its path must await its pleasure.

Even if the fellahin should wish to live tranquilly and alone, they will never be able to do so, as their country happens to be an international highway. This circumstance may be a trump card or it may be a peril, but it is always there. It did not fail to attract the attention of the great sovereigns who governed Europe in the nineteenth century, when the map of world communications was beginning to take its present form.

Mehemet Ali, who was alive to the complications which the piercing of the Isthmus would bring in its wake, said in his wisdom, 'I do not wish Egypt to become a second Bosporus'. The Khedif Ishmail, on the other hand, was delighted to see his kingdom enter the international circuit. When he solemnly inaugurated the Suez Canal, he proclaimed that Egypt was no longer African, but would henceforth play its part among the Mediterranean powers. Foreseeing a danger which also had not escaped Mehemet Ali, this Ishmail was wise enough to tell Ferdinand de Lesseps that although he was as much of a 'canalist' as was de Lesseps himself, yet he wanted 'the canal to belong to Egypt, not Egypt to the canal'. One can well understand Ishmail's desire, but it can never be granted. From the moment that the canal came into existence, it became an international undertaking, and could never be purely Egyptian. There is even a possibility that the situation may react against the interests of Egypt. As she is inseparable from the canal, does she not therefore run the risk of being mortgaged so that she cannot enjoy the full benefits of political independence? Such limitations, resulting from her unique geographical position, may have been written into her destiny.

CHAPTER III

THE CANAL IN ANCIENT EGPYT AND THE ROUTES TO THE EAST

I

THE ancient Egyptians were remarkably well equipped to carry out great public works, and as they were particularly expert at building canals, it was only natural that they should have concerned themselves with the linking up of the Nile and the Red Sea. Nature herself seemed to suggest it, and after all it only meant building one more canal. From inscriptions and the accounts of contemporary travellers, we know that this task was achieved, and we can still see traces of the old earthworks.

Several facts stand out as probable from a mass of conjecture. According to a Greek legend the canal must have been begun as early as the Middle Empire, most likely under the 12th dynasty between 2000 and 1800 B.C. It was undoubtedly in existence at the time of the 19th dynasty between 1350 and 1200 B.C. Its course began on the Nile at Bubastis (near the modern Zagazig) and ended at the Great Bitter Lake, which at that period was still part of the Gulf of Suez. When the Great Bitter Lake was more or less cut off from the sea by a ridge of sand that had piled up, Necho, a pharaoh of the 26th dynasty (609-593 B.C.), tried to carry the canal on as far as the Red Sea, but 120,000 labourers died at their work without finishing it.

Darius the Persian (521-486 B.C.) took up the task and this time it was completed. Nevertheless it was Ptolemy

Philadelphus (285-246 B.C.) who really gave it its final form. It ran from the Nile to Arsinoe, the site of the present town of Suez, where a lock or 'diaphragma' held the waters in check.

The last of the Ptolemys neglected the canal, but the Emperor Trajan (A.D. 98-117) re-established it. From then on it was called Trajan's River, just as it had previously been called Ptolemy's River. Once more it was neglected, but under Constantine and Justinian there was a last period of activity before it finally fell into disuse at the end of the Byzantine period in the reign of Heraclius.

It was not destroyed, however, for during the Arab regime Amr, who was governing Egypt in the name of the Caliph Omar, reconditioned it in A.D. 642 with very little trouble. He even wished to open up direct communication between the two seas, but the Caliph refused, fearing to provide a route for the Infidels. In the end the canal actually was blocked up by the Abasside Caliph, Aben-Jafar-al-Mansour, in order to cut off Mecca and Medina,

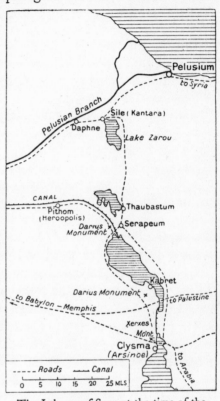

The Isthmus of Suez at the time of the ancient Egyptians

which were then in revolt. Perhaps he also hoped to injure the Isthmus route, and so favour the overland road which led by the north to the Gulf of Persia.

However, the section from the Nile to the Bitter Lakes was in use for a long time, until sand eventually drifted over the entire structure. So the canal died, after having lived for a thousand years and more. It was destined to wait another one thousand and one hundred years to be reopened by Ferdinand de Lesseps.

Many contemporary travellers have described it as it existed under the Ptolemys and the Romans. Herodotus, who visited Egypt about 460 B.C., some half-century after Darius had completed the work, says that the canal was wide enough to allow two triremes to pass abreast and that it took four days to make the journey. 'It is filled with water that, coming from the Nile, enters the canal above Bubastis, a town on the Pelusiac branch of the Nile. This town was the capital of Egypt under the 22nd Dynasty.'

Diodorus, who travelled about 60 B.C., at the time of Ptolemy Dionysus, left the following description: 'A man-made canal stretches from the Pelusiac branch of the Nile as far as the Arabian Gulf of the Red Sea. Necho, the son of Psammetichus, was the first to undertake it; Darius the Persian continued the work but did not complete it, for he was told that if he cut through the isthmus he would inundate Egypt. It was proved to him that the Red Sea was at a higher elevation than the ground level of the Delta'. This legend seems to die hard. 'Ptolemy was the last to try his hand at it, and at the most favourable point he had a very artistic and practical lock gate constructed. It could be opened when one wished to sail through, and closed again immediately afterwards.'

About A.D. 40 Strabo said that 'the canal was 100 cubits

wide and deep enough to admit the largest boats'. Pliny the
Elder, who was to meet his death in the eruption of Vesuvius
in A.D. 79, tells us that the canal, as excavated by Ptolemy,
was 100 feet wide, 40 feet deep, and 37,500 paces in length
as far as the Bitter Lakes. He adds that the Egyptian rulers
had not continued the work farther for fear of floods, for it
had been discovered that the level of the Red Sea was three
cubits above the ground level of Egypt. Others, however,
did not attribute the interruption of the work to this danger,
but rather to the fear of the sea water ruining the Nile, which
was their only source of drinking water.

Lucian, who lived in Egypt in the second half of the
second century, tells of a young man who, after having
embarked at Alexandria, sailed up the Nile and on as far as
Clysma (Arsinoe) on the Red Sea.

From all these descriptions we gather that it was a fresh-
water canal fed by the Nile and functioning only at high
water. Cleopatra was unable to use it when she wished to
send her fleet from one sea to the other, and was obliged to
have her ships hauled overland across the isthmus. The
canal was 100 miles long, over 70 feet wide, and 10 to
15 feet deep, which was sufficient for the boats of that
period.

It originally left the Pelusiac branch of the Nile at Bubastis,
but later started at Babylon, no doubt to attain greater
height. It then made use of the depression of Wady Tumilat
along the course taken by the fresh water canal of the present
day. It ended up at the northern extremity of the Great
Bitter Lake. In the time of the Pharaohs there were several
channels, some no doubt natural ones, leading towards the
Red Sea, which in those days penetrated much farther into
the Isthmus than it does to-day.

As for the Ptolemys' canal, it went from the Little Bitter

Lake near the ford used by the Hebrews, and terminated at
the Clysma lock. Bonaparte himself rode over the traces of
this canal, which are still remarkably well preserved. At
this historic spot what seems to be the withered arm of a
river stretches away for several miles. The outline is perfectly clear cut, and it looks as if it could easily be flooded
anew, even though it is filled with the accumulation of
centuries.

II

The ancient Egyptians maintained important trade
relationships with Arabia, Ethiopia and the shores of the
Red Sea. They imported spices, perfumes, ivory, precious
woods and wild beasts. As a result a maritime trade grew
up. In those days the canal was used for Egypt's own
imports and exports, and not as to-day merely as a route of
transit. It could not in any event have acted as a link between far off continents, for civilization was too rudimentary
and many lands were still undiscovered.

In spite of the advantages of sea travel, most people
preferred to go overland because of the risks of navigation
on the Red Sea, where the winds are contrary and the rocks
treacherous. The alternative route was to go up the Nile as
far as Koptos just north of Thebes or to Edfu. From there
one crossed the desert and reached the shores of the Red
Sea, either at Myos Hormos opposite the southernmost
point of the Sinai Peninsula, or at Leucos Limen near
Kosseir, or even at Berenice which lies on the Red Sea shore
about as far south as Aswan. Thus several routes led from
the delta to the Red Sea, and the one through the canal was
not necessarily the most important. The contrary winds in
the Gulf of Suez were too much for the ancients, for not

merely were their ships' rudders too small, but also they did not know how to tack.

After Alexander the Great had broken down the barriers which subdivided the Orient, a very considerable amount of commerce began to develop. This international trade linked up the Mediterranean, the Greek Empire, and India and China, which were the three principal centres of civilization at that time. Greek and Arabian merchants were employed by the Romans, who, though they were large buyers of Oriental products, had personally little taste for trade.

During the Roman occupation of Egypt there was a flourishing transit traffic. Goods were stored in the ware-houses at Alexandria and Pelusium after having been imported either by the canal, or by transhipment across the isthmus.

In his book *La Route des Indes* M. Paul Morand gives a spirited account of the infinite variety of merchandise which Rome sought from the East:

'Slaves and Ethiopian eunuchs, trained monkeys and parrots were brought for the ladies' boudoirs; for the circuses there were lions from Nubia, leopards from Afghanistan and tigers from the Punjab; and for the pro-consuls' tables they imported pheasants and other game, poultry, honey (sugar was still unknown), bananas, apricots, and coco-nuts. They also brought in fabrics from Medea, wool from Kashmir, silks and skins from China, furs from Thibet, shells from the tropics, gold from Ethiopia, pearls from the Persian Gulf, wood from Lebanon, sandalwood, aloes and cloves from Persia. For their Roman clients the merchants of Alexandria laid in stocks of white and black pepper, ginger, cinnamon, spikenard and incense from Hadramut, gums, dyed cottons, cosmetics and camphor. India sent her finest weapons and all sorts of gems, diamonds, chalcedony, onyx, quartz, rock crystal, amethysts and the opals beloved by the patricians, sapphires from Ceylon, aquamarines, lapis lazuli, and precious metals. Pliny draws a picture of the "Golden Isles" set in the Bengal Sea. . . .'

From this we see that it was a luxury trade, reflecting the fabulous wealth of the Orient. Now, because of her excessive needs, Rome had few products to send back in exchange. She paid to the best of her ability by shipping lead, zinc, glassware, hides and wine. But the trade balance was unfavourable, and in the end she had to settle the account in gold, which steadily drained all the gold out of the west.

If we compare the products we have just enumerated with the composition of the north-bound traffic through the Suez Canal to-day, we realize the immense difference there is between our commerce and that of the ancients. Instead of this diversified list of extravagances and luxuries, we now import in bulk vast quantities of foodstuffs and the raw materials without which Europe, over-populated and over-industrialized, could not survive. And yet the same danger is threatening our present economy. Like the Romans we are experiencing increasing difficulty in finding products to export, and so in our turn we find our gold draining away.

While the western half of the Roman Empire was ruining itself and disintegrating, the eastern part remained prosperous. It still controlled, up to the time of the Arab invasion, the whole of the Eastern Mediterranean. However, after the new conquest commercial activity in all these regions was at first considerably reduced, and for three centuries it was almost entirely dried up. Later on, during the Middle Ages, Egypt became once more the great intercontinental distributing point. At Pelusium or at Alexandria the Western merchants coming from Genoa, Venice or Catalonia got into contact with traders from Asia and Africa. The whole aspect of this trade was similar to what it had been during the time of the ancients. The East still offered its spices, porcelains, aloes, camphor, pearls and perfumes in exchange for timber, clothing, furs and metals. But the canal could no longer be used, so they transported their goods either from the Red Sea ports across the desert to the Nile or by the overland routes from Arabia and the Isthmus. Egypt levied a toll on all that passed by and waxed prosperous. . . .

III

Neither in ancient times nor during the Middle Ages did the Red Sea route to India attain the unique importance that it had in the nineteenth century. The perils of navigation were no myth, so people preferred to travel by land whenever possible, particularly as their trade did not involve handling bulky materials. When goods are expensive and not very heavy the cost of transhipment does not become prohibitive as it would be to-day. No decisive advantage was thus to be gained by water transport, so the alternative overland route, farther north towards Central Asia and India, was destined to compete with the Suez route. The struggle between an east-west flow of traffic across Syria, with a north-south current through the Red Sea, seems to be the essential feature of the problem of communications in this part of the world.

In the same way political rivalry has always existed between the power controlling the Isthmus of Suez, and the one that dominated the upper reaches of the Tigris and Euphrates. Thus any government with imperialistic ambitions was bound to take a deep interest in both Mesopotamia and Egypt. This observation is as true to-day in the age of the motor car, the aeroplane and the pipe-line, as it was in the days of the trireme and the camel.

On the historic roads of Western Asia the means of transport have not altered in thousands of years. Across the desert we still have the camel and the caravan, and in the mountains the pack animal and the light cart. On the Mesopotamian rivers we still see the *kelel*, or raft buoyed up on goatskin bottles, as well as the flat-bottomed boat or *chartouche*, and even the *gouffah*, the peculiar gourd-shaped basket of reeds that is propelled by a paddle. The adaptation of these various means of transport to the geographic structure of the country has little by little created the main traffic routes, though the extent to which they could be used and protected has altered throughout the centuries. On the mountain roads where the population is stable, and also along the rivers, it has been possible to sub-divide the journeys into definite stages and to establish a police service.

The desert, however, is like the open sea; here long stretches are empty and undefined, and the oases are few. The natives are such natural born thieves that it has been impossible to organize any police similar to the naval patrol of the high seas. This can be done either in the grand manner like the *Pax Romana*, or it can be carried out by a subvention policy in which one negotiates with the highway robbers and tacitly recognizes them. Neither the creation of a barrier similar to the Roman walls or *limes*, nor the attempt to protect each individual convoy was any more successful in the past than it would be to-day. The solution of the problem is really political.

Various types of towns and cities have been called into being as the result of different kinds of transport. On the sea coast we have ports, and on the edge of the desert bazaars and caravan towns, where convoys are organized and trade

is carried on. Along the route itself are villages marking
the different stages. These may be likened to maritime
ports of call. Finally there are the capital cities, which like
magnets attract the routes towards the centres where the
political power of the moment is entrenched.

From earliest history three main highways have thus been
defined across Western Asia. The first linked up Samsun on
the Black Sea with Mesopotamia and the Persian Gulf,
passing by way of Sivas, Diarbekr, and the upper Tigris
Valley. The fact that Xenaphon and his 'Ten Thousand'
retreated on a neighbouring road was a great military
achievement, but without commercial importance. The
second highway leaves Constantinople or Smyrna, and after
passing Konia and Adana touches the port of Alexandretta.
Then it goes on to Nisibin, Mosul, and Baghdad. This is
approximately the line followed by the Baghdad Railway.
An alternative route goes through Angora to the upper
Tigris. The third main highway joins up the Syrian coast
with Mesopotamia, passing across the desert either from
Homs towards the Upper Euphrates via Palmyra, or from
Damascus towards the Lower Euphrates.

As one proceeds farther east from Mesopotamia towards
Persia, Central Asia and India, the main road is the famous
silk caravan route. This starts from the Caspian seaports
and climbs towards Ispahan, where one branch goes towards
Kashmir and another to Kabul and India. Farther to the
north a parallel route leaves the Black Sea and passing south
of the Caucasus Mountains goes towards the Caspian Sea
and Turkestan.

The relative importance of these highways varied throughout the ages as the political centres of gravity altered. So
long as truly imperial powers existed, the highways were
stabilized and organized. Even the deserts were held in

check. However, the moment the ruling authority weakened or became incompetent and divided, the desert regained its lost territory. The roads were then forced to make long detours in order to keep within settled areas.

In the end, however, there appeared to be a certain permanence in the main highways, whether it was the Royal Road of the Persians, the path followed by Alexander the Great's armies, or the network of Roman roads. From the time of Alexander to the third century A.D., the Hellenistic East was no longer a frontier between different civilizations, but a common meeting ground. The Romans kept the desert in order by a policy of buffer states, but after the fall of Palmyra in A.D. 272, their control over its traffic once more eluded them: the *limes* which they then began to build were nothing more than barriers, simply marking the limits of an empire which was thenceforth to be on the defensive. Later on, the security of the desert was confided to the nomads themselves, and not without a certain measure of success. Under the Arabs, communications were improved between Baghdad, Damascus and Mecca, and in this system politics, religion and commerce all found their place. During the latter half of the Middle Ages, Europe and Asia were in contact across the eastern Mediterranean, the Black Sea and the Red Sea.

But a sudden and totally unsuspected competitor was about to arrive from an entirely different point on the horizon. This competition was to prove equally fatal to both the overland and the sea routes in the Near East.

CHAPTER IV

FROM VASCO DA GAMA TO FERDINAND DE LESSEPS, 1498-1854

I

In the second half of the fifteenth century two events of outstanding historical importance took place. The capture of Constantinople by the Turks in 1453 blocked the overland route towards Asia, which meant that the desert was again abandoned to the nomads and so reverted to its previous condition of insecurity. Almost at the same time, in 1498, the discovery of the Cape of Good Hope opened up a new route to India, an event of tremendous consequence. Instead of being a highway, the Mediterranean became a blind alley. The pattern of world communications was transformed, and the whole balance of the continents was upset.

It was during this amazing period that Europe, stimulated by a mysterious urge for expansion, launched forth into the outside world. Missionary zeal, the appeal of curiosity, and the hope of fabulous reward inspired these pioneers. The exotic products of Asia still maintained their prestige, particularly her famous spices. From ancient legends, explorers had learned that it was possible to reach India by rounding the continent of Africa, so they set out on this route to seek for pepper, ginger, nutmeg, cloves, cinnamon, aloes, amber and precious stones, pearls and mother of pearl, and all the tissues and embroideries of China and the East.

The countries possessing outlets to the Atlantic were best

situated for such explorations. About the middle of the
fifteenth century the Portuguese, who, even more than
the Spaniards, possessed a genius for navigation as well as
being less aloof with foreigners, descended from island to
island and from cape to cape towards the southernmost
point of Africa. Finally in 1498 Vasco da Gama reached
the 'hope of the Indies', the greatest cape of them all.
Setting out from Belem near Lisbon he eventually landed at
Calicut, thus attacking in the rear the whole Venetian commercial system which, as a result, was destined soon to disappear. A page of history had been turned!

The immediate consequence was that a Portuguese
monopoly of eastern trade replaced the previous Venetian
one. The new maritime route was very much longer but it
was easier to navigate the ocean than the Red Sea, where
reefs were frequent and winds irregular. Above all it did
not involve transhipment and this enormously reduced the
cost of transport. Spices set down at Lisbon cost only a
fifth of what they did in Venice. So in a very few years the
pepper trade passed into the hands of Portugal, even the
Venetians themselves being obliged to go there and buy!

The ancient traffic through the Mediterranean was thus
diverted at its two main sources, the Red Sea and the
Persian Gulf. Aleppo and Alexandria were ruined at the
same time as Venice, whose decay was irremediable once her
trade was limited to that of the Levant. The centre of
gravity of the whole world had shifted towards the west, and
the powers of the future became those bordering the Atlantic
— Portugal, France, Spain, Holland, and England, while
the eastern Mediterranean went to sleep for three centuries.

The atmosphere of Lisbon well expresses this contact
between the Atlantic and the Orient — a new contact in so
far as Europe of the Middle Ages was concerned. Situated

on a rough and uneven plot of ground like Rome on her
seven hills, this city, white as a Levantine seaport, looks out
over the Tagus, here as wide as a lake. But she is under the
influence of the ocean, which, though invisible from the town,
makes its presence felt by the sea breezes, the open sky, and
the western horizon which stretches away in its immensity.
Looking at certain sections of the city with their teeming
undisciplined masses, we might classify it as the last of the
Mediterranean ports. But it is also the first city of Latin-
America. It is a foretaste of Rio and Bahia, and curiously
resembles San Francisco, that other gleaming and somewhat
Latin city which also is situated on the western edge of a
continent. A glance at a map of world. communications
reveals that it is just outside of Lisbon that the maritime
routes open out like a trident towards South America, the
Cape, and through the Mediterranean to the Far East.

II

Vasco da Gama's discovery heralded in a four-century
struggle between two groups of powers: those profiting
from the Cape route, Portugal, Holland and England; and
those suffering from it, Venice, Egypt, and Marseilles (in so
far as Marseilles stands for France). The old route seemed
to be condemned for ever. The insecurity of the Isthmus
during the regime of the Mamelukes, quite apart from their
prohibitive tariffs, was enough to drive away any traffic.
Turkey, for her part, dreamed chiefly of keeping the
Western world away from these Eastern territories. However, in the face of the fatal competition of the Cape, the
Mediterranean Powers tried to pull themselves together.
From then on the hope of restoring their old route by bringing its equipment up to date became an obsession, which

was increasingly manifest throughout the centuries up to the time of de Lesseps.

At the beginning of the sixteenth century the Venetians proposed cutting a canal across the isthmus, in the hope of regaining their lost trade. The Turks, at the end of the same century, thought of organizing a commercial highway overland towards Baghdad and the Persian Gulf — still following the path of the time-honoured caravan route. Ali, the Renegade, the Beyler-Bey of Africa, also conceived the idea of a canal at about this time, particularly to facilitate the passage of the Turkish fleet into the Red Sea. Pope Sixtus V was also interested in the project, for it would shorten the voyages of the missionaries — but naturally nothing was done!

The French monarchy had conflicting interests in the matter. Marseilles played a considerable role in the Levantine trade, but Lorient, an Atlantic port, was also the harbour of the East India Company and benefited from its monopoly. The Old Regime nevertheless took a keen and persistent interest in the route to India, and even though nothing came of it the tradition, thus created and maintained, prepared a future which otherwise might not have been realized. Colbert thought of creating a company for the Near Eastern trade to which he intended giving the monopoly of French commerce in the Red Sea, and for which he hoped to get a preferential tariff in Egypt. During the entire reign of Louis XIV French diplomacy was diligently negotiating with either Turkey, Egypt or Persia in the hope of obtaining commercial advantages in connection with the development of the route to India.

Several projects for canals across the isthmus were considered, of which the most celebrated was that of Leibnitz in 1672. Jacques Savary, in *Le Parfait Négociant*, visualized a direct link between the two seas.

Benoist de Maillet, French Consul in Egypt, made a great effort 'if all the circumstances were favourable' to assure the transport of letters from Paris to Surat in 50 days, and was thus in a way a precursor of Waghorn and his 'overland route'. Activity redoubled under Louis XV during the conquest and the loss of India. The Marquis d'Argenson, a forerunner of St. Simon and of de Lesseps, dreamt of a canal which would be 'for the common good of all Christians', but M. de Perdriau, Consul at Aleppo, and the Duke of Praslin, on the contrary both favoured an overland road, from Aleppo towards Basra on the Persian Gulf.

The reign of Louis XVI and the revolutionary years should be considered as one, in so far as this affair is concerned. The traffic in Indian textiles and Arabian coffee that was passing overland through Suez was becoming more and more important. At the same time the presence of the English in the Indian Ocean was making the whole question steadily more political, more especially as the French also were studying the problem of opening up a route either by Suez or by Baghdad and Diarbekr.

The French missions multiplied in number: Montigny went out in 1776, and Choisseul-Gouffier in 1777. The Truguet-Magallon Treaty in 1785 obtained guarantees for the security of caravans and also certain tariff concessions. Volney, who visited Egypt in 1783-84 and whose book caused a sensation at the time, believed that a canal was feasible not in a direct line across the isthmus, but by using the ancient route via the Nile. In 1790 the merchants of Marseilles addressed a memoir to the Constituent Assembly asking, 'that the ports of the Red Sea should be open to French ships; that their commerce there should not be subjected to hindrance; that they should be allowed to bring Indian merchandize to Suez; that their transport from Suez to Cairo should be protected by the ruling Bey; Cairo, they felt, would soon become an entrepôt, for the East Indies, and the collossus which the English had erected in Bengal would thus be overthrown'. Already we have the atmosphere that led to Napoleon's expedition to Egypt.

III

The Egyptian question had never ceased being a live issue, and so it could be taken up at a moment's notice without fresh studies being needed to bring it up to date. In fact it was ripe. When the idea was pursued under the Directory it gripped the imagination of several leading personalities, and insinuated itself into Government departments where old plans were dug out. Talleyrand, who inherited the traditions of the Old Regime, here played a role of first importance, basing his policy on the following underlying arguments: 'Opening up the Suez route will react on England in the same fatal way that the discovery of the Cape of Good Hope ruined Genoa and Venice in the sixteenth century. If France is in possession of the Suez route, it matters little into whose hands the Cape of Good Hope may fall.'

This was in keeping with the belief held by many Frenchmen, including Bonaparte, that great deeds could only be done in the East. The Egyptian Expedition aimed at acquiring a route to India, such in fact being the real meaning of the instructions which the Directory issued. 'The Army of the Orient shall take possession of Egypt. The Commander-in-Chief shall chase the English from their possessions in the Orient, which he can reach, and in particular he shall destroy all trading posts in the Red Sea.

He shall have the Isthmus of Suez cut through, and he shall take the necessary measures to assure the free and exclusive possession of the Red Sea to the French Republic.'

So Bonaparte was instructed 'to cut the isthmus'. On December 24th, 1798, he visited the area, accompanied by Generals Berthier and Caffarelli, Admiral Ganthéaume, J. M. Le Père, his Chief Engineer, Monge, Berthollet, and Costaz. The little expedition discovered the relics of the ancient canal, the long empty ditch which I could not contemplate without emotion. Then the Commander-in-Chief and Berthier rode along it for some twenty miles. After a stay at Suez where he was busy organizing a base for an expedition against India, and then inspecting the wells at the Fountains of Moses, Napoleon returned to Cairo, this time following the depression of Wady Tumilat.

'The question of the canal is of the greatest importance,' he finally said to Le Père. 'Publish a memorandum, and force the Turkish Government to construct it, both in their own self-interest and in the hope of glory.'

Le Père proceeded to make a technical examination on the spot, in spite of almost insuperable difficulties such as lack of both water and equipment, insufficient transport, insecurity, floods, etc. His famous report was presented to the First Consul on August 24th, 1803, but was not published until 1808.

In his estimation the canal could be built without major difficulties at a cost of some 25-30 million francs. He turned down the idea of a direct route, for he believed in the old theory that there was a difference in the levels of the two seas, which he thought would be about 29 feet. Laplace and Fourrier, however, did not agree with him on this point. He also thought that it would be impossible to make a harbour out of the beach at Pelusium. His plan was to build a

round-about canal with locks roughly along the old track
followed by the ancients. Thus it would go from Alexandria
to Suez, passing by Bulaq (near Cairo), Serapeum, and
Shalûf. Although he seems to have exaggerated the difficulties of navigation on the Red Sea, this collaborator of
Bonaparte's clearly saw the conditions under which a new
maritime route could be created. In the introduction to his
memorandum he wrote: 'By means of the canal the Egyptian
route would become as continuous and uniform for navigation as that of the Cape of Good Hope, and at the same time
it would be more exclusive for those who would be in control.' He may have misled the public in his belief that the
two levels of the seas required an indirect canal and locks,
but that really is only of secondary importance. The main
thing is that for the first time we now have an engineering
plan exact enough to provide a basis for technical discussion.
It was on Le Père's memoir that Ferdinand de Lesseps
eventually based his great work, even though he decided to
adopt the other or direct route.

IV

Modern Egypt, in which the undertaking and completion
of vast projects was to be possible, was born with the reign
of Mehemet Ali (1805-1849). He re-established order,
created a state, called in experts from Europe, and set on
foot a vast policy of public works. He thus produced those
stable conditions in which Ferdinand de Lesseps was destined
to work. This genial sovereign feared lest his country
should suffer from being an international highway, although
it actually was his own reforms that were bringing it nearer.
He was afraid that the Isthmus of Suez might become a

second Bosporus, and yet it was during his reign that the problem of transit across Egypt began to be so urgent that it had to be dealt with. The English backed a railway, the French a canal. Egypt had been 'discovered', and the West was never to leave it alone again.

The trip to India around the Cape was desperately slow. Gradually, however, the Red Sea route came into the limelight, especially for those who were pressed for time, and it was realized that it was much quicker, once transhipment had been properly organized between Suez and Alexandria. This was first appreciated by the English, for they were more directly concerned. As early as 1829 Lieut. Thomas Waghorn was speeding up the mail services by routing across Egypt duplicates of dispatches sent to Calcutta. Ten years later the P. & O. organized this overland route by working two shipping services in conjunction. They demanded the immediate construction of a railway, which actually was carried out in stages between 1850 and 1860. About this time travellers began to desert the Cape route.

The French, who were then competing with the English in practical as well as political affairs, tackled the problem in a different spirit. First of all there were the followers of St. Simon, with their ideals of social regeneration through work, and their ambition to serve universal peace by undertaking public works of international importance. There were some to sneer and remark, 'industrial popery', and others to deprecate these 'illusions of visionaries'. Nevertheless, their desire for progress represented nineteenth-century idealism at its best. In his programme St. Simon included interoceanic canals at Suez and Panama. Prosper Enfantin, who inherited his ideas, left for Egypt in 1833 accompanied by a large staff of technicians. He was not imperialistic, not even tinged with selfish nationalism. He believed that the Suez Canal should be European and universal, and, let us not forget, de Lesseps was imbued with the same humanitarian motives. Enfantin's group remained four years in Egypt and twelve of them died there, but they achieved nothing practical.

It was only in 1846 that a company was incorporated to explore the whole problem. Among its members were Enfantin, Arlès Dufour, Paulin Talabot, and Stephenson, the latter being the son of the famous inventor of the locomotive. After completing a fresh technical survey, and consulting with the principal European Chambers of Commerce, Paulin Talabot drew up a plan in 1847, but to tell the truth it did not show much advance over the earlier plan by Le Père. However, the new survey definitely established that the two seas were on the same level. The direct route across the isthmus could now be considered, but the idea was abandoned owing to the difficulty of building a port on the beach at Pelusium.

So this company too came back to the plan of an indirect canal like that of the pharaohs.

After leaving Alexandria it was to cross the Nile by a bridge about half a mile long and 65 feet above the level of the river. It was to join up with the Bitter Lakes by the depression of Wady Tumilat, covering in all a distance of 250 miles and at a cost of 300 million francs.

After delivering themselves of this project, which certainly was not feasible, the company drifted into internal discussions. Stephenson, being a Scotsman and the heir of a railway inventor, finally declared his natural preference for a railway rather than a canal. Enfantin rebelled both against British intrigue on the one hand and that carried out by Turkey and Russia on the other. So again nothing practical was accomplished.

On November 7th, 1854, Ferdinand de Lesseps disembarked at Alexandria, and in his pocket was the plan for the canal which he intended to submit to the new Viceroy, Mohammed Said. From this point the biography of the man, later to become The Great Frenchman, and the history of the canal were to be one and the same thing.

v

At this stage of its long career, the problem of the canal was swept clear of non-essentials. It had already been admitted that the Suez route was infinitely shorter than that of the Cape, and would be preferable if adequately equipped. Europe had become the workshop of the world, and the rapid transportation she was demanding had come to be a vital necessity. Also the nature of Eastern trade had changed from spices and other luxuries to heavy bulky products which did not lend themselves to transhipment. So a maritime canal was needed, more especially as steamships, which were just beginning to become important, were likely to derive great benefit.

The political conception of the canal was also taking shape. It was no longer to be the monopoly of any single power, but rather a work of international importance which would be placed at the service of Europe, of civilization, of the entire human race. It would have been most regrettable if its construction had been directed against any one, by France for example to harm England who as Mistress of India was destined to be the principal user. From this point of view it would seem that Napoleon's expedition to Egypt was on the wrong road, and that Thiers' anti-English manœuvres in Egypt in 1840 were even more unwise.

The ideals that were destined to triumph were first formulated by d'Argenson, Enfantin and Lamartine, because they viewed the enterprise from its humanitarian aspect. This policy was political wisdom on the part of France.

'England', said Lamartine, 'would fight to her last ship before she would allow a French Power to close the Suez Canal directly or indirectly against her ... The whole of mankind is interested in this Eastern question ... It is essential that the Mediterranean, this great lake which is neither French nor European but international, should once more become the theatre and the vehicle of an incalculable volume of commerce and ideas. Finally in the background stand the immense empires of India and China, which will be brought five months nearer Europe as a result of the Suez route and the discovery of steam. They will renew their contacts with us through Asia Minor and Africa, and so we will help to weld the whole universe into one great unit, politically, industrially, and religiously.'

The canal as eventually achieved by de Lesseps was very close to St. Simon's inspiration, and corresponded to his humanitarian ideals which were among the finest things produced by nineteenth-century Liberalism in its most glorious period.

CHAPTER V

FERDINAND DE LESSEPS AND THE CONSTRUCTION OF THE CANAL

I

FERDINAND DE LESSEPS was born at Versailles in 1805. He belonged to a family that had been distinguished in the French Consular Service. His father, Mathieu de Lesseps, had had a long career, entirely in the Mediterranean countries, and on one occasion had personally assisted Mehemet Ali in his extraordinary ascent to power. At Malaga he married into the Montijo family. He died without fortune, but not before he had persuaded his son to enter the same profession as himself.

After having occupied various posts in Tunis, Alexandria, Barcelona, and Madrid, Ferdinand became Minister Plenipotentiary at Rome in 1849. He was there at the delicate moment when the legislature was reversing the policy of the Constitutional Assembly. Ferdinand was accused of being too favourable to the Roman Democrats, and was accordingly asked to retire. He was then forty-four years of age, and his career seemed to be over.

To believe that, however, would be to misunderstand the man entirely. His vitality — his dynamism we should say to-day — was extraordinary. He was bursting with physical energy, was a keen sportsman, and delighted in spectacular exploits. Once, when still a mere child, he swam across the Seine in a spirit of bravado. He was a good horseman, an excellent pistol shot, an indefatigable dancer, and charming company socially. In addition he had amazing courage. Extremely sober in his personal habits, he fasted on occasion from choice. He was always perfectly at ease in an oriental atmosphere, for he believed in omens and prophesies and used to amuse himself by trying to read in the stars what Destiny had in store for him. He was endowed with sound intuition, and once he was convinced about the soundness of a venture, he would proceed with reckless temerity. He was, in short, a veritable tower of strength.

While he was consul at Alexandria in 1832, he became the close friend of Mohammed Said, the Benjamin of the thirteen sons of Mehemet Ali. The latter transferred to Ferdinand the gratitude which he had always felt for Mathieu de Lesseps: 'It was your father who made me what I am,' he would say.

Mehemet Ali requested Ferdinand to give riding lessons to his young son, Mohammed, who was inclined to become fat. His father wished to see him slim at all costs, so he tried to ration his son's food. The young Prince used to go to the French Consulate, however, where a succulent dish of macaroni would be given to him in secret. His friendship for de Lesseps was sincere, and lasted all his life. Perhaps among the trump cards which contributed to the success of the canal, we should place a modest dish of macaroni!

When he was thirty Ferdinand de Lesseps had married a Mlle Delamalle, who presented him with five sons. He worshipped his mother-in-law, a woman of great intelligence, and at the time of his diplomatic disgrace, he sought refuge in the Château de la Chesnaie which she had acquired near Berri at his suggestion. His wife died shortly after, and he then began to lead the life of a retired gentleman farmer. The days of his great ambitions seemed to be ended.

Nevertheless his thoughts kept turning towards the Orient. Back in 1832 a friend had sent him a packet of books to help him while away the tedium of a fortnight's quarantine in the lazaret of Alexandria. Among these books was the report by Le Père on the question of the Suez Canal. From then on he became passionately interested in the project, which he once had discussed at great length with several followers of St. Simon. During his leisure at La Chesnaie he re-examined and classified his notes on the subject, and sent a memorandum to the Viceroy, Abbas Pasha, who meanwhile had succeeded Mehemet Ali. He also sent a copy to the Turkish Government, but neither effort met with success. How often is not this the fate of private initiative appealing on behalf of some great enterprise! A stilted acknowledgment — or possibly no reply whatever, for the proposition has been immediately consigned to the waste-paper basket.

On September 15th, 1854, the double tidings of the death of Abbas Pasha and accession of Mohammed Said suddenly reached La Chesnaie.

'On learning of the accession of my former pupil', writes de Lesseps, 'I sent him a note of congratulation. In his reply he begged me to come to see him immediately. During my retirement I had studied completely everything pertaining to the Suez Canal. I was thus perfectly familiar with the isthmus, and had even persuaded myself that to cut through it was quite a practical proposition. The idea had captured my imagination when I first read the memorandum written by Le Père, who was the chief engineer in General Bonaparte's expedition. So once more I took up my old work, fully convinced that I should obtain the concession.'

On November 7th he disembarked at Alexandria, where a princely welcome awaited him. The Viceroy treated him as a close personal friend, installed him magnificently, and presented him with a fine charger. He was then invited to accompany Mohammed Said on a military expedition, with ten thousand men, from Alexandria to Cairo by way of the desert.

In his pocket de Lesseps had the plans for the concession, for he felt that this would be an excellent occasion to propose it. However, he bided his time, for in affairs of this nature, depending almost entirely on personal relationships, any false move would be irreparable. A week later, out in the open desert, he risked it. According to his custom he had previously consulted the oracles in the Egyptian sky, and that morning there had been a rainbow of brilliant colours which seemed to him to be a happy omen. Mohammed Said listened with interest to his proposals, and then replied:

'I am convinced. I accept your plan. We will spend the rest of the trip discussing how it can be carried out. You can count fully on me.'

On their arrival at Cairo, the Viceroy convened a formal meeting on November 25th of all the consuls-general, who attended in full dress uniform. He then announced to them that he had decided to have a canal cut through the isthmus by a public company with capital subscribed by all nations, and that M. de Lesseps was commissioned to form the company. Then, turning to the latter who was standing at his side, he added, 'This is what we intend to do, is it not?' In a letter in which he describes the scene, the new concessionaire remarks that the British Consul-General seemed to be rather upset.

II

The essential details of the enterprise, such as it exists and functions to this day, were drawn up in an edict which was signed on November 30th, 1854. The concession was personal, and was granted to 'our friend, M. Ferdinand de Lesseps'. (Sometimes the Viceroy also refers to him as 'my devoted friend of high birth and lofty rank'.) He received the exclusive right to organize and manage a universally owned company, formed for the purpose of cutting through the isthmus and exploiting a canal between the two seas.

The profits were to be divided in the proportion of 15 per cent to the Government, 10 per cent to the founders, and 75 per cent to the shareholders. As The Company was described as 'universal', this clearly expressed the wish that it should be completely removed from the dangers of selfish nationalistic schemes. The tolls were to be the same for all nations, none of which were to obtain special advantages of any kind. All this was evidently due to the inspiration of the St. Simonians, of whom de Lesseps was to a certain extent a disciple, although politically he was not connected with them in any way at that time.

The length of the concession was to be 99 years, starting from the date of the opening of the canal. At the end of this period the Egyptian Government was to inherit the canal, after paying The Company an indemnity, to be fixed by arbitration, for any stores on hand at that time. Every contingency was foreseen, and everything was very well arranged. One important reserve was annexed: the work could not commence until the concession had been ratified by the Sublime Porte, which, theoretically at any rate, had sovereignty over Egypt.

De Lesseps immediately set to work. The first costs were to be borne by an exploration syndicate, in which a hundred founder members, recruited from among his friends, were each to pay 5000 francs. In addition he could count on the support, material as well as moral, of the Viceroy.

Without further delay he set out for the Isthmus, accompanied by two French engineers, Mougel and Linant. Both men were in the employ of the Egyptian Government, but Mohammed Said put their services at his disposal.

Once on the spot he decided in favour of the direct route across the isthmus. According to his method of procedure, which never varied, he listened first to the experts, but in the end he drew the actual line himself with a sureness of judgment, or perhaps with an intuition, which was rarely at fault — at any rate, not at Suez. He realized, however, that the approval of technical men was necessary, and therefore he called in an international commission of experts at the end of 1855. They visited the isthmus, and confirmed his plan to construct a direct canal.

The project adopted at the beginning of 1856 was the result of these preliminary studies. It was many years since any one had worried about the difference in the level of the two seas; also, the difficulty of constructing a port in the swamps on the Mediterranean shore no longer appeared insurmountable. The so-called Talabot plan was therefore abandoned, in favour of a direct maritime canal from the Red Sea to the Mediterranean, passing through the Bitter Lakes. The depth was to be 26 feet, and the width about 80 feet across the bottom.

The first indispensable task was to construct a subsidiary canal to bring fresh water from the Nile, as otherwise the isthmus would not be habitable. It was estimated that the whole work would require six years, and that the cost would be about 200 million francs. The traffic through the canal was expected to be some three million tons annually, and this guess the future has more than ratified. The toll of 10 francs a ton authorized by the concession seemed to make it reasonably certain that the venture would be financially profitable. The stage thus was all set, and de Lesseps was ready to begin the work, but in this great enterprise the technical details were the least of the difficulties that had to be overcome.

When the new concessionaire arrived at Constantinople in the beginning of 1855 to obtain his permit, he was given a good reception by the Turks. However, the British ambassador, Lord Stratford de Redcliffe, insisted that before the Porte gave its consent the British Government should be consulted. The centre of the discussion was thus shifted to the West, and with the sure instinct that this splendid fighter always possessed, de Lesseps betook himself at once to the very heart of the battlefield. The assistance of French official circles was easily acquired, for, being a relative of the Empress, de Lesseps always had an *entrée* to the Tuileries. 'Be strong and everyone will help you,' the Emperor said to him. 'I am sure you will succeed.'

It was England that had to be convinced. De Lesseps went there in June 1855, and again in April and May of the following year. His campaign of propaganda was simply magnificent! First he sent out a series of open letters addressed to Parliament, to the East India Company, to the City merchants, to the Chambers of Commerce, to the mining finance houses, to the great industrialists, to bankers, and to the merchants who traded with India, the Far East and Australia . . . Then followed meetings with a great display of maps and graphs, not merely in London, but also in the big industrial towns.

There were visits to influential personages — first the Queen and the Prince Consort, then Palmerston, Gladstone, and Cobden. Then a great deal of social activity, in which this man of tact and culture was at his best. Invited and fêted everywhere, he was the veritable lion of the season.

Wherever he went he left a favourable impression, and success seemed assured. Nevertheless he was up against a blank wall — the opposition of the Government, which was absolutely in accord with true British traditions.

Palmerston's hostility is historic; the violence of his language was almost comic. He said in a speech on July 7th, 1856:

'It is an undertaking which, I believe, in point of commercial character, may be deemed to rank among the many bubble schemes that from time to time have been palmed upon gullible capitalists. I have been informed, on what I believe to be reliable authority, that it is physically impracticable, except at an expense which would be far too great to warrant any expectation of any return.'

Speaking again on August 14th in the same year, he invoked another argument, namely that the principal and only motive which had caused him to advise the Turkish Government not to accept the proposed plan, had been the possible damage to Turkey, not the damage to England. He felt in fact that the proposed canal was an attack on the integrity of the Ottoman Empire.

Thus, as so often happens, the British statesmen kept the real reasons for their attitude in the background. It was not a question of protecting some gullible capitalist, nor even the integrity of the Ottoman Empire, but in reality the safeguarding of England's lines of communication. Their preoccupation was essentially imperial. The route to India by the Cape was long undoubtedly, but it was safe, and England could easily control it. The passage by Suez certainly was direct, but if Egypt, which was the key-piece, should fall into the hands of some European power, there could no longer be any question of British control. Now it was France that was proposing to construct the canal. Palmerston's arguments were so grotesque that de Lesseps might well have wondered whether he was discussing the matter with a statesman or a maniac. But the reasons which the Foreign Minister refrained from stating were sound enough from the British point of view, and even to-day there are certain Englishmen who believe that he was right, and that it would have been better if the isthmus had never been cut.

As a result of diplomatic conversations, the Governments of England and France finally agreed not to interfere with any decisions made by Turkey and Egypt, but to leave the whole affair to follow its industrial and commercial course. However, British hostility persisted and could not be ignored, especially by Turkey who timorously would not ratify. Four years had passed since the concession had been granted. Finally de Lesseps, weary of waiting, decided to take matters into his own hands, and go ahead in spite of everything.

'With regard to the political aspect of the Suez Canal, the British have agreed to defer to the wishes of the French Government, and the tacit consent of the Porte has been sufficiently clearly expressed. All I have to do now is to prepare the organization of The Company.'

That is what he wrote on August 18th, 1858, to Bar-thélemy Saint-Hilaire. As the legal basis of his argument was singularly lacking, one can easily understand that his correspondent was a bit anxious and refused to follow him any further. However, the intrepid fighter continued on his way, unpardonably irresponsible if he had failed. But he was to succeed! As we are unable at this late date to decide what were his virtues and what his defects, we can only admire and exclaim, 'What pluck the man had!'

He then set about raising the required capital of 200

million francs, divided into 400,000 shares of 500 francs each. The cost of the work was estimated at 160,000,000 francs, and to this was added 40,000,000 francs, for interest during construction. It was then expected that the canal would take nine years to complete. De Lesseps, the owner of the concession, agreed to surrender it free to the new company, thus emphasizing his disinterestedness — a point well worth noting! His one aim was to bring the task to a successful conclusion.

But how to find the 200,000,000 francs? He was alone, he was not a financier, and he had a concession of doubtful legal value. In his excellent biography of de Lesseps, M. Robert Courau recounts the picturesque meeting with the bankers:

'De Lesseps appealed to Rothschild. He explained his plan for an international subscription. The financier congratulated him, and offered to put the Rothschild banking organization at his disposal, both in France and abroad. De Lesseps thanked him warmly, but as he was about to leave, a doubt crossed his mind. Turning towards Rothschild, he said:

' "What do you wish in exchange?"

' "Good Lord! It's easy to see that you are not a business man! It will be the usual five per cent." "Five per cent!" said de Lesseps, "but on two hundred million francs that is ten millions! Do you propose to take ten millions of money away from my shareholders in payment for the use of your dingy corridors? No, thank you. You may keep your bank. We will make the issue without you. I will hire some suitable office for which I will pay twelve thousand francs a month, and it will do me quite well."

' "You will not succeed."

' "We shall see!"[1]

[1] ROBERT COURAU, *Ferdinand de Lesseps* (Grasset), p. 84.

70

' "The bankers wished to lay down the law to me," said de Lesseps afterwards, "but I would not give in. I decided to do my business quite alone and go direct to the public." '[1]

That is exactly what this extraordinary man did. He rented an office in the Place Vendôme, and by himself toured Europe in a whirlwind of propaganda. His success was amazing, for 25,000 subscribers applied for the issue which took place from November 5th to the 20th, 1858. In France they were chiefly middle class and professional people, though some working men brought along their savings as well. Public opinion was almost sentimental. No doubt they hoped to make a good investment, but they were also proud to collaborate with this Frenchman in a great humanitarian enterprise, and the fun of teaching the English a good lesson had something to do with it as well.

In the end it was the savings of the French people that furnished most of the capital, for they took up 207,111 shares out of a total of 400,000. The Ottoman Empire, including the personal subscription of the Viceroy of Egypt, took 96,517 shares. After making allowance for various small subscriptions from other countries, there remained a bloc of 85,506 shares, which The Company had reserved for England, the United States, Austria, and Russia — but they all abstained entirely. So Mohammed Said, who was a great gambler, took the whole bloc for his own account, and thus became the principal shareholder. Later this accumulation of shares in the possession of the Viceroy was further augmented until it amounted to almost half the capital; it was this bloc that Disraeli bought in 1875.

The Company was finally incorporated on December 15th, 1858, and naturally Ferdinand de Lesseps was elected President of the Board of Directors. But England was not

[1] J. CHARLES-ROUX, *L'Isthme de Suez* (Hachette), p. 285.

ready to make peace. In an editorial on November 30th, the *Globe* commented as follows on the issue of shares: 'If the canal should ever prove practical, it will of course be quite unable to make a profit . . . The subscribers are mostly waiters from the cafés who have been deceived by the newspapers which they find lying around, or else they are grocers' boys who are accustomed to read advertisements in the old papers with which they wrap up their parcels . . . The whole business is an obvious fraud . . . for no one will ever collect a farthing of tolls from this impossible canal.'

III

The Company approached the Viceroy for authority to begin its work. The latter was very embarrassed, for the three legal experts with whom he had consulted, namely Messrs. Dufaure, Jules Favre, and Odilon Barrot, had made no attempt to conceal their view that, as the concession had not received the visa of the Porte, it had no juridical status. De Lesseps produced a further legal opinion, and once again Mohammed Said was content to be guided by his intimate friend. After all, they argued, Turkish permission was possibly not absolutely essential, for had not England done without it when she built the railway from Alexandria to Cairo?

The first shovelful of sand was dug up on April 25th, 1859, and thanks to the forced labour of 20,000 fellahin, furnished by the Egyptian Government, progress was rapid. By February 2nd, 1862, the fresh water canal was finished, and on November 18th of the same year the waters of the Mediterranean flowed into Lake Timsâh. Ferdinand de Lesseps was then promoted to the rank of Commander of the Legion of Honour.

In January 1863 Mohammed Said, the faithful supporter during all these early days, disappeared. His successor, the Khedive Ishmail, was not an adversary, for he maintained that he was 'as much of a canalist as de Lesseps himself', but still he was not a friend in the true sense of the word, and as for Nubar, his Foreign Minister, he was a British agent. At the instigation of the English, Nubar obtained authority from the Porte to reduce the number of forced labourers to only 6000 and to compel The Company to return all the lands that had been granted to it. A violent moral campaign against forced labour was let loose in England. Finally an injunction was sent to The Company ordering it to suspend work, and it had to give way.

The dispute again escaped from Egypt, for it was in Paris that Nubar and Ferdinand de Lesseps now pursued their struggle for influence. They eventually agreed to submit the whole matter to the arbitration of Napoleon III.

On July 6th, 1864, Napoleon gave his verdict, in which he revised the original contract in several essential points. The Company lost the right to employ labour requisitioned from Egypt; it was compelled to give back over 150,000 acres of land which it held under the original concession; it forfeited the ownership of the fresh water canal although it still had the right to use it. In compensation it received an indemnity of 84 million francs, and, above all, and this was the essential point, the concession was declared to be valid. After various supplementary negotiations, the Porte finally gave its visa on March 19th, 1866, twelve years after the initial firman had been promulgated by Mohammed Said.

Irrespective of what the price might be, Ferdinand de Lesseps was quite justified in considering this decision to be a great victory. As he said at the general meeting of shareholders on August 1st of that year, the project was no longer merely a hope, but an incontestable reality.

Work was begun again, and this time there were no further set backs, but it was carried out on a new basis. Owing to the shortage of labour, a recruiting campaign was launched throughout the whole of the Mediterranean region, and 15,000 free workmen — French, Italians, Dalmatians, Arabs, and Syrians — were obtained. Also, recourse was made to intense mechanization which incidentally resulted in considerable improvements in the use and design of machines of this nature. Under the direction of Voisin Bey the work proceeded steadily towards its final stages. On March 14th, 1869, the waters of the Mediterranean were let into the Bitter Lakes, and August 15th, truly a memorable date, saw the junction of the two seas.

Yet right to the very end Ferdinand de Lesseps had to struggle against the nightmare of further checks. As a result of all these successive delays, interest charges during construction had steadily accrued.

At the same time the original estimates were found to be inaccurate, partly owing to the suppression of forced labour, and partly because of the high cost of the mechanical equipment which had thus become necessary. In 1868 a further sum of 85 million francs was required, but the resources of The Company were exhausted, as well as its credit. A malicious speculative raid against the shares was made from London. An issue of 100 million francs of bonds failed, only a third being taken up. The Company was *in extremis* when the French legislature authorized a lottery loan. Although this saved the situation the financial position of The Company was not really healthy until about 1873, but by that time at least one could say that the canal was an accomplished fact.

The inauguration, which took place on November 17th, 1869, was a real oriental fête. The Khedive acted as host at a grandiose reception. Among the distinguished guests were the Empress Eugenie, the Emperor of Austria, the Prince of Wales, the Crown Prince of Prussia, as well as a cruiser full of kings! On the fourth day of the celebrations 80 vessels, of which 50 were warships, passed through the canal and out into the Red Sea.

A few days afterwards Ferdinand de Lesseps, then sixty-four years old, married Mademoiselle de Bragard who was twenty-one. By this second marriage this amazing man was to have six sons and six daughters.

He became the most decorated man in Europe. In July 1870, England, always a good loser, received him in triumph, and *The Times* itself, which had fought him so bitterly, made honourable amends in an editorial filled with wit and grace.

'Mr. de Lesseps has arrived in a country which did nothing to help in the construction of the canal, but which since its opening has had more ships passing through it than all the other nations of the world put together. It is this country that will provide him with almost all the dividends which his shareholders will cash. Let that be the compensation which we offer for all the wrongs which we have managed to inflict on him in the past.'

IV

One can hardly pay too great a tribute to Ferdinand de Lesseps, for it was he and he alone who made the canal. He personally was the whole canal, the creator of a new world route. He ranks with Magellan and with Vasco da Gama. And yet this man who achieved so much was not a specialist, nor an engineer, nor a financier, nor even an administrator. He was essentially something which was much more difficult: he was the inspiration, the man who conceived the idea, worked upon it, and carried it to completion.

Above all, he had faith. It was his zeal which, after first being passed on to a few close collaborators, in the end carried away the multitude, enthused the shareholders, and convinced or frightened the politicians. He understood how to influence public opinion and even governments by practices which have since become completely in line with modern ideas of publicity and propaganda. A born diplomat — more than a diplomat — he was always where he was needed, always at the very centre of the storm, one day in Cairo, and the next in Paris, Vienna, Constantinople, London, or else at Suez or Port Said. Always perfectly at ease and never allowing himself to be intimidated, he spoke as an equal with Ministers, with Princes, and even with Sovereigns.

Perhaps his real strength lay in the fact that he was not interested in money. On several occasions he could have sold his concession to a group of financiers, and so realized a fortune at a single stroke. But he could only see the work which he had set out to accomplish. It was a work of humanity, and one by which he felt that he could serve France better than in any other way.

CHAPTER VI

THE CANAL AND POLITICS
FROM 1869 TO 1914

I

Now that the Suez Canal has been born, its history begins.
This history is going to be as full of adventures and vicissitudes as was the long period of its conception.

Both Ferdinand de Lesseps and Mohammed Said undoubtedly wished to accomplish a work of peace, *aperire
terram gentibus*, but with no underlying nationalistic motives.
Palmerston had complained that Thiers' whole policy in
Egypt in 1840 was aimed at obtaining a transport monopoly,
but a similar accusation could not be levelled against de
Lesseps.

In the first memorandum which de Lesseps handed to
the Viceroy on November 15th, 1854, he expressed the
thought that all the nations of the world were equally
interested in opening up a new passage across the isthmus,
as well as in maintaining its strict and inviolable neutrality.
Such were the principles contained in the firman of November 30th, 1854, and confirmed by the details of the
concession of January 5th, 1856.

The canal was not a political enterprise, but a private
company with its chief administrative office in Paris and
registered statutory office at Alexandria. The board of
thirty-two directors represented the principal nations
interested, and from the beginning included eleven
foreigners: one American, one Austrian, one Portuguese,
one Spaniard, one Russian, one Englishman, one Belgian,

one Dutchman, one Egyptian, and two Italians. Feeling that the administration should be international, the founder had chosen his foreign collaborators from the nations that had contributed to the creation of the canal, without bothering about whether they were likely to use it or not.

Still, the principles of equality and universality inscribed in the concession bound only the signatories, i.e. the Porte, Egypt, and The Company itself. Ferdinand de Lesseps apparently wished the Powers to guarantee the neutrality of the canal in perpetuity by means of some international diplomatic document. Such in fact was the sense of the resolution which he tried to have adopted at the Conference of Paris in 1856, and in 1864 he had submitted a proposition in the same spirit to Drouyn de Lhuys. These suggestions remained sterile, however, with the result that while the canal did in fact benefit from a regime of neutrality, as was proved during the Franco-Prussian War of 1870 and the Russo-Turkish War of 1877, it had no international status.

One Power, however, watched over the canal with a particularly attentive eye, and this was England. Being satisfied that she was receiving perfect equality of treatment commercially, she did not seek any special favours. Yet logically the situation was bound to arouse a desire for a special position politically, for the canal lay on the route to India, and she used it far more than any other nation. After having fought against its creation with all her might and main, she finally accepted it as inevitable, and now tried either to insinuate herself into its administration or else to acquire some measure of political control. By two strokes of genius as daring as they were astute, she eventually achieved her ambitions: she purchased the shares of Ismail Pasha in 1875, and secured the military occupation of Egypt in 1882.

11

The Khedive Ismail, who was a great spendthrift, found himself on December 1st, 1875, faced with a maturing debt of some 80 to 100 million francs, and as practically all his assets were already mortgaged the banking fraternity was beginning to shun him. As the value of the Suez Canal shares was now beginning to be recognized it was suggested that he should sell them. The bloc in his possession came from the initial subscription of Mohammed Said, plus various later purchases. It amounted to 177,000 shares out of a total of 400,000, or almost half the total capital of The Company. There was one serious difficulty, it is true. In 1869, being already short of cash, he had detached and sold back to The Company the dividend coupons for the next 25 years, and consequently lost the right to vote during that period, though a friendly agreement allowed him to delegate his voting power to the president of The Company at the general meetings. Nevertheless his shares, even without coupons and voting rights, still had a certain commercial value.

About the beginning of November 1875 a Frenchman named Edouard Dervieu, who formerly had been a banker in Alexandria, became interested in the matter. Having obtained from the Viceroy an option good until November 16th, he went at once to Paris. The big banks there gave him a reception that was anything but cordial, so he changed his plans and instead of trying to sell the shares he sought to raise a loan on their security. De Lesseps took an interest in the affair as one can well imagine. He begged the Duc Decazes, then Minister for Foreign Affairs, to intervene at the Credit Foncier, the quarter from which most of the opposition was coming. The political aspect of the negotiations was then clearly apparent.

79

If the shares were purchased by a Parisian group, from then on The Company would become an entirely French enterprise. There were no objections to this in France, but what would England say to such an important change in ownership of the canal? So it seemed to Decazes, who felt isolated in Europe, being still under the shadow of his country's recent defeat in the war of 1870. He also was anxious not to fall out with a government which, though not genuinely friendly, had nevertheless supported him in his difficulties with Germany. He therefore took upon himself to discuss the matter with Lord Derby, who firmly expressed his disapproval. It was a disastrous blunder! The purchase of the shares would have been quite in order, providing it was not talked about. Now that so much fuss was being made, it began to look as if France was being discourteous to her great neighbour.

England for her part showed less delicacy, for she started negotiating while the French were still wavering. On November 18th the British Government made a firm bid, which the Khedive accepted on the 23rd. The price was one hundred million francs, which worked out at £3,976,582 sterling. The contract was signed on the 25th, and next day the shares were delivered to the British Consul General at Cairo. The negotiations had been conducted at lightning speed, and the French were dumbfounded.

True, it required great courage and decision on the part of Disraeli, the British Prime Minister, as well as a certain amount of parliamentary audacity, for as payment had to be made on the spot there was not sufficient time to procure from the House of Commons the usual appropriation of a credit. Disraeli in fact arranged everything directly with Rothschild, borrowing from him the £3,976,582 necessary at an agreed commission of 2½ per cent, plus 5 per cent interest for 96 days. Parliament would have to vote later; meanwhile the important thing was to proceed quickly and not miss the boat. England in fact was most anxious to get a finger in the pie in order to have some say in fixing the tolls, and in the general administration of The Company. Of course she was acquiring a substantial financial interest as a shareholder, but at the time that fact was only of secondary importance for her. The transaction was purely political.

In any event the Prime Minister could be quite sure of parliamentary ratification, for British public opinion did not fail to greet, and with reason, this fine haul as a brilliant diplomatic victory. A few qualms were expressed by the more scrupulous. 'I don't like it', murmured Sir Stafford Northcote, secretary to the Chancellor of the Exchequer; 'not quite gentlemanly'. However, the two adroit personages who had carried the affair to its successful conclusion looked only to the result, and England as a whole thought they had done well.

In France, on the contrary, the reaction was humiliation and bitterness. 'Oh you French people!' wrote John Lemoinne. 'All you understand is how to pull someone else's chestnuts out of the fire!' When I think back to my own childhood, I seem to remember something of the affair. There was a grudging admiration for the cunning neighbour who, having taken no part in building the canal, had now been able to purchase it under our very noses.

Ferdinand de Lesseps, wiser and more of a statesman, saw the matter in quite a different light. 'This, to my mind, is excellent,' he declared. 'The powerful solidarity which has now been established between the French and British capital invested in the affair will insure that this international canal will be run on purely businesslike and peaceful lines.'

Without delay he began negotiating with his new share-holders, who had in truth purchased less rights than was realized at first sight. There were no coupons to cash until the year 1894, and for the time being there was no repre-sentation at the annual general meeting. Furthermore, there was Article 51 in the statutes of The Company, which specified that every owner of 25 shares should have one vote, and that no single shareholder could have more than ten votes.

The British Government now found that it was the sole proprietor of 177,000 shares. Some arrangement with the canal management appeared inevitable, and the originator of the canal lent his support with good grace. The British Government was allowed to vote at the Assembly, and was given three seats on the board. Later, in 1884, The Company admitted seven additional English directors, who were to be regarded as special representatives of British commerce and shipping. As a result of this friendly arrangement, which is still in force, it was also understood that one of the three British Government representatives should have a seat on the Executive Committee.

The founder of the canal made no mistake when he received the newcomers graciously. The presence of England as an associate in the great enterprise helped to consolidate it, more especially as her representatives were always strictly loyal in their collaboration. In the long run the Suez Canal became a binding link between France and England, and as such proved to be a valuable factor in the Entente Cordiale.

III

Palmerston had predicted that if the canal ever were built, England would sooner or later be obliged to annex

Egypt. A feeble State situated on a great world highway could hardly remain completely independent. There was no lack of pretext for intervention, and actually it was about this time that the interference of the Western powers increased; for example the formation of the 'Caisse de la Dette' in 1876, the Franco-British financial control in 1878, and in the deposition of Ismail in 1879. An explosion of local nationalism followed inevitably.

The protests were directed partly against the foreigners who were monopolizing the government jobs, and partly against the Palace where the atmosphere was still Turkish. The Proclamation of Arabi Pasha, expressing the popular indignation, was characteristically Egyptian and nationalist. Arabi became Minister of War in February 1882, and on June 11th in the same year an anti-foreign riot occurred in Alexandria. The military had to be called out, and fifty Europeans were massacred.

The British fleet bombarded the town and re-established order, but the French fleet retired. England proposed joint action with France to protect the canal against any eventuality, but when de Freycinet's Cabinet weakly asked the Chambre des Deputés for the necessary credits, they were refused. The Chambre was not only afraid of dispersing the armed forces of the nation, but they had also inherited a fatal timidity as a result of the defeat of 1870. It was the same sort of thing which in 1875, seven years earlier, had paralysed Decazes. So a second time France failed to act, and the British fleet and army advanced alone. They occupied the canal with the consent of the Khedive. Arabi fled after being beaten at the Battle of Tel-el-Kebir. The British army entered Cairo, and it is there to this day. Under the pretext of a simple military occupation, England began to exercise absolute political control in Egypt.

British intervention in the canal zone provoked a categorical protest from Ferdinand de Lesseps. He described it as a violation of the neutrality which was inscribed in the concession. When London replied that the Khedive had agreed to their intervention, there followed a period of extreme tension between The Company and the British Government.

'The old devil is playing tricks on us,' said Lord Granville, 'but we will get him yet.'

Granville did in fact launch a double attack against the old fighter. On the one hand he threatened to have the concession withdrawn, and on the other he talked of constructing a rival canal from Alexandria to Suez via Cairo. De Lesseps felt that he must come to terms, so he signed the Accord of January 15th, 1884. By this agreement transit was to be facilitated, tolls were to be reduced, the British were to have the seven additional directors already referred to, and the canal was to be enlarged. So peace was declared between the 'Universal Company' and the new masters of Egypt.

IV

The events of 1882 seriously modified The Company's position in Egypt. From then on it was no longer merely confronted by the Khedive or in extreme cases by the Sultan, but instead by England herself. The latter, it is true, accepted the principle of neutrality for the canal, but at the same time she wished to obtain any privileges that might accrue from her military occupation. As for France, she was jealous of the British success, and hoped that some international statute might be adopted which would remove any excuse for England to remain in Egypt. It was under these conditions that preparations for the future Convention of Constantinople began.

The leading Powers were more or less in agreement with the general principles laid down by M. de Lesseps. France and England, who had been asked to prepare the work, signed a preliminary convention in 1887, which at the outset embodied a significant reservation on the part of England. She agreed to the proposed dispositions only 'in so far as they should be compatible with the transitory and exceptional state in which Egypt found itself at the moment, and that they should in no way restrict the liberty of action of the British Government during the occupation of Egypt by Her Majesty's Forces'. It is interesting to note that forty-two years later when she signed the Kellogg Pact, England made almost the same reservation. The Convention of Constantinople was signed in 1888, and to this day it still governs the international status of the Suez Canal.

The principles of neutrality and particularly of freedom of use were generally adopted, though not entirely in every case. The canal was to be for ever free and open, in time of war as in time of peace, to all ships of commerce or of war, without distinction of flag. No attack was to be made against its free use, whether in war or peace. No permanent fortifications were to be erected, and it was never to be occupied or blocked up. (The same also applied to the fresh water canal.) In time of war no hostility likely to interfere with free navigation was to be permitted, either in the canal itself or in the ports at either end, or even within a radius of three nautical miles. (This was to apply even if Turkey was a belligerent.) Warships were never to be allowed to remain for more than twenty-four hours either at Port Said or Suez, nor were they to be permitted to take on stores beyond their immediate needs. Obviously this was a special sort of neutrality, or, to quote Baron de Courcel, one created for this particular transaction.

'This is a special pact,' he told the Board of Directors of the canal on May 16th, 1904. 'It has been concluded between all the high contracting parties in order to maintain here, contrary to ordinary rules of conduct and over and above the usual rules of neutrality, absolute freedom of transit.'

Should the canal ever be in danger the Khedive's Government was to be responsible for carrying out these rules, and they were to call on the Ottoman Government for help in case of need. The duration of the Convention was not to be limited to that of the concession, but was to stand for all time.

If one reads between the lines, which is easy enough, one perceives that since 1882 the Khedive's Government had in reality become Great Britain. The latter, however, insisted on her previous reservations, and this prevented the Convention from coming into force. Actually, it was applied in 1888, but it was only after 1904 that the situation was regularized as a result of the Franco-British reconciliation. Britain then gave up her reservations, and finally accepted the Convention, which after all practically entrusted her with the military protection of the canal. France on her side forgot her ill humour and, compensating herself in Morocco, ceased to protest against the British occupation of Egypt. So a stable regime was at last created, relying on the Entente between the two great Western Powers. It was in fact exactly what Ferdinand de Lesseps had always desired.

Throughout her long history France has often displayed her creative genius, while England shone in the political sphere. The story is not over, however, for the Great War has now placed the whole question on an entirely new basis.

CHAPTER VII

THE CANAL AND POLITICS DURING AND SINCE THE GREAT WAR

I

EVER since the canal was opened, the guiding principle of British policy has been to ward off any power that might menace the security of this route to India. For many years France had been considered the chief danger, but she was now appeased, and since 1904 has been occupied in other directions. England had long been in the habit of worrying about the possible occupation of Constantinople by Russia, but since 1905 Russia had been paralysed because of her defeat in Manchuria, and the agreement of 1907 finally ended her long rivalry with England. And yet the danger was not ended, for each generation brings a new adversary. From the beginning of the twentieth century a grave German menace began to emerge.

A traditional road to the East has always existed overland across Western Asia. Turkey is the key to this route, just as Egypt is the key to the route to the Indies via the Red Sea. In her *drang nach osten* policy Germany began to look in this direction, particularly as she was admirably equipped politically to obtain a foothold in the Turkish Empire. In 1903 she obtained the concession of the Baghdad Railway, and this meant a double menace for England. It threatened India through the Persian Gulf and Egypt via the Hedjas Railway.

Foreseeing trouble as far back as 1899, the British Government had established a Protectorate over Koweit, which commands the approach to Mesopotamia. In 1906 she had to protect Egypt's interests against the pretensions of the Turks, when the Sinai frontier was being surveyed. She was particularly suspicious of a projected strategic railway which was planned to run in the direction of the isthmus and the Red Sea. She scored a further point in that year by acquiring from the Sultan the control of the section of the railway to be built between Baghdad and Basra, for this barred German expansion towards the Persian Gulf. In any case, England had long since taken precautions to protect her interests in these territories by occupying a whole series of strongholds: Cyprus in 1878, Aden in 1839, the island of Perim in 1857, the island of Socotra in 1886, and the Somaliland coast between 1884 and 1886. Thus, like the Persian Gulf, the Red Sea had become practically an English lake.

In any event England's policy with regard to Turkey had been progressively changing. Since her military occupation of Egypt, the integrity of the Ottoman Empire interested her less and less. Eventually she even approved of Turkey's dismemberment, for she relied instead on the control or friendship of Egypt, Palestine, and Arabia. Turkey, which had previously been a shield against Russia, was now becoming a source of danger, owing to her alliance with Germany. Let us see what the Herr Professors have to say, for in countries where politics are planned in detail, the professors must be consulted if we wish to discover the long-term trend of national policy.

'England can be attacked and mortally wounded at only one point, and that is Egypt', says Paul Rohrbach in his book *Die Baghdad Bahn*. 'The loss of Egypt would signify not only the end of her control of the canal and the route to India, but it would probably also bring in its wake the loss of her possessions in Central and Eastern Africa. The conquest of Egypt by a Mohammedan power like Turkey would also imperil her rule over her sixty million Mohammedan subjects in India . . . The stronger Turkey becomes, the greater the danger for England, for in any war between England and Germany, Turkey will be on the side of Germany.'

England did not put much faith in the neutrality of the isthmus, even though guaranteed by an international convention. As a protection against this growing menace she preferred military occupation. Further, she was not sure of the Viceroy, Abbas Hilmi. He was at Constantinople when the war broke out in 1914; he did not return, and scarcely concealed his hostility. In his absence the Regent, who was subjected to British influence, declared that Egypt would remain neutral, and at the same time he undertook measures of defence which placed her among the countries fighting on the British side. Later, when Turkey declared war against the Allies on November 5th, the position of the Khedive, who was openly pro-German, became frankly impossible. On December 18th England proclaimed a Protectorate over Egypt, and so ended Turkish sovereignty. Hussein Kamel replaced Abbas Hilmi, not now as Viceroy, but as Sultan, and instead of a simple Consul-General (who, however, had had full powers) a British High Commissioner was nominated.

In so far as the canal was concerned, England and The Company came to an agreement to maintain the freedom of transit in conformity with the concession of 1854 and the convention of 1888. But that meant nothing whatever, once enemy navigation was driven off the high seas by the Allies. However, the British respected the letter of the law in the measures they took against German and Austrian vessels which had sought refuge in the Isthmus. True they did not seize them in the canal, but they obliged them to come out and captured them immediately they left territorial waters. The British thesis, which was confirmed by the prize courts of Alexandria, was that the canal ports were ports of transit and not of refuge, and that no user could demand the right to remain in them indefinitely. Such was to be the ruling applied throughout the whole of the war. Ships belonging to the Allies and neutrals passed freely, but enemy ships naturally ceased to present themselves.

The defence of the isthmus itself fell upon Egypt, or, in other words, upon England, and in this The Company willingly associated itself. No permanent fortifications were constructed, but provisional defences were set up, especially between the Bitter Lakes and El Quantara. This was done in case of a Turkish land attack from the north-east, which in fact did take place later on.

This expedition was organized by Djemal Pasha, the commander of the Turkish 4th Army, with headquarters in Syria. He had the assistance of two senior German staff officers, Colonels von Frankenberg and von Kress. The objective was the canal and Egypt, and for this purpose an important amount of war materials — pontoons, waggons, camels, pipe-lines to conduct water, etc. — was assembled at Damascus, where an army of 30,000 men was concentrated. The plan adopted was to make a night march across the desert in the direction of Tussûm. This village is in reality the key to the isthmus, being near the junction of the fresh-water and Suez canals. Once master of this strategic point, the whole of the canal zone would be in their grasp, and they could then attack and conquer Egypt.

The English, who had organized a rather weak defence, were entrenched behind the dykes alongside the canal, which they used as a gigantic moat. In addition to various

British naval units, they had with them two French warships, the *Requin*, which lay broadside on near Lake Timsâh, and the *Entrecasteaux* in the Great Bitter Lake. Both these ships played an important part in the defence. In spite of repeated warnings the British command did not really believe that an attack would take place. Nevertheless it was made on February 3rd, 1915, and at first partly succeeded thanks to surprise. A few troops crossed the canal, but twenty-five enemy pontoons were sunk, while the naval artillery shelled the assembly points in the desert and rendered them untenable. The attack failed, and Djemal departed without being pursued.[1] The lesson, and it will not be forgotten, is that the desert in itself does not constitute a protection, but rather a dangerous quarter from which surprise attacks may come; also it can be crossed with modern military equipment.

The canal was saved, Egypt was saved and would not be threatened further. But very soon, actually in the following year, another peril appeared, namely the submarine. Thus for the second time since 1914 we see that the use of the canal was inseparably bound up with the freedom of the high seas. The way in which the British parried this new thrust was most significant. They altered the course of their traffic, and sent it around the Cape, especially supplies of foodstuffs from the Far East and Australia. It was an improvised makeshift, however, for the equipment at intermediate ports of call such as Durban and Capetown proved insufficient. Therefore in 1917 they returned to the old itinerary, but they now used the convoy system. Once more ships passed through the Suez Canal, but not without heavy losses in the Mediterranean.

[1] A full account of this battle is given in a book by Commandant Douin, *L'Attaque du Canal de Suez* (Delagrave), 1922.

This lesson from the sea was quite different from the one learnt in the desert at Tussûm. The route to India via the Mediterranean in time of war is no longer safe, and in future it will become even less so, not because of the canal itself, but because the narrow Mediterranean Sea is poisoned by the new enemies which lie in ambush along its course. The route via the Cape, which had been neglected since the days of de Lesseps, now reappears as the alternative. So, for the second time since Vasco da Gama we turn another page in the history of communications.

We look in vain in the Treaty of Versailles for a reference to this serious change in the *status quo*. By Article 152 the authority of the Porte in so far as the protection of the canal is concerned, was transferred to England. The principles laid down in the Convention of 1888 were reaffirmed, and continued to be strictly enforced, i.e. that no Power shall forbid either access to or transit through the canal, even to naval vessels of belligerent nations; all hostile acts are forbidden, both in the waters of the canal and in its ports. However, no one has any illusions about the value of these provisions, for in the case of a conflict all that counts is to possess the isthmus and Egypt and to be able to defend them.

II

At the end of the war England's position in the eastern Mediterranean was decidedly stronger than it had ever been before. She had nothing to fear from her old rivals, Russia and Germany, or even from France. The canal seemed as solidly guaranteed as possible, between the Egyptian protectorate on the one side and the Palestine mandate on the other. And yet fresh difficulties were about to begin.

The war had a profound effect on the Egyptian mentality. In the first place it had imposed a heavy burden on the country. There had been requisitions, military occupation, martial law, etc., all of which had been borne with growing impatience. The British also were imprudent in allowing themselves to be too much in evidence. There had been too many highly paid functionaries, and too many troops passing through on their way to the Dardanelles or to the Western Front. These troops stopped over in Egypt, and some, particularly the Australians, behaved with a regrettable lack of restraint. Otherwise order was almost too strictly maintained.

No doubt Egypt profited from this military inundation, which, like that of the Nile, left behind it a certain amount of silt. All the same her profits had remained limited, partly owing to the numerous requisitions of man-power that she had had to meet, and also because wages were not raised to keep pace with rising prices. Furthermore, President Wilson's appeals for the self-determination of peoples did not fall on deaf ears in Egypt, but aroused a new nationalism, recalling the earlier outbursts of Arabi, but immensely stronger.

The English did not appear to realize what was happening. They forbade the Nationals or Wafd to send a delegation to Versailles to explain the Egyptian point of view. They maintained the protectorate, and let it be understood that they were preparing to remain permanently. The Nationalists were exasperated by the English attitude, and when Zaglul, their chief, was deported by the foreigners, they made a martyr of him. Thus, instead of being solved by the establishment of the protectorate, the Egyptian question became even more critical.

England is seldom stubborn in her mistakes; so she

decided to negotiate with the opposition. A first conversation took place in 1920 between Zaglul and Lord Milner. Milner was a great statesman. He clearly foresaw the correct solution when he suggested substituting an Anglo-Egyptian alliance for the protectorate, and that is what came about sixteen years later. He would not, however, agree to withdraw British troops from the canal. A second conversation between Lord Curzon and Aldy Pasha also failed.

Finally the High Commissioner, Lord Allenby, who realized that a policy of repression could not succeed, concluded a treaty on February 22nd, 1922. Egypt was recognized by Great Britain as an independent sovereign state, but with four explicit reservations, which were bound to have an important bearing on future history.

First, Great Britain could not disinterest herself either from the security of her Empire communications through the Suez Canal, nor from the defence of Egypt; secondly, she would not permit any other Power to get a foothold there; thirdly, she would not disinterest herself in the protection of foreign minorities — in other words, 'capitulations' were to continue. Her last point was that she would not give up the Sudan, which lies on the route from the Cape to Cairo. A British declaration, to which Egypt did not agree, was annexed to the treaty a few days later. It notified the Powers that nothing was changed in so far as their relationships with Egypt were concerned, and that any intervention on their part would be considered by England as an unfriendly act.

However, Egypt accepted the new regime. Fuad became the first king, a great king. Zaglul was nominated Prime Minister.

Yet even this settlement did not provide the complete solution. It had come too late, and the country remained unsatisfied. The situation was further envenomed when in November, 1924, Sir Lee Stack, Sirdar of the Egyptian Army and Governor of the Sudan, was assassinated in Cairo. As a measure of reprisal, England suppressed the Anglo-Egyptian joint sovereignty over the Sudan, and made her strength felt by a policy of repression.

Soon, however, she felt that it would be better to start negotiating afresh. For twelve fruitless years conversations were to be kept up between the various parties in power, who were constantly changing in both London and Cairo. All the negotiations failed, whether they took place between the Wafd and the Labour Party in 1924 and 1930, or between King Fuad and the Conservatives in 1927, or between him and Labour in 1929. They always failed because the opposing theses seemed to be irreconcilable.

Egypt demanded the end of the military occupation, whereas England declared that it could not possibly be given up. It is true that the Labour Party might even have gone so far as to content itself with the occupation of the isthmus; but the Conservatives insisted that neither El-Zagazig, where the fresh water canal branches off from the Nile, nor Cairo, which was a centre of anti-British intrigues, could be prudently evacuated.

The Egyptian demands did not halt there. They went further and insisted that British control over their foreign affairs should cease, that the protection of the Suez Canal should be entrusted to the League of Nations, and that Egyptian rights over the Sudan should be recognized anew. One or other of these demands always brought negotiations to an end. No doubt in the long run the two points of view were gradually approaching each other, and at times they were almost in accord. But the right atmosphere was still lacking, more especially as there was no burning urgency driving the negotiators to come to an agreement at any cost. As a result of long experience, England mistrusted the future and was on her guard against possible outside interference. As for Egypt, she feared no other foreign Power, for, as in the fable, she could well say 'our enemy is our master'. However, all this was destined to change completely in 1935, at the time of the Abyssinian War.

III

The Italian conquest of Abyssinia profoundly altered the problem of the Sudan as well as that of the Upper Nile Valley, and even the defence of Egypt itself. This was suddenly appreciated in 1935, not merely by the Wafd leaders but indeed by all the Egyptian people. For the first time they feared another Western Power more than they feared England. If they had to be dominated, then let it be by the country that enjoyed the greatest prestige.

Now it must be confessed that the Italians have absolutely no prestige amongst the local populations of the Orient. Another point, more trivial perhaps, is that although the Italian colony in Egypt is by far the most numerous after the Greek colony, it is composed of the lower classes, whom the Egyptians regard as competitors. Now an Englishman is a haughty ruler whose ambitions are limited to the upper social levels, and the same applies to the French and the Belgians. One meets them on boards of directors or in the higher administrative posts. If Italy were to obtain political influence, then an army of job-seekers would descend upon the country. So a curious solidarity is growing up between the English and the Egyptians, in spite of their antagonism of over half a century.

La Bruyère has written, 'There are certain families who, by the laws of this world or by what we may call decorum, seem destined to remain in perpetual enmity. Then suddenly we see them united, for where religion has failed in its efforts, self-interest comes into play and instantly succeeds'. Psychologically this is the sole foundation of the Anglo-Egyptian Treaty of August 26th, 1936. A few weeks of discussion produced agreement where fourteen years of bitter negotiating had failed — but this time they were uniting against a third party!

By the new treaty Egypt was recognized as an independent sovereign state. She was to be a member of the League of Nations. Military occupation was to terminate, and be replaced by a permanent military alliance. In these conditions, however, every facility was to be given to the great ally in collaborating in the defence of the·country. British military experts were to be allowed to circulate freely in the Libyan Desert. British military aeroplanes could fly over Egyptian territory, while a corresponding privilege permitted Egyptian aeroplanes to fly over British territory. The special character of the British position in Egypt was explicitly recognized, that is to say no treaty was to be concluded by the Egyptian Government that was inconsistent with the new alliance. The British Ambassador was to replace the High Commissioner, and was to enjoy right of precedence over the heads of all the other diplomatic missions.

The Suez Canal was specified as being part of Egyptian territory, and at the same time was recognized as constituting an essential piece in the system of British Imperial communications. Britain was authorized to station 10,000 troops and 400 air pilots, not as an army of occupation, but as collaborators in the defence of the country. The barracks for their use were to be built at the cost of the Egyptian Government, who further agreed to link up the isthmus and the delta by a network of roads, of which the strategic importance is self-evident.

In so far as the Sudan is concerned, the system of joint responsibility of 1899 was reaffirmed on the understanding that there would be no discrimination between the English and Egyptians. The question of sovereignty, however, was held in reserve. Finally, England promised to use her good offices with other capitulary Powers to obtain a prompt abolition of the system of capitulations, which she admitted was no longer in accord with the spirit of modern times, or with the present status of Egypt. The capitulations were abolished at Montreux on May 8th, 1937.

In twenty years' time the position is to be reviewed to see if the Egyptian Government alone can then undertake the defence of the canal, but it was mentioned that any revision of the treaty must leave the alliance between the two countries intact.

The treaty is a monument of political wisdom, for both parties showed their readiness to sacrifice secondary interests in order to assure what was essential. England obtained what she valued most, namely, her right to defend the canal. By her occupation of the isthmus and by the alliance, which after all is only a euphemism, she has even preserved her political and military control of Egypt. Being fully aware of this, she agreed to abandon the military occupation of Cairo, although this has not yet actually taken place. Possibly the occupation of Cairo is no longer necessary, as she is not contending now with a hostile country; in any event, with a network of adequate roads, sufficient communications between the isthmus and the delta are assured for all military purposes. She also renounced the right to interfere in local Egyptian affairs, but we must not forget that her position as the Power in occupation will necessarily give her certain privileges. The country will certainly be less well administered than under Lord Cromer, but that is not the point. Finally, there will be no more capitulations, but as there are more French investments in Egypt than British, in this concession England was paying with other people's money — a clever move of hers that is almost aesthetic! The present war has not altered this agreement in any way for, after all, it was based on fundamental aspirations.

For her part, Egypt's honour was satisfied. Though the military occupation of Suez, and even of Cairo continues to exist under the name of an alliance, it ceases to wound the self-respect of the nation; the country has become master in its own house without there being any restrictions. Certainly the concessions have been paid for by submitting to a form of protectorate, but in Egypt the necessity for this is tacitly admitted. As we have already said, Egypt may demand independence, but being located on an international highway she is not likely to get it.

When the Khedive Ismail wished that the canal might belong to Egypt, and not Egypt to the canal, he read the situation aright. Alas, it is impossible, for Egypt will always belong to the canal. There is a maximum of independence beyond which she cannot go, and frankly this is not complete independence at all. Our French author, Quercy, is often quoted for the wisdom of his peasant's remark that 'great rivers and great highways are always bad neighbours'.

CHAPTER VIII

THE ORGANIZATION OF THE CANAL

I

In 1869 Ferdinand de Lesseps finally succeeded in finishing the Suez Canal, after a fifteen-year diplomatic struggle extending from 1854 to 1869. The completion of the canal also marked the culmination of the engineering and technical work that had gone on for some seventy years since the time of Le Père, and of economic and political desires that had existed for three and a half centuries since Vasco da Gama had discovered his new route and the Venetians had reacted against it. The canal also carried on a tradition over 4000 years old, dating back to the first canal constructed by the pharaohs.

And now, having examined the Anglo-Egyptian Treaty of 1936, we have brought the story up to date, and so are ready to study the enterprise as it functions to-day.

The legal basis of The Company has not altered since its inception. The concession was for 99 years; it was given to Ferdinand de Lesseps personally, and he transferred it to The Company. It is an exclusive concession, which means that a rival canal may not be built, not on Egyptian territory at any rate. The Company is Egyptian in theory, but French in fact, and its shares are listed with other purely French securities on the Paris Bourse, although the French fiscal authorities rank them as foreign. Nevertheless it is genuinely French in its capital, its staff, and its management. Its head office is in Paris at 1 rue d'Astorg.

The capital is the same as it was at the beginning, 200 million francs. It was originally divided into 400,000 shares of 500 francs each, but in 1924 they were split in two, so that there are now 800,000 shares of 250 francs each. There are 100 founders' shares, each divided into 1000 sub-units. The 15 per cent share of the profits that was initially reserved for the Egyptian Government was sold in 1880 to a French syndicate, and is now owned by a company called the 'Société Civile'. This company has outstanding 84,507 shares of its own. Each of these shares has been divided into fifths, each fifth thus being about one-third the value of one share in the Suez Canal itself. As a result of this the Egyptian Government has no further direct interest in the profits of The Company. One can understand that it feels rather bitterly on this point, but the fault lies not with the French, but with its own imprudent predecessors.

The statutory division of the profits remains practically the same as in the beginning: 71 per cent goes to the ordinary shareholders as against 70 per cent up to 1871; 10 per cent goes to the founders' shares; 15 per cent to the Egyptian Government, that is to say, now to the French company; 2 per cent to the Board of Directors as compared with 3 per cent originally; and 2 per cent to the employees.

A little over half of the shares belong, as we have said, to the French public, whereas the English bloc, which was purchased from the Khedive Ishmail in 1875, corresponds to about three-sevenths of the total. Except for this one bloc, very few other shares are at present in non-French hands, so the business is therefore practically Franco-British in its composition, but with a French majority. As the statutes have never been amended, this gives the control to France. England is represented on the Board of Directors as the result of a friendly arrangement, and she has accepted the situation without trying to obtain further advantages. The reconciliations brought about by de Lesseps in 1875 and again in 1883 have thus been crowned with success, for in so far as The Company is concerned they have resulted in an Entente Cordiale in the true sense of the term.

The Board of Directors which meets in Paris consists to-day of 21 Frenchmen, 10 Englishmen, and 1 Dutchman, but recently The Company has agreed in principle to nominate 2 Egyptians. As the latter will take the place of two of the Frenchmen, the French group will in future have only 19 members. The president has always been French: first, Ferdinand de Lesseps from 1858 until his death in 1894; then Guichard, 1894-1896; Prince d'Arenberg, 1896-1913; Jonnart, 1913-1927; and since then the Marquis de Vogüé.

The president has many duties to perform, for the canal is an international enterprise, treating the great Powers as equals, and defending its own interests as if it were a State. The president must not only be an able administrator, but also a diplomat and a statesman — and this de Lesseps was in the highest degree. The head office of The Company is in Paris, and the technical headquarters at Ismailiya, but it is Paris which governs. The spirit, the methods, and the tone are those of the finest type of French company; indeed the whole enterprise does credit to France. I doubt if a better administration is to be found anywhere — or one that maintains as high a level of efficiency.

It is interesting to analyse the composition of the personnel in the canal zone. There we find a stratification corresponding to the various racial and social levels of the Near East. This evidently has occurred without any deliberate effort on the part of The Company, but simply from the nature of things. The higher executive is chiefly French — French,

59 per cent, Italians 14 per cent, Greeks 8 per cent, English 7 per cent. The intermediate personnel is principally Italian or Greek, and as for the workmen, they are 52 per cent Egyptian, 20 per cent Greek, 18 per cent Italians. By an agreement dated 1937 The Company promised to admit 33 per cent of Egyptians on to its permanent staff, and this was to continue until the end of the concession.

When we visit the eastern Mediterranean, we soon see that if inefficiency is to be avoided the executive posts must be confided to Westerners. They alone have a sense of order, and the ability to look into the future and see things as a whole. But we also soon learn that, if we wish to get things done, we must have recourse in practical matters to the intermediary elements that are to be found in these parts of the world, to the Greeks, Italians, Syrians, and sometimes the Jews. Their intelligence is quicker than ours, and though less reliable they are more subtle in character, and oh, how useful they are! Until I personally visited the Levant I did not appreciate what was meant by a Greek. With all the qualities of Ulysses — and even some of his defects which are almost as valuable — this Jack-of-all-trades comprehends in a word, is ingenious, practical and swift: in short, he is indispensable. Both at the canal and in Egypt it would be difficult to get along without him.

Suez Canal shares are now among the most highly esteemed securities in France, but financial success did not come immediately; also the concession ends in 1968. We are therefore dealing with a share that has had an exceptionally brilliant Stock Exchange history, but one whose future is necessarily limited. Certain weaknesses have begun to be apparent, especially during the past few years. The 500 franc shares were quoted only 163 francs in 1871, but then from 1873 to 1875 when success was assured the quotations rose. It reached 1000 francs in 1880, and 5000 francs in 1914.

These stocks are now to be found in the portfolios of most middle-class investors, and many sons, who have grown up with them, now congratulate themselves that their fathers' daring and financial idealism has brought them such magnificent results. After the post-war crisis the shares had their finest period on the Bourse. After being cut in two, they attained and even passed the 8000 franc level in 1924 and in 1929 they touched 26,000. Then after having fallen to 11,250 in 1931, they rose again, and on February 4th, 1937, they touched what will probably prove to be their all-time high, provided one adjusts for the fall of the franc after 1936. This price was 28,300 francs.

The receipts of The Company were collected on a gold basis until 1935. This meant that in the post-war years the value of the shares moved in France in sympathy with the rate of exchange. The shares were then no longer considered as merely a good holding for prudent middle-class investors. Though still well thought of, and benefiting from nineteenth-century stability, they now became the kind of guarantee that clever people were seeking as a hedge against the monetary uncertainties of the times.

Since 1935 the tolls have no longer been levied in gold but in Egyptian shillings. Nevertheless the maximum level to which The Company was authorized to raise them was limited to the equivalent of ten gold francs. This allowed adequate protection against monetary fluctuations.

As ill-luck would have it, however, since the Abyssinian crisis the Mediterranean has become the centre of a political depression which is giving great anxiety. The Suez route has lost the enviable security that it enjoyed before the Great War, and which it seemed to have recaptured after the victory of the Allies. To-day at the slightest sign of trouble on this tortuous and vulnerable short-cut, the cost of marine insurance increases, and the threatened traffic turns to the Cape route. A war, as we have seen, can dry it up entirely.

And so, after having ranked as gilt-edged, this share now tends to become a security that is influenced by international politics, and as a result, since 1937 its quotation has been halved. Also, the end of the concession is beginning to loom in sight, so even taking into account the possibility of renewal, it can no longer be considered as a good investment for the future. However, come what may, the Suez Canal will have been one of the finest French ventures, and one that has always been truly national in its management, in the inspiration of its creator, and in the enthusiasm of its first subscribers.

II

The length of the Suez Canal is about 100 miles, and if we add the two miles of extension in the harbour of Port Said, the five miles of dredged channel into the Mediterranean, and the one of about two miles jutting out into the Red Sea, we get a total supervised length of about 109 miles. The Panama Canal by contrast is only 50 miles long. There are no locks at Suez, and the waters of the two seas mingle in the canal without causing any inconvenience. The belief that the two seas were at considerably different levels — a fear that had been handed down throughout the centuries and which still existed at the time of Napoleon's expedition to Egypt — has been proved to be unfounded. However, certain works carried out by The Company since the war have shown that the Mediterranean actually is about 25 cm.

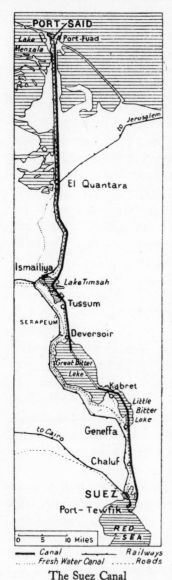

The Suez Canal

higher than the Red Sea. So after all, the legend had a modicum of truth in it.

One can better understand the course of the canal by looking at a map than by reading a description of it. Let us say simply that there are two principal sections: from Port Said to Ismailiya, and from Ismailiya to Suez. At the entrance to the first section, on the mole of Port Said, is a statue of Ferdinand de Lesseps with outstretched hand pointing towards the isthmus as if he were inviting the traffic of the world to pass through it. *Aperire terram gentibus!* It has been maliciously suggested, however, that the great Frenchman is in reality directing ships to the cashier's office where tolls are paid!

Proceeding southwards the canal first traverses about twenty-five miles in Lake Menzala, between the artificial dykes formed from the sand excavated when the channel was being dredged. At the 28th mile we reach El Quantara on the eastern shore, which is the terminus of the railway from Palestine. It crosses the canal by a ferry, for The Company has

106

always been averse to the construction of a bridge, and after the Armistice it even demolished the temporary bridges built by the British military authorities.

Then, after passing the ridge of El Gisr the canal enters Lake Timsâh at the 47th mile. The administrative headquarters are situated in the town of Ismailiya on this lake. Here also is the outlet of the fresh water canal, which has travelled from the Nile along the old depression of Wady Tumilat. Between Lake Timsâh and the Great Bitter Lake the canal crosses the ridge of Serapeum at the 57th mile, a little to the south of Tussûm. At Deversoir it finally opens out into the Great Bitter Lake. There are two of these lakes, the Great and the Little Bitter Lake, and together they are about twenty miles in length and have a maximum width of seven miles. The canal course runs through both of them until it reaches Geneffa at the 84th mile. Then cutting through the ridge of Shalûf it goes for seventeen miles in a straight line until it finally reaches Port Tewfik where it enters the Gulf of Suez.

During construction no serious technical difficulties were encountered. The three principal ridges — at El Gisr, Serapeum and Shaluf — are respectively only 50 feet, 37 feet, and 23 feet, above sea level. The whole area is flat and sandy, and Nature herself seems to have indicated which depressions to use. The contrast is striking between this and the great trench 260 feet deep that had to be cut through solid and treacherous rocks at Culebra.

In 1869 the width at the bottom of the canal was 72 feet, but it is now 200 feet and in several places 250 feet. It is never less than 270 feet at its thirteen curves. At the surface it is between 400 and 500 feet wide. Since 1935 the old passing points or 'garages' have been suppressed, for ships can now pass each other anywhere and get out of each other's way.

The initial depth was 27 feet, but to-day it is 42 feet for
the greater part of the canal, and about 40 feet in the rest.
Vessels drawing up to 34 feet are allowed, which gives a
6 foot margin. A certain margin is necessary, because when
a ship travels at more than a certain speed it settles down
deeper into the water. As a matter of practice the canal will
admit all ships that are not over 34 feet in draught, 860 feet
long and 97 feet broad. This is an important point that
must be considered well in advance by maritime architects.

The maintenance of the auxiliary equipment which the
canal itself has necessitated has created a colony out in the
desert. We must first of all consider the two termini at Port
Said and Port Tewfik, both of which were constructed from
zero. Port Tewfik has been built on an artificial mole
opposite the town of Suez, but on the Mediterranean shore
when de Lesseps arrived, there was nothing but space and
silence — less than nothing indeed, for on the lagoons of
Lake Menzala navigating and building were equally awk-
ward. The difficulty of establishing a port at such a spot had
frightened Paulin Talabot and Le Père, and was one of the
reasons that discouraged them from advocating a direct route
for the canal. De Lesseps, being more courageous, was not
deterred by this objection, and so Port Said was born.

There is, however, one difficulty, which even to-day has
not been overcome, and that is the perpetual deposit of
alluvial silt brought by a current coming out of the delta.
To oppose a barrier to this current and protect the entrance
to the canal, a mole has been built which juts out perpendicu-
larly into the sea, but as the silt continues to fill up beyond
it the mole is always being lengthened. This jetty, which is
not a breakwater as one is inclined to think, now extends for
over three miles and beyond that below the water level for
another mile and a half. At Ismailiya, the administrative

centre of the canal, de Lesseps hoped to establish a great entrepôt centre or warehouse, for which he foresaw much commercial activity; this, as we shall see, has never been developed.

The equipment on the isthmus also includes the fresh water canal, which is navigable for Nile barges as far as Ismailiya, and semi-navigable on the two forks which go towards Port Said and Suez. A railway joins Port Said to Cairo, passing via Ismailiya, and there is a direct line from Cairo to Suez, but up to the last war there were no roads. About three or four hours are required to go by launch from Ismailiya to Port Said, and about the same time from Ismailiya to Suez. A fine roadway, which was begun during the war by the British Army, now links up the two seas, and along this, one can go from Ismailiya to Port Said by car in an hour and a quarter, and from Ismailiya to Suez in an hour and a half. Here, as elsewhere, distances have been overcome.

Port Said and its suburb, Port Fuad, on the other side of the canal, together have 130,000 inhabitants. Ismailiya, with its 40,000 inhabitants, is one of those charming colonial establishments such as one finds in British India. Suez, Port Tewfik and Port Ibrahim together form a group with a population of about 53,000 souls. Ferdinand de Lesseps has thus brought life and activity to a district which before his time was one of the emptiest stretches of desert in the world.

III

The chief function of the canal is to assure the passage of ships from one sea to the other, with the regularity of trains on a railway. Thus the way in which transit is organized is of great importance, both as regards pilotage and also the general supervision of the traffic.

Ships passing through the canal are guided by the 110 pilots on The Company's staff. One-third are French, one-third English, and one-third belong to various other nationalities such as Greeks, Jugoslavs, Italians, and so on. Piloting a ship through the canal is delicate but not really difficult. A ship may be troublesome to steer in a canal if its dimensions are too great, if it is badly designed, if its rudder is too small, if there is a current, and when it is passing another ship. Also as we have said, its draught increases in proportion to its speed. Since an accident might occasion a serious blockage, one can well appreciate that The Company feels the need to maintain a corps of excellent pilots. It has also taken the precaution of drawing up a register of the ships which form its regular clientele. This register gives all sorts of useful information, and above all indicates the ships that are difficult to steer. In some cases a false rudder is affixed, rather like a false nose!

The passage is divided into two sections, and the pilots are changed over at Ismailiya, without, however, forcing the boat to stop. I once made the trip from Lake Timsâh to the Great Bitter Lake on a ship returning to Madagascar. I stood on the bridge of the liner alongside the pilot, the captain, and a representative from the transit office of The Company. My impressions were very clear and quite different from what I had expected. I had thought that navigation would be easy, simple and without complications, but that was by no means the case. Though the bow of the ship always kept in position and followed along a straight line, the stern on the other hand wobbled in the most alarming way. At first I felt sure that we were going to graze the sides of the canal. Then I perceived that the ship corrected itself alone, or almost alone, and that nothing serious happened. The movement had a sort of automatic elasticity.

However, to be a good pilot one needs to be phlegmatic, and be adaptable by instinct — the same as a good chauffeur. The qualities of a successful pilot are many and various, and some men have tried in vain to acquire them. Technique comes with experience and with knowledge of the canal, but the pilot must also have natural ability, a capacity for detail, and above all no nerves. Some, it appears, always suffer from the nervous strain. The pilots too must be diplomats, for certain captains, being supreme on their own ships, are anything but easy to get on with, and the helmsmen are sometimes touchy, sometimes bad, and sometimes sheer brutes. A single false touch at the helm and the ship would land high and dry. Yet accidents are extremely rare, and in any case are less dangerous on these sandbanks than on the rocks at Panama. All things being considered I got the impression that the pilots were giving magnificent service.

Transit problems involve both tactics and strategy. The pilot undoubtedly guides the ship, but he does not direct it. A whole series of problems connected with the general conduct of vessels cannot be settled by the pilots but are decided by the management of the canal. Since 1887 ships have been allowed to proceed not only by day, but also by night, when The Company places its own searchlights on them. This doubles the capacity of the canal. As the first limitation is, of course, speed, it must be strictly controlled. Except in the big lakes, the maximum speed is nine miles an hour, but seven or eight is preferred. The ideal speed would be fast enough for the ship to be steered easily, and yet not so fast as to produce an excessive draught or create waves that might damage the dykes. The second general rule is that two moving ships may not pass each other *en route*, as is done at Panama, except of course on the Bitter Lakes. Since the canal has been enlarged and the old 'garages' or passing points have been done away with, ships can now pass anywhere, but one of them must be moored. It is usually the one with the current against it that waits, for manœuvring with the current astern is more difficult. Every eighty yards on both sides there is a mooring post — actually 3000 in all.

Then, in order to insure rapid and safe transit, there is the more general problem of controlling the passage of each ship, much as the trains on a single-line railway are dispatched. For this purpose a special transit office that plans and orders the movements of every ship, decides which shall moor and where, and which on the contrary shall pass and in what order; it also gives instructions to the pilots. They try to reduce the moorings to a fixed minimum, by organizing the ships in convoys, and also by sending through mail boats and those liable to be dangerous as quickly as possible. Otherwise they try to avoid any arbitrary preference for the rest. There is always the old English legend that the French are specially favoured, but I personally do not believe there is the slightest foundation for this story.

The general staff of the transit department is situated at Ismailiya. It has a central control office which issues its orders through sub-stations spread along the canal. Experience has shown that completely automatic control does not work, for ticklish problems are always occurring which give rise to an infinite variety of combinations. Running the canal is an art requiring great executive skill, and those responsible for the service at Suez seem to carry out their duties with a fine enthusiasm. The time required for a ship to pass through is the result of these many and complex factors, depending on the speed allowed, the moorings, the halts, etc. In 1882, when ships stopped at night, it took 53 hours; in 1938 the average time that a ship spent in the canal zone was only 13 hours 23 minutes, and of this the average time *en route* was only 11 hours 31 minutes.

The maintenance of the high level of our civilization demands that services of this kind shall be carried out to perfection. One feels that the Suez Canal Company is succeeding in this respect.

CHAPTER IX

THE CANAL AND WORLD COMMUNICATIONS

I

THE discovery of the route around the Cape of Good Hope by Vasco da Gama meant an immense step forward, particularly as the ancient road across the isthmus was so difficult, uncertain and dangerous. From then on until 1840 the Cape route was the regular and only practical one.

We must think back to the stage that navigation had reached at the time when Ferdinand de Lesseps obtained his concession to build the canal. Sailing ships still accounted for almost the entire merchant marine, for in 1846 out of 11,128 ships only 102 or 0.9 per cent were steamers, and by 1855, when there were 391, the proportion had only increased to 3.5 per cent. Moreover these steamers were really composite vessels, having both paddle wheels and sails, as steam was still considered an auxiliary. In 1829 the P. & O. ship *Hugh Lindsay* could take only one passenger, for all other available space was filled with coal.

The trip around the Cape in those days must have seemed interminable, for in 1840 it required 120 to 150 days to sail from London to Bombay. Even in 1860 a Dutch commission that was preparing a report on the Suez Canal project estimated that a voyage in a sailing ship from Marseilles to Ceylon would take 109 days. The first steamships did not go much faster, for in 1826 an auxiliary vessel belonging to the P. & O. Company required 113 days to go from London to Bomaby. In 1842 the *Hindustan* of the same line took 91 days and made twenty-eight calls between Southampton and Calcutta, and yet this voyage was considered rapid. The Dutch commission found that an auxiliary steamer would require 81 days to go from Marseilles to Ceylon.

In view of such discouraging slowness, there was naturally a great temptation to cut the trip short by going via Suez, even at the additional cost of transhipment. The rapid progress made by Egypt under Mehemet Ali allowed this solution to be taken seriously, and indeed after 1830 it became the order of the day. The hero of this affair was an ex-Indian Army officer named Waghorn, who was rather like Jules Verne's character Phileas Fogg. He made a great effort to carry the dispatches to India quicker by the overland route than could be done by the traditional mail boats around the Cape. When he succeeded in doing so in 1835, it was considered a great achievement. Then he organized a private company for the rapid transportation of letters, which had to be addressed 'c/o Mr. Waghorn, Marseilles'. This courier was dispatched either by Suez or by Kosseir, and in a way it was a forerunner of the modern travel bureau.

With Waghorn's help the P. & O. started in 1840 to organize a service for passengers travelling from Southampton to Bombay via Egypt. The transhipment conditions were unbelievable. The passengers went from Alexandria to Rosetta in eight or ten hours by canal in a rowing barge called a *dahabiah*, then from Rosetta to Cairo up the Nile in sixteen hours for the first stage. After twelve hours' wait at Cairo, where Shepheard's Hotel had just been built (and with a bath!), they set out for Suez across ninety miles of desert. They rode in a two-wheeled omnibus which took another eighteen hours *en route*, plus twelve hours' delay at intermediate halting points. So the whole trip took about seventy hours, and at the end of it each traveller was given a teacup of Nile water — not to drink, for that would have been suicidal — but to wash with. Surrounded by thousands of mosquitoes, they quenched their thirst with luke-warm beer, for there was no ice. Meanwhile the luggage arrived as best it could on baggage camels.

Such transhipment was a great adventure, but it was considerably improved when a railway was built in 1854. My father, Jules Siegfried, went to India in 1862 to found a cotton exporting firm, and in his diary he gives the following description of his trip across Egypt:

'After having passed several days at Marseilles, I embarked on December 5th (1862), on the S.S. *Valetta* belonging to the P. & O. Company. The *Valetta* was a little ship of only 800 tons, and presently she danced around so skittishly that our trip was anything but pleasant. After six days of very rough sea, broken by a short stay at Malta, we finally saw the lighthouse at Alexandria loom up. Not long afterwards we dropped anchor as close to the shore as possible.

'We disembarked at eleven o'clock in the morning, and were supposed to leave for Cairo at four o'clock the same afternoon, for with P. & O. tickets no time is lost anywhere . . . At four o'clock I was at the station, where a train had just come in from Cairo. The result was unbelievable confusion. Until one has actually seen these foreign races rushing around in every direction, scurrying to the right and left, talking and screaming all at once, everybody replying without listening to the question, one can have no idea what confusion means. All the coaches were bursting with humanity, and instead of sitting on the seats the Arabs squatted on them, smoking their pipes and chattering. They wore the most varied of costumes. After much shouting and gesticulating, we managed to get into the train.

'The darkness unfortunately concealed most of the countryside from us. At one of the many stations where we stopped, they announced that there would be a halt of half an hour, and that dinner would be served at the expense of the P. & O. Company. Everyone rushed to get this free meal, rather fearing, however, that as it was not being paid for it would not amount to much. As a matter of fact in a neighbouring hall we found a superb repast set out for us. I made inquiries from an attendant who replied, "Sir, only the gentry dine here. The first service is for the English — but you know what barbarians they are when it comes to cooking!" Finally at about midnight we arrived at Cairo, and left it at nine next morning for Suez.

'Immediately on leaving Cairo one enters the desert, and does not leave it again until Suez is reached. Though it produces a feeling of desolation the desert has a certain amount of interest at first ... There is not the slightest vegetation, nothing but fine sand and shingle, scorched by the sun. It is extremely unpleasant to cross the desert, for whenever a strong wind blows, the fine sand penetrates everywhere, and irritates the eyes and throat. The glare also made me suffer cruelly. Everything is tinted a fiery red ... at first you admire it but it soon begins to pall.

'From time to time I saw in the far distance a caravan of camels marching one behind the other, and could distinguish the drivers crouched on the camel's backs with their legs crossed on the animals necks. Happily for us the time required to cross the desert was not long, and soon we reached the Red Sea with its beautiful clear water — not, however, before mirages had several times deceived us into thinking that we had finally arrived.

'*En route* I was soon aware of the corruption which exists among the employees of the railway, and also of the pitiful state of its administration. Half the travellers did not have any tickets, but gave a bribe to the conductor who pocketed it with the best will in the world. I met one fellow who was in the habit of going twice a month from Cairo to Suez, and he had not bought a ticket for several years!

'After we had passed a few hours at Suez in a good hotel of the European style, a little tender came to take us on board the *Yeddo*, the steamer which was to conduct us to Bombay. This proved to be a magnificent ship, one of the finest in the company's service. It was built entirely of iron, and the cabins were large and comfortable. It was very steady and made splendid progress. It had 460 horse power engines and propellers, and its total tonnage was 1600 tons.'

Being very methodical my father gives in his diary the exact time spent on the trip. He left Marseilles on December 5th, arrived at Alexandria on the 11th, and after taking two days to cross the isthmus was able to leave Suez on the 13th, and so arrive at Bombay on the 25th, the journey taking twenty days in all.

Ten years later, in 1872, the record trip of Phileas Fogg shows us what new possibilities had resulted from the opening of the canal in 1869. Though the book *Around the World in Eighty Days* is pure fiction, there is no doubt that Jules Verne had collected his facts with great care. Here then is the time-table of the phlegmatic hero: He left London on October 2nd at 8.45 p.m., and travelling via Paris and Brindisi arrived at Suez on the 9th at eleven in the morning, after having passed through the canal. He left Suez on the same day at 6.30 p.m., and passing by Aden arrived at Bombay on October 20th. The trip had thus required eighteen days, and was a record.

According to the *Morning Chronicle* of about this date it required twenty days to do the trip, seven days from London to Suez and thirteen from Suez to Bombay. Phileas Fogg, however, thanks to his famous 'handful of bank notes', was able to do the latter half of the trip in eleven. Since then progress has been important though not sensational (if we except aviation). By 1887 the length of the voyage had been reduced to sixteen and a half days. In 1900 I myself, travelling P. & O., required exactly fifteen days from Bombay to Marseilles, and nowadays the trip is done in twelve days in ships of 15,000 and 23,000 tons. This fairly eclipses the 1600 tons of the *Yeddo*, that 'magnificent ship, one of the finest in the company's service'.

From these comparisons we see that very little is gained by going through the canal as compared with the previous overland route — at least if we consider nothing but time and speed, and that only for passengers. So from this point of view the problem of the route to India by the Red Sea had already been solved before 1869. The chief advantage of the canal lay in doing away with the cost of transhipment. This fact, together with the saving in time, caused the complete displacement of the Cape route. We realize to-day that a stupendous change in the trade routes has resulted from the canal, but when Ferdinand de Lesseps began his work it was not at all certain that such would be the case, for there was considerable doubt as to whether the navigation of that period was capable of using the new route. The success of the canal has been the answer.

When we examine the length of the principal voyages we find that the canal route has a decided advantage over the Cape, though of course this advantage varies and in some cases is not very great, as the following table shows:

From Liverpool	Via The Cape	Via Suez	Percentage gain
To Bombay (maximum advantage)	10,680	6,223	42
To Yokohama (fairly good)	14,436	11,113	23
To Melbourne (minimum advantage)	11,890	11,018	8

India thus gains more in proportion than the Far East, which in its turn gains more than Australia. In the same way at the other end it is the Mediterranean countries which enjoy the greatest reductions. From Constantinople to Bombay there is a reduction of 70 per cent in distance, from Genoa to Bombay 58 per cent, but only 42 per cent from Liverpool to Bombay. Thus at first sight south-eastern Europe seems to have benefited greatly from the canal, and at the expense of western and Oceanic Europe. Such we remember was the way the Venetians reasoned at the beginning of the sixteenth century. Experience has proved that they were wrong, but that is because many factors other than distance have come into play.

For example, when Ferdinand de Lesseps was first planning his great work, steam power was only just beginning, and its future was by no means assured. Now, would the canal have been successful if there had been nothing but sailing ships to use it? At a meeting of the Havre Chamber of Commerce on October 1st, 1858, the contrary opinion was expressed. They gave as their view that precious and valuable merchandise such as gold and silver, silk and indigo, could afford to use steamers between India and Europe, but such articles constituted only a small proportion of the traffic, the greater part being made up of bulky and low-value merchandise like wood, rice, sugar, coffee, etc., which could be transported only by sail. Now it is difficult to navigate sailing ships in the Red Sea owing to the prevalence of both adverse winds and flat calms. This was proved by the fact that marine insurance by the Cape route ranged from $1\frac{1}{4}$ per cent to 3 per cent, while by Suez it went as high as 10 per cent or even 18 per cent. In spite of its praise of M. de Lesseps, one felt that Havre was fundamentally hostile, no doubt fearing that the canal might favour the rival French ports of the Mediterranean.

An opinion which was current at this time was that though it would be quite feasible to construct the canal, it would never pay, because sailing ships would hesitate to use it. Such views were common right up to the time of the canal's opening, and were shared by my father, for in 1864, after having made several trips to India, he wrote in his diary, 'I believe that it is quite possible to build the canal, but I do fear that it will hardly become useful. When I see by M. de Lesseps' calculations that he is counting on three million tons of freight annually, paying ten francs a ton, or in other words a revenue of thirty million francs, I say that profits of this sort are very easy to make in theory, but very difficult to obtain in practice, at any rate until we have discovered some motif power other than the steam engine. No sailing ships from India or China will pass through the canal coming to England, and that means that only steamers and a few ships from the Mediterranean will take this route'.

Now for the views of the sailors whom my father met at this time. 'The captain and the first mate of our ship do not believe that the Suez Canal can be constructed, at least not for ships of large tonnage. They maintain that even if the isthmus is open to big ships, the Red Sea will always be an immense impediment to navigation by sail because of the feeble winds. Out of five ships, they told me, two will never arrive, and the sailing boat captains who have once succeeded in making the voyage will never want to undertake it again, in spite of the enormously high freight-rates that may be offered for this route. Therefore they will continue to prefer rounding the Cape, for though this course may be slow, at least it has the advantage of being cheap and easy. For steamers the Red Sea is excellent, but then transport by steam is still much too expensive.'

The author of this diary, I should emphasize, was a man of progress, exceptionally daring and full of initiative, and yet he did not believe in the canal! And possibly he might have been right, had navigation continued to depend on the sail. It was a providential chance that steamships had just begun to develop seriously at the time that this great enterprise was about to be exploited. To-day sailing ships amount to only 1.53 per cent of the world's fleet — but could de Lesseps have foreseen this? No, fate undoubtedly had a share in his achievement.

II

The financial success of the canal also depended on the establishment of a fair tariff. If it had been too high it would have discouraged traffic, but if too low the share capital would not have been sufficiently remunerated. Experience was soon to prove that in the matter of fixing the tolls The Company would have to consider very seriously the interests of the users of the canal, for they were likely to be backed up by their governments.

Article 17 of the Concession permits a maximum tax of ten francs a ton of 'tonnage of capacity' and ten francs per passenger but does not go into details; as the definitions of tonnage were numerous and varied some interpretation had to be given. In 1868 The Company set up a commission to study the different measures of tonnage commonly employed at the time. This commission recommended adopting the tonnage shown on the ship's papers, without making any distinction for nationality. After the canal was opened The Company decided to apply a system of gross tonnage, such as was used in England, for this was to their advantage as it considerably increased the tolls. The British and French

Governments acquiesced, but the shipowners protested and the Messageries Maritimes started a law suit.

Ferdinand de Lesseps appealed to the Khedive who referred him to the Porte, and the latter proposed convening an international conference to decide the question. This was the Conference of Constantinople of 1873, and as it was under the influence of the shipowners, it decided in favour of nett tonnage modified by certain deductions in accordance with a set of rules known as the Moorson System. Since this method had a very unfavourable effect on the tolls, the conference authorized the canal to recoup itself by adding a surtax of four, and in certain cases of three francs per ton. This surtax was to be decreased as the traffic through the canal increased. The decision was given to Ferdinand de Lesseps as a direct command. He protested, then negotiated, but refused to submit. In 1874 the Turkish Government finally imposed the decision of the conference, but only after sending a force of 10,000 soldiers to the isthmus.

This method of calculating the tolls is still in force. The tax is levied on nett tonnage, as defined by the rules drawn up by the International Conference of Constantinople. Before a ship goes through the Suez Canal a special certificate, giving these rules in detail, will be delivered to any captain asking for it by his own national authorities attached to the transit office of the canal.

Thus such incidents brought to light the peculiar characteristics of this enterprise within less than five years of its inauguration. It could not be administered privately like any other company, because it affected interests — commercial, political, and international — which were more important than the rights of its shareholders. The complexity of the situation increased when the British Government itself became a shareholder in 1875, and seven years later when the British military occupation of Egypt took place matters were still further complicated.

If, in face of all this, Ferdinand de Lesseps had tried to insist on the letter of the law and to demand the rights to which he was entitled according to the terms of the concession and the by-laws of The Company, he probably would have been crushed by opposition from England. However, he showed his wisdom by always negotiating and by realizing that in such cases rights, even when incontestable, are worthless if the Powers refuse to acquiesce. This observation is as true to-day as it was yesterday. Since 1935 the tolls have been calculated in Egyptian pounds expressed on a gold basis. The present tariff, which was issued on December 15th, 1938, is 5s. 9d. per ton for loaded vessels and 2s. 10½d. for those in ballast, and 5s. 9d. for passengers, whether civil or military. In 1874, just after the conference of Constantinople, the tolls were ten francs a ton plus three francs surtax. Ever since then the tendency has been to revise the tariff downwards and the present rate of 5s. 9d. was equivalent to 4.08 gold francs per ton at the time when the tariff was fixed on the eve of the present war.

Fixing the tariff is a delicate task so far as The Company is concerned. The shareholders have the right to demand that their capital be adequately remunerated, for they took the risk when success was by no means assured. One might even say that the guarantee of efficient management depends on these profits. On the other hand the canal might lose its clientele if the latter felt they were being held up to ransom, especially as, contrary to general belief, the canal is not a monopoly. Excessive tolls, especially during troublous times when marine insurance is dear, would quickly divert part of the traffic around by the Cape.

Again, one must not forget that The Company is subjected to the constant jealous supervision of the British shippers who for years provided three-quarters, and still provide over half, the tonnage passing through the canal. Although relations with the Government in London are good, British public opinion at heart is jealous, for this French enterprise works on behalf of its shareholders, the majority of whom are French, and causes the British Merchant Marine to pay tribute. Every now and again certain Englishmen protest against the dues, which they declare are strangling British shipping for the benefit of the canal shareholders. They point out that British exporters to the countries on the Red Sea and the Indian Ocean are being handicapped in competition with the Japanese who do not have to pay the canal tolls. Such complaints are loudest whenever freight rates are low, or when, during periods of depression, the canal dues weigh heavily on the half-empty ships. Italy's protests have been of a more political nature, for since establishing herself in Abyssinia she has sent whole armies through the canal, and has been obliged to pay the ordinary passenger rate for every soldier.

The Company has had to display great judgment in determining how far it was wise to resist such demands for lower tariffs. It could not ignore them completely, and that is why, since the historic quarrel of 1873, it has never pushed matters to extremes. It is natural for the user to protest, but I as a Frenchman cannot see that there is anything to get indignant about if the country which built the canal should make money out of it. After all, as the years pass and the end of the concession approaches, the interests of the shareholders diminish in comparison with those of Egypt. Thus it is the Egyptians who are beginning to put up a vigorous resistance against any further lowering of the tariff.

CHAPTER X

THE TRAFFIC THROUGH
THE CANAL

I

IN the memoir which he submitted to Mohammed Said on November 15th, 1854, when they were in camp together at Macarius out in the Libyan Desert, Ferdinand de Lesseps estimated in the following way what the traffic through the canal would probably be:

'The Pilgrimage to Mecca will become easy for Musulmans at all seasons. The canal will give an immense impulse to steam navigation, and also to long distance voyages. The Mediterranean and northern Europe will be brought more than 3000 leagues nearer to the countries bordering on the Red Sea and the Persian Gulf, as well as to the east coast of Africa, India, the Kingdom of Siam, Cochin China, Japan, the vast Chinese Empire which alone has over 300,000,000 inhabitants, the Philippine Islands, Australia, and that immense archipelago towards which emigration from old Europe is already beginning to take place. Such are the sudden and immediate results that would come from cutting through the Isthmus of Suez.

'It has been calculated that navigation from Europe and America around the Cape of Good Hope and Cape Horn annually accounts for about six million tons of shipping, and that on only half of this, the commerce of the world would realize an extra profit of about 150 million francs a year if ships could pass through the Arabian Gulf. That is a large amount of shipping, but let us count only on three million tons, though without doubt the Suez Canal will give

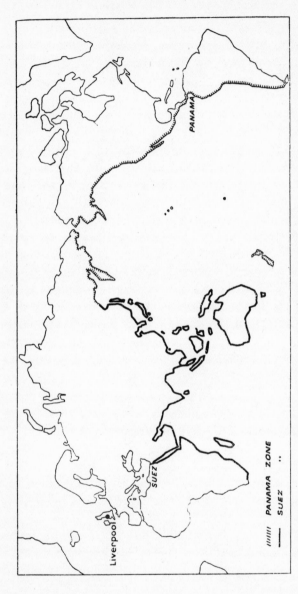

The respective zones of the Suez and Panama Canals, based on traffic to and from Liverpool. (Reproduced from 'Le Canal de Panama', a report issued by George-Edgar Bonnet and Louis Lucas)

rise to a great increase. So we will obtain an annual income of about 30 million francs if we levy a toll of 10 francs per ton. As navigation increases we should be able to reduce this toll.'

Later on in 1867, de Lesseps increased his estimate to six million tons a year, for the outlook had improved with the rapid progress being made in steam navigation. Perhaps also he felt obliged to predict a greater volume of business in order to encourage his shareholders, since total expenses had been heavier than he had foreseen. Be that as it may, these prophecies appear very modest when we see that in 1937 the traffic through the canal reached the figure of 36,491,332 tons. His predictions were 'conservative', as the English would say, and no one can accuse de Lesseps of having drawn too rosy a picture of the future.

On page 129 we give a graph of the nett tonnage through the canal. This indicates the activity of navigation as a whole, and at the same time reflects the prosperity of the canal, for the tolls are reckoned on this basis. It also enables us to see at a glance the economic history both of the whole world and of the canal. The following table is a resumé of the statistics that indicate the various stages:

	Tons[1]
1870	436,609
1879	2,263,332
1908	13,633,283
1912	20,275,120
1914	19,409,495
1917	8,368,918
1919	16,013,862
1929	33,466,014
1932	28,340,290
1937	36,491,332
1938	34,418,187

[1] Figures obtained from the Bulletin of the Compagnie Universelle du Canal Maritime de Suez.

Here we have a splendid temperature chart of the planet, and from it we can draw several interesting conclusions. First of all the year 1879 was of historic importance, for it marked the beginning of an immensely important development in inter-continental relations. It was then that large quantities of non-European products began to reach the Old Continent, which also for the first time began to feel the shock of this new competition. The prosperity of Europe was to continue for another thirty years, but this stage marks the end of her triumphant nineteenth century.

In this graph we can also see the effect that the three great economic crises of our time have had on world traffic. The first, from 1890 to 1896, was masked and long, being connected with the declining tide of world prices. Its effect on the canal was to create a sort of marking time. The second,

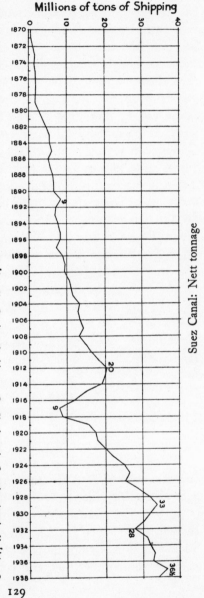

Millions of tons of Shipping

Suez Canal: Nett tonnage

129

caused by the war, produced a decided shrinkage in traffic. The third came with the brutal crash of 1929, and by 1932 had reached the bottom of a significant depression; since then convalescence has definitely set in. We should note that these sudden blows do not in the long run prevent steady progress, for every time traffic has recovered to a point higher than that from which it fell. In comparison with the past, the figures for 1937 are an all-time record.

A graph giving the number of passengers would be less significant, because military traffic at times predominates. Yet it is interesting to follow the constant progress that has taken place since the opening of the canal. It started with 26,758 passengers in 1870, and by 1937 had reached the record figure of 697,800. During the ten-year period 1900-1910 the average annual number was 242,000 passengers, and during 1910-1920 it increased to 298,000, falling again to 262,000 in the decade 1920-1930. Finally, from 1931 to 1938 the figure has climbed again to 454,000.

Obviously the figures increase during years of great troop movements, as for example during the Great War and the Italian expedition to Abyssinia.

Year	Passengers
1919	527,500
1935	625,465
1936	781,929
1937	697,800

When we break down the 1937 statistics, we find that out of a total of 697,800 passengers, 365,790 were soldiers and 332,010 civilians. Out of the 365,790 soldiers no fewer than 300,079 were Italians, while there were only 48,270 British, and 16,219 French. In the matter of passengers, the Suez Canal is struggling, as we shall see later, with direct and efficient competition, and yet we may conclude that there is no likelihood of its being abandoned by passenger traffic.

The canal has become — or has 're-become' — the main route from Europe to the East. No competition and no circumstances can seriously divert this current of men and goods, for the traffic evidently is based on a natural necessity. When in 1854 Ferdinand de Lesseps foresaw three million tons of shipping, he kept his figure much below what later was to become a reality, and yet this three million level was not reached until 1880.

This explains the singularly precarious position of The Company's finances at its inception. When the canal was opened the costs of construction had already reached 432 million francs, and the president was forced, arbitrarily it must be admitted, to increase his estimate to the six million ton level. At that time eleven million tons were passing around the Cape, he said, and it was necessary only to attract half of it, and yet they had to wait until 1888 before they realized this six million.

The delay was not without risk, for The Company was being attacked by hostile speculators. In 1872, when a bond issue failed, the Board of Directors considered liquidation, although the canal was functioning well technically, and economic victory seemed to be in sight. Lebaudy saved the day by means of a generous credit, but immediately afterwards the Conference of Constantinople had to authorize a surtax, as we have already said. It was only little by little that the traffic increased, became established, and afforded a guarantee of durable and eventual success. The jealous nation that has profited so much from this enterprise, after refusing to collaborate in its creation, will do well to remember these early beginnings. The risks of these first years are a fine illustration of what private capital must overcome when it initiates new ventures.

The curve giving the number of ships passing through the canal is a good measure of its activity, and follows more or less the curve of nett tonnage. In 1870 only 486 ships passed through the canal, a striking contrast with the record figures of 6,635 and 6,171 attained in 1937 and 1938. On this curve we can observe the effects of the same vicissitudes that influenced the other curves we have discussed. We must not forget, also, that the average size of the ships has tended steadily to increase.

Year	Average Tonnage of Ships
1890	2,877
1910	5,086
1920	6,047
1930	7,628
1938	7,747

Since the post-war recovery, that is since about 1924, the size of ship that has passed most frequently through the canal is 7000 to 8000 tons. Actually vessels of between 4000 and 10,000 tons gross accounted for 77 per cent of the total, but those of more than 20,000 tons did not even amount to 2 per cent. The biggest ship that has ever gone through the canal is the *Empress of Britain*, 42,745 tons. Monster tonnages such as one finds in the North Atlantic are not in their proper setting here. The Suez is not a route for record-making, but for practical every-day transport.

It is rather interesting to classify the ships by their motive power. Sailing ships originally were the rule, but they have disappeared to-day even from the statistics of the canal, and now coal-burners in their turn are meeting with competition. Oil-burners appeared in 1908 and motor-ships in 1912. In

1931 for the first time oil-burners and motor-ships combined exceeded coal-burners. In 1938 the different methods of propulsion were as follows:

	Suez Canal
	per cent
Coal-burners	40.9
Oil-burners	27.8
Motor-ships	31.3
	100.0

In the total of the world's mercantile marine the proportions are approximately the same, although in the Panama Canal oil plays a much more important role:

	World Totals
Sail	5.1
Coal-burners }	
Oil-burners }	72.6
Motor-ships	22.3
	100.0

The last quarter of a century has brought many changes in the design of ships, and when I think back to

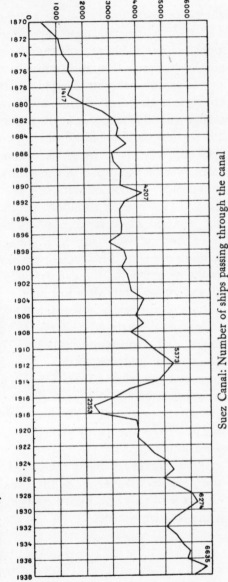

Suez Canal: Number of ships passing through the canal

the types that I used to see at Havre in my childhood about
1880, I seem to recall an entirely different and infinitely remote
world. Even in those days there were paddle boats with tall
smoke-stacks as thin as cigarettes, and in addition to steam
power there were complicated masts and rigging and spars
covered with sails. Modern ships have funnels only by
courtesy, and their masts, now purely symbolical, are erected
chiefly for the benefit of their wireless aerials. I cannot
accustom myself to these new forms. Just as the Chinese
paint eyes on the prows of their junks to enable them to see,
so I really cannot imagine motive power without smoke-
stacks. However, for modern youth speed is symbolized by
the pedal on which he presses his foot.

Tankers account for 18.6 per cent of the total traffic
through Suez, so this special type of ship has provided a new
source of profit for the canal. Sails now scarcely appear at
all, except for a few slow but poetic dhows, whose enormous
masts and top-heavy sails catch the lightest breeze and seem
to remain unchanged in form throughout the ages. Ferdinand de Lesseps would certainly be amazed if he could see
his company's clients to-day. Yet, by comparison with the
ships of 1832 when he was Consul at Alexandria, those that
he saw in 1880 had already undergone an even more
astonishing revolution for they had passed from sails to
steam. It was this revolution that really assured the success
of the canal.

If we divide up the tonnage according to flag, we find
considerable changes since the canal's first decade. In the
ten years 1870-1880 the four principal users were classified
in the following order:

	Percentage of Total Nett Tonnage
England	76.1
France	8.3
Holland	4.1
Italy	2.7
	91.2

By 1938 this classification had been considerably modified:

	Percentage
England	50.4
Italy	13.4
Germany	9.1
Holland	8.7
	81.6

France is only fifth with 5 per cent and Norway comes next with 4.3 per cent. Though England's traffic is still to-day by far the largest, in the nineteenth century it was positively overwhelming. Indeed one might almost say that in those days the whole world was an international mercantile republic, operating under Britain's flag and protection. Since then the relative decline of British shipping in the canal has been unabated, except during the military occupation of Egypt and in the Great War, and on both these occasions this decline was only temporarily suspended due to purely military reasons. Britain used to enjoy what was virtually a monopoly, but it was impossible to preserve it once other Powers began to take an active part in international trade.

We must admit, however, that the British merchant fleet could have defended its interests better if its new rivals had played fair. But more often than not the newcomers were assisted by subsidies, for their governments were determined to build up a shipping industry artificially and at all costs, due more to their desire for power than to any natural economic needs. Such applies in particular to Italy's progress, which for some years has been remarkable. Owing to these methods her share in the canal's traffic has been pushed up from 6.3 per cent in 1934, to 18.5 per cent in 1935, and 20 per cent in 1936, though it fell again to 16 per cent in 1937 and 13.4 per cent in 1938. In these figures one easily perceives the repercussions of the Abyssinian War, with its considerable movement of ships and men. This was not normal traffic — if one may use the term 'normal' at all these days.

To explain the reduction in the British percentage, we must take into account the change which has occurred in the balance of world trade now that Europe is no longer the sole centre of gravity. An independent market has grown up in the Far East and the Pacific, where Japan is becoming a dangerous rival for England. Nevertheless, the British proportion of the traffic through the Suez Canal remains unique and unchallenged. In this classification according to flag, Japan in 1938 accounted for only 1.9 per cent and the United States for 1.1 per cent. These figures are significant, for they are not the result of chance. There is a zone of American economic influence, but it does not extend as far as Suez; similarly Japanese influence is centred in the Far East.

England, acting in concert with certain Western countries, is the only nation able to straddle the various continents. She acts as a connecting link, and the traffic which results passes to a large extent through the Suez Canal. In a highly interesting report on British shipping in the Orient, published by the Imperial Shipping Committee in 1939, it is estimated that out of total gross receipts of about £66 millions the British merchant marine drew at least half from its trade with the Far East, Asia, Australia, etc., and half of this in turn came from ships passing either through the Suez Canal or around the Cape. It will be long before any other maritime Power is likely to play such a part in international commerce. Therefore, in a world organized as it is to-day, it is natural that the first place at the canal should be occupied by Britain.

III

The economic sphere served by the Suez Canal is largely dependent upon the inter-relationship of Europe on the one hand with the Indian Ocean, the Far East, and Australia on the other. Suez is a return to the traditional route of the past, and is the most direct and the most practical one now that transhipment is no longer required. However, vast territories lie outside the canal's domain, such as the Atlantic with all the commerce between the Old and the New Worlds, and the Pacific in so far as it forms an autonomous trading centre between America, Asia and Oceania. In part of the territory which it is already serving, the canal also has to meet the competition of two other international highways, the Cape and Panama.

All the eastern coast of Africa south of the Mozambique Channel, for example, belongs to the Cape route. Under certain circumstances the Cape can also compete in the Australian trade. Competition from the Panama Canal is encountered only much farther off, that is to say east of a line drawn from Sydney, Australia, northward to Kamchatka. This applies particularly to ships embarking from Liverpool. The Panama Canal also has a slight advantage for ships leaving New York, and bound for any of the ports

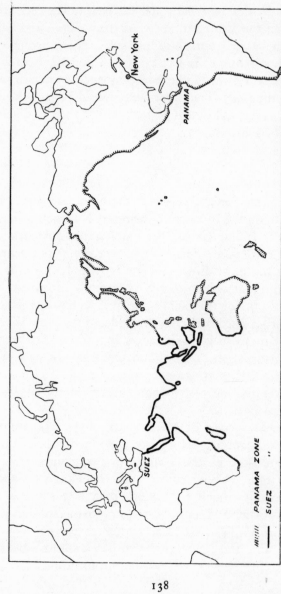

The respective zones of the Suez and Panama Canals, based on traffic to and from New York
(Reproduced from 'Le Canal de Panama', a report issued by Georges Edgar Bonnet and Louis Lucas.)

on the Asiatic side of the Pacific Ocean. Overlooking this limited American competition, the domain of the Suez route embraces the shores of the Indian Ocean, Australia, and the Orient. Its importance derives from the fact that these are the most densely populated areas of the world, where three-quarters of the human race is congregated. From this point of view, cutting through the Isthmus of Suez in 1869 was a world event of the greatest significance, greater even than the opening of the Panama Canal in 1914.

The Suez Canal statistics give us the exact geographical divisions of the nett tonnage. In the following table we have an interesting comparison between the present and the pre-war period:

NETT TONNAGE OF SHIPS TRADING WITH PORTS EAST OF SUEZ

	1913		1938	
	Per cent	Per cent	Per cent	Per cent
With India and the Far East		79.7		61.2
India, Burmah, Ceylon	45.4		25.4	
China, Japan, Philippines, Siberia	22.1		20.4	
Dutch East Indies, Malaya	9.1		10.9	
French Indo-China, Thai (Siam)	3.1		4.5	
With the Near East		7.8		31.1
Persian Gulf	1.4		16.6	
Red Sea and Gulf of Aden	1.3		7.6	
East Africa and the Islands	5.1		6.9	
With Australasia		9.9		6.5
With the American Coasts of the Pacific		2.6		1.2
		100.0		100.0

The relative decline in the traffic with India has been very accentuated and to a lesser degree with China, Japan and Australia, while marked progress has been made on the contrary with the Persian Gulf and the Red Sea. When we examine actual figures as well as relative ones, we find that, thanks to oil, the traffic with the Persian Gulf has increased nineteenfold since before the war, whereas the Red Sea traffic has grown sevenfold owing to the Italian military activity. Traffic with East African ports and the Far East has about doubled, but Australasia has scarcely progressed, due to the competition of the Cape route. There has been a recession in the traffic with India both actual and relative.

Distances cannot vary but a host of other factors, some very changeable, come into play. Tariffs, for example, can divert part of the traffic, and the rate of marine insurance when it is high can make re-routing imperative. The changing nature of the cargoes and whether they are urgent or not must be considered, also the varying attractions of intermediate ports of call on both the canal's itinerary and on the competing routes, the facilities of replenishing coal and fuel oil, the kind of ships employed, etc. All these complex factors, whose repercussions are so difficult to follow, eventually influence the total volume of nett tonnage as well as its geographic distribution.

Here we have the temperature chart of international trade, showing its depressions and its fevers — in a word its state of health. But our study is not complete if we do not go farther and examine in detail the nature of the goods that are being carried through the canal.

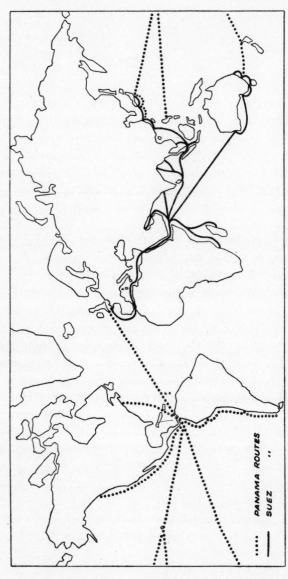

PANAMA ROUTES

SUEZ   ,,

Sketch map showing the principal maritime routes served by the Suez and Panama Canals

CHAPTER XI

TRADE THROUGH THE CANAL

I

THE total volume of merchandise that passed through the
Suez Canal in 1938 amounted to 28,779,000 tons weight,
and in 1910 to 22,435,000 tons. (Unfortunately earlier
figures are not available.) We must distinguish clearly between these tons which record the actual weight of the
cargoes, and nett tonnages which is used as a measure of
shipping.

The volume for 1938 was not a record, for higher levels
had been attained in the past, but the interesting point to
note in the curves on pages 129, 133 and 143 is that in their
essentials they are the same for volume of goods, for nett
tonnage, and for the number of ships using the canal. This
shows that the life of the canal is a unit, and that it corresponds to world economic fluctuations. It is impossible to
imagine the canal prospering during a depression, because
shipping cannot be active when commerce is anaemic.

Our graph on page 143 gives an exact reflection of the
tides and seasons in economic history. It shows first of all a
steady rise during the pre-war years, and then the catastrophic
fall from 1914 to 1917, when about three-quarters of the
traffic was lost. The actual figures were 25,775,000 tons in
1913 and 6,775,000 in 1917. The recovery that now set in
was almost as rapid as the fall, and by 1925 the former level
had been reached and passed. As in everything else, 1929
marked the peak with its 34,516,000 tons. It was immediately
followed by a drop of about a third, being the direct effect of
the 1929 crash. The bottom was reached in 1932, and since

then there has been undoubted recuperation, although in fits and starts. Still, it is obvious that in comparison with the pre-war period there has been no decline. When we reflect on the number of states that are trying to develop an autarchic or self-sufficient economy, and so are trying to divide the

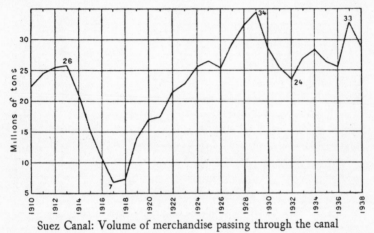

Suez Canal: Volume of merchandise passing through the canal

world up into compartments, and also on the modern tendency to manufacture raw materials on the spot, we really must congratulate ourselves on the astonishing amount of international trade that has survived. Nevertheless, if the war of 1914 had never taken place and if the conditions prevailing in the nineteenth century could have continued, world trade would have been very much more active. So I fear we must conclude that this graph is not as optimistic as appears at first sight.

The difference between the northbound and southbound traffic through the canal enables us to examine the nature of the trade that is taking place. The southbound current is always lighter in weight, and averages about 30 per cent to 35 per cent of the total traffic. This proportion is always lower during an economic depression — only 19 per cent in 1917 and 26 per cent in 1932 — whereas prosperity has the opposite effect — 43 per cent in 1913 and 37 per cent in 1929. The types of cargo naturally explain this disparity, for we are now considering weight only and not value.

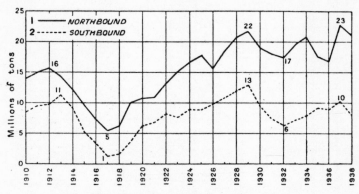

Suez Canal: Northbound and southbound traffic

Europe exports chiefly manufactured articles, which are expensive and relatively light, whilst she imports heavy raw materials. The complementary character of most of this trade is evident, though of course there are some exceptions. One can understand how the Old World is apt to see its exports fall away during a depression, whereas its imports, which represent more or less constant needs, do not shrink in the same proportion. Once recovery sets in the relation of exports to imports quickly rises again, partly because the latter, having shrunk less, do not expand so fast. (See graph on this page.)

The principal headings under which the southbound traffic could be classified in 1938 are quite different from those of 1913:

SOUTHBOUND TRAFFIC THROUGH THE SUEZ CANAL

1938	Per cent
Metals, machinery, railway equipment	28.3
Fertilizer	8.4
Cement	7.2
Wood pulp	5.0
Salt	4.5
Oil	3.6
Beverages	3.6
Chemical products	3.0
Coal	2.6
Timber	2.0
Sugar	1.9
Textiles	1.6
	71.7

1913	
Metals, machinery, railway equipment	25.5
Coal	10.5
Oil	4.5
Salt	3.9
Cement	3.8
Sugar	1.6
Fertilizer	0.5
	50.3

Though in both cases metallurgical exports stand at the top of the list and their percentage has even increased, the next two headings under 1913 have ceased to play so important a role. Coal has fallen from 1,190,000 to 208,000 tons, although by the end of each period of prosperity — for example in 1929 and again in 1937 — it will be found that coal shipments through the canal have recovered somewhat. Yet owing to certain fundamental reasons this traffic is drying up. The decline of the steam engine especially on the high seas has reduced the demand for bunker coal at marine coaling stations. Furthermore, shipments of British coal to points beyond the Red Sea are being cut into by the competition of new producing countries such as Australia, South Africa, China, Japan, Indo-China and India. As for oil, undoubtedly it has won the day, but it is in the opposite trade current that its importance is so marked. Fertilizer,

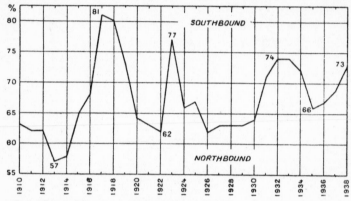

Suez Canal: The proportion of the total traffic accounted for by the Northbound current

cement, wood pulp and salt, have on the contrary made considerable progress, and so have certain other categories which the earlier statistics do not mention, namely beverages, chemical products, wood and textiles.

There is a certain individuality about this southbound current, as the following approximate classification shows:

	1938	Per cent
Foodstuffs		11.3
Raw materials		32.7
Manufactures		33.3
Sundries		22.7
		100.0

As most of the 'sundries' are manufactured goods, we can say that manufactures account for a little more than half, and that the outstanding characteristic of this traffic is to furnish other continents with industrial goods which, for years, Europe alone used to produce. Yet a change is now taking place, for all over the world countries are equipping themselves to manufacture their own current needs. European exports are bound to be hit, although fortunately as new countries industrialize themselves, so they develop new needs for machinery and spare parts, and for cement and other things required in the construction of factories. This is one reason for the stability of the category 'metals, machinery and railway equipment', and for the significant progress made by cement. It is quite likely that in these conditions Europe, together with the United States, can long remain the world's chief producer of capital goods, but perhaps this may be the last phase of the Old World's historic superiority in the heavy industries.

The trade current flowing northwards is entirely different:

NORTHBOUND TRAFFIC THROUGH THE SUEZ CANAL

1938	Per cent
Petroleum	24.8
Vegetable oils	18.6
Cereals	15.0
Foodstuffs	10.8
Ores and metals	7.6
Raw fibres	6.5
Oilcake	3.0
Rubber	2.4
	88.7
1913	
Cereals	27.0
Vegetable oils	18.0
Raw fibres	12.0
Ores and metals	10.0
Petroleum	2.0
	69.0

We see at once that this current is chiefly composed of bulky products, generally in the raw state. The 1938 statistics may be further classified as follows:

1938	Per cent
Foodstuffs	44.4
Raw materials	47.9
Sundries (mostly manufactures)	7.7
	100.0

In a general way this represents natural products, for after all Asia and Australasia are still fundamentally agricultural. In the vegetable oil category we have peanuts, soya beans, copra, linseed oil, colza oil, cottonseed and castor oil. Under cereals we have rice, maize, wheat and barley, while foodstuffs include sugar, tea, coffee, edible oils, tapioca, fruit, butter, vegetables, molasses and chilled meats. As raw fibres we have cotton, wool, sisal and hemp. Ore and metals, which are of secondary importance, represent above all manganese, brass, bauxite, copper, lead, zinc and tin. As for manufactured goods, their role in this traffic is still mediocre, even when we add semi-manufactures. Nevertheless it is increasing. Although industrialization has been rapid in parts of Asia, it has as yet had little effect on the northbound traffic through the isthmus. Thus the complementary nature of the trade between Europe and the other continents still exists almost the same as before.

Nevertheless, a comparison with 1913 indicates certain important changes. The stability of the vegetable oil traffic is striking, and so is the relative unimportance of ores and metals. The progress of petroleum is sensational, having risen from 2 per cent to 24.8 per cent. On the eve of the Great War coal still enjoyed a crushing superiority over oil, and in any case the petroleum industry in the Persian Gulf was only then beginning to be developed. Note also the decline in cereals and raw fibres, for we are here touching on a significant change in the direction of certain trade currents which must not be overlooked.

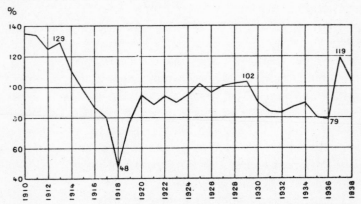

Suez Canal: The relationship between nett tonnage and the volume of goods. (The volume of goods is expressed as a percentage of nett tonnage)

In the nineteenth century Europe's role in world trade might have been likened to both a suction and a force pump. She was still the main buyer; and also the main seller of any and every product. Everything came from her or ended with her, which meant that few direct relationships existed between non-European countries. Since the war much of this trade has been short-circuited.

Owing to their recent industrialization, many countries are now in the market for raw materials and foodstuffs, and accordingly certain trade currents which used to flow towards Europe have been reversed. Also many of these countries are now getting into direct contact with one another, quite independently of the Old Continent.

In the five years 1924-1929 Europe absorbed 83 per cent

of Australia's wool exports, but in the five years 1931-1936 she took only 75 per cent. On the other hand Japan and India are purchasing direct, and now account for 24 per cent instead of 11 per cent. The same thing applies to raw cotton from India. Before the war Europe took 55 per cent, but only 42 per cent in the five years 1927-1932. Here again Japan and China, who previously bought 45 per cent, now take 57 per cent. Thus we have a current which used to flow chiefly towards the west, but which now goes towards the rising sun. Australian wheat furnishes still a third example. Since the post-war period purchases for the Far East — Japan, China, the Dutch East Indies — have increased from 23 per cent to 41 per cent in the period 1932-1936, whereas at the same time Europe's share has declined from 77 per cent to 57 per cent.

These displacements do not necessarily mean a decline in the traffic of the canal, nor yet the economic decadence of Europe, but rather indicate a change in the relationship of the continents themselves, accompanied by a change in the characteristics of their commerce. Many products which formerly passed through the canal now stay in the Indian Ocean or on the Pacific. Yet the total volume of world traffic keeps up, with a stability arising from its very diversity. Each region furnishes products of a certain type. The Near East supplies petroleum, ore and metals, and phosphates; Australia supplies wheat, wool, meat, and ores and metals; India supplies cotton, peanuts, jute, manganese, pig-iron, rice, tea and linseed cake. The Far East supplies soya beans, raw fibres, and even certain manufactured goods; the Dutch East Indies and Indo-China supply rubber, copra, rice, petroleum, etc.

Among these bulky imports there is no trace of the spices, precious stones and all the other costly luxuries which for centuries the West sought from Asia, that fabulous realm of prodigious pomp and alluring fantasy. What we now require are those standard foodstuffs and weighty raw materials which European workshops devour like insatiable ogres. Sir Charles Dilke in his book, *Greater Britain*, coined the mythological term, 'omphalism', to describe the extraordinary ascendancy of this tiny Europe, which has succeeded in swallowing up the whole of the non-European world. The new Hercules has now imposed its own methods and rhythm of work, and has paid in terms of modern comfort which the rest of the world has really never wanted. The system of complementary trade which was born of this collaboration still continues to form the fundamentally healthy basis of the canal's activities.

I I

'Ptolemy's Road' undoubtedly established communications between the two seas, but in actual practice it had much the same economic effect as any other canal in ancient Egypt. The modern canal is entirely different, for it is mainly important as a means of through transit, not as a centre for local distribution. When de Lesseps was trying to reassure Ismail that the new enterprise was not likely to have a dangerous effect, he remarked that all it meant was that Egypt would have one more canal. By minimizing in this way he was simply pretending to misunderstand the true character of the maritime route which he was trying to create, not to re-establish. We do know, however, that when he first studied the matter he thought that the Suez Canal would have certain purely Egyptian activities. He believed that Ismailiya was capable of becoming a great warehouse centre, from which merchandise would be distributed either to the delta via the fresh water canal, or to the neighbouring shores of the Eastern Mediterranean, or even to the countries bordering on the Red Sea. At first sight it seemed as if considerable local trade might be centred on the isthmus, as this corridor was to be the sole passageway between the East and the West.

These expectations have not been confirmed in actual practice. One need only live for a very short while on the banks of the Nile to realize that the Suez Canal pursues its own life far away on the Egyptian borderland. No one contests the fact that it goes through Egyptian territory, but it is easy to see, especially from an aeroplane, that its course, parallel to that of the Nile, is entirely foreign to the life of the delta with which it is connected only by the slender umbilical cord of the fresh water canal.

One can live for weeks in Cairo without ever hearing the canal mentioned . . . We discuss cotton, sugar, the problems of the mortgage bank, finance and politics. At Alexandria we talk cotton, shipping, Mediterranean commerce, and then more cotton. But in the canal zone our interests are neither commercial nor financial, they are purely technical and maritime. We feel much closer to great international movements than to the atmosphere of Egypt itself — in which to tell the truth I found it rather difficult to breathe!

By its very nature the canal traffic is world-wide. One might say that it unites the ends of the earth — Western Europe with the Far East, Australia, India, and so on. There is almost no Egyptian traffic, for most ships pass through without disturbing their cargoes. Like a needle through cloth, they go in one side and come out the other. The proportion of the traffic that requires transhipment does not reach 5 per cent. For example in 1937, out of a total

movement of 32,776,000 tons, the transhipments and re-
distributions of cargo made at Port Said totalled 4,394,000
tons, or about 13 per cent. But when one deducts fuel for
the ships themselves, such as 3,418,000 tons of oil and coal,
there remains only 976,000 tons of general cargo, or about
2.9 per cent. Obviously the isthmus has not become a
warehouse centre.

In this respect it is instructive to compare the different
Egyptian ports with those of the canal. Alexandria is a
great harbour for cotton exports, and also for importing
goods for Egypt's own consumption. Here are carried out
all the commercial, maritime, financial and Stock Exchange
transactions which are connected with the foreign trade of
the country, and particularly with the cotton trade which
gives this town its own special personality. Cairo, on the
contrary, is the distributing centre for merchandise destined
to be consumed in the delta and in Upper Egypt, and therefore it has an entirely different type of trade. As for the re-
exports, they are divided between Alexandria and Port Said,
but their volume is limited. Egypt's former role as half-way
house between the East and the West seems to have died
out.

In the canal zone itself all important transhipments are
made at Port Said, and even there they do not amount to
much, as is evident from the equipment of the harbour.
There are no wharves along which large ships can tie up,
no doubt because they have never been needed. Goods are
of course distributed from Port Said along the Syrian and
Turkish coasts, but in comparison with the total tonnage of
the canal the figures are insignificant, for the eastern
Mediterranean is poverty stricken, and with its low purchasing power can absorb very little.

Merchandise coming from the Indian Ocean or the China

Seas makes straight for the great ports of Western Europe, and it is there and not in Egypt that we find the enormous docks and warehouses situated near the industrial regions, where dense masses of humanity have congregated and where vast capital wealth has been accumulated.

All this means that the canal is international. Egypt can equip Port Said and Suez if she wishes, in the hope of making them centres for her own foreign commerce. Eventually this may be justified, for the new roads now being built between the isthmus and the delta are bound to stimulate traffic. Nevertheless, in spite of such possibilities, Egyptian trade will always be a bagatelle in comparison with the great transit traffic through the canal.

Look at these ships as they pass between the rectilinear walls of sand . . . we are not deceived. These are birds of passage from the high seas; they belong to the great oceans. They never dream of slowing down, and one guesses in advance that they are on their way to China, India or Australia. Then if one stands at Port Tewfik and watches them emerge into the limpid waters of the Red Sea, one feels the *wanderlust*, and longs to follow them to the ends of the earth. No, they would never be tempted to halt at a warehouse here. On the contrary it is they who beckon to us, as they sail away.

III

As the canal is fed by the trade currents of the whole world, its traffic rises and falls in cycles with the great economic tides, so there can be no better barometer to measure world activity. But how can we make use of this barometer? M. Raymond Jullien's excellent book, *Le Traffic du Canal de Suez* (Sirey, 1933), gives many valuable pointers.

Of the two traffic currents the northbound is the more illuminating, for being chiefly made up of raw materials it is simpler to analyse, and responds more quickly to the movements of wholesale prices. The southbound traffic is more complex, as it comprises not only manufactured goods, but also fuel and certain raw materials that have been partly processed. The shipping which serves this traffic is equally mixed. It includes tankers, which naturally are empty when they leave and therefore of no commercial interest; and ships in ballast embarking on distant voyages in quest of cargoes, and therefore foretelling economic events yet to occur. In a word this current coming from Europe is controlled by commercial activities in other parts of the world. Many trips are made with the holds more or less empty, but they are justified chiefly because these ships will later bring back cargoes to the Old World. It is the return trip which will be profitable, so shippers are ready when they send their boats off to accept any outward bound freights they can get.

This practice indirectly reflects the decline of Europe as an industrial exporting centre. As the southbound traffic becomes to some extent a function of the contrary current, it loses its intrinsic importance. It is really instructive only when studied from a particular angle. It is the relationship between the two currents that interests us more directly. In periods of prosperity or recovery, the southbound traffic (measured by volume of goods) rises to as high as 30 per cent of the total, but it falls again as soon as there is a depression or even an economic readjustment.

The question is which of these canal statistics is likely to be the best indicator of the general trend of economic activity? The nett tonnage figure mainly discloses the level of shipping activity, whereas the volume of goods corresponds to commerce in its strictest sense, and, as we have seen, it is the northbound current that will serve us best here. A more sensitive curve is obtained by plotting the relationship between nett tonnage and the volume of goods, i.e. ships *v*. cargoes. The latter is apt to exceed the former in prosperous times when the ships' holds are fully laden, but

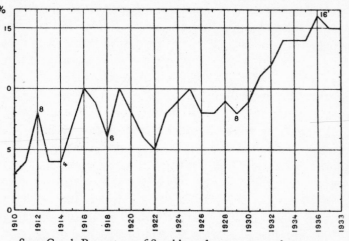

Suez Canal: Percentage of Southbound nett tonnage that went through in ballast

when trade is bad and the ships are half empty then the cargo curve falls below the shipping curve. More delicate still is the curve showing the tonnage of the southbound traffic that goes through in ballast — indeed this is the most prophetic of all for it announces the first signs of recovery.

Finally, it is important to compare the level of traffic with the level of prices. If possible wholesale prices should be expressed in the most international of currencies, and for this purpose I am inclined to prefer the pound sterling even to gold prices, for although the pound fluctuates it is the most generally accepted medium in international trade. The close relationship between wholesale prices and the total canal traffic is soon apparent, as high prices, or more correctly rising prices, stimulate business, and the contrary depress it. It is the trend rather than the level which we must consider, and we shall then see our graphs running in surprisingly parallel lines.

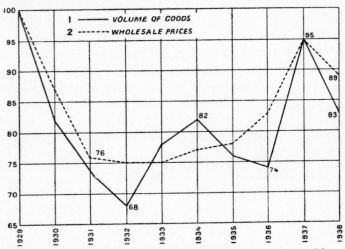

Suez Canal: Volume of goods and wholesale prices (expressed in sterling) in comparison with 1929 levels

Thus it is not only remarkable but also most significant that no matter from which point of view we prepare the graphs, they all give the same result. Whichever curve we study we find it reflects the same outstanding events of economic history, the same periods of rise and fall — or to use a musical metaphor, passages played in the major key and others in the minor. In every curve we see the heavy decline that occurred during the war years and again after the 1929 crisis, and always the year 1932 marks the lowest point of the depression. The milestones and signposts on this great economic highway can be determined with accuracy, or to employ still another metaphor, all these economic phenomena seem to breathe a common atmosphere.

So we invariably come back to the international or world-wide character of the canal, for therein lies its true personality. During the nineteenth century it was the canal which drew the continents more closely together and stimulated the industrial expansion of Europe, by putting at her disposal practically unlimited sources of raw materials, and at the same time immense outlets for her products on three other continents. But in revenge it again was the canal which, through this very contact, hastened to awaken Asia, that wonderful Sleeping Beauty. In any event the canal has played a stupendous part in the evolution — or shall we say the revolution? — of the world as we see it to-day. Ferdinand de Lesseps thus stands out in history in his full stature alongside Vasco da Gama and Magellan.

CHAPTER XII

WORLD TRADE ROUTES THAT COMPETE WITH THE CANAL

I

THE Suez Canal does not enjoy a monopoly of the communications between the East and the West. On the contrary it has to struggle against a great deal of diverse and constantly changing competition. For example, one can to-day reach India, the Far East or Central Asia by travelling overland on the Baghdad Railway, the Trans-Siberian Railway, or even the motor bus service across the Syrian desert. To reach the Pacific or the Indian Oceans there are also rival maritime routes through the Panama Canal and around the Cape of Good Hope. Then in recent years air transport has developed with lightning rapidity, and finally we must even class the oil pipe-lines as competitors.

Nothing could be more subtle than the interplay of the various factors entering into this competition. Geography is at the base of the structure, as distances still have to be reckoned with, although technical progress is freeing us more and more every day from such limitations, and is presenting mankind with unlimited possibilities of travel. The scale of fares, being still mainly based on distances traversed, is of course worked out with mathematical precision. But this is only the beginning of the problem, for many other complex economic arguments have still to be considered, though military risks are apt to override them all. Finally, politics have now introduced imponderable elements into this domain, which used always to be regarded as purely practical. However, Nature always has the last word, so in the end each route gets the traffic to which it is entitled.

Travelling from Europe to Southern China, Indo-China or the Dutch East Indies, the sea route is almost imperative. Geography affords no other choice. For India, Eastern Siberia, Northern China and Japan, however, the overland routes offer alternatives to the Suez Canal which are all the more attractive as their axis lies farther to the north. As trade is nowadays made up of bulky commodities, land transport is infinitely more handicapped in comparison with sea transport than it was in former epochs. Yet even when there are not sufficient economic reasons to create a new route, the ambitions of a great Power are often enough to do so for purely political purposes. Such new routes are in turn likely to generate traffic. Still it is curious to see to-day how the railway, the autobus, and even the aeroplane have picked up the most ancient caravan trails.

Before the Trans-Siberian Railway was built, the journey to the Far East across Siberia can only be described as a great adventure. The broken and erratic trail across the Russian Steppes has been admirably described in Jules Verne's famous novel, *Michel Strogoff*, where he tells how it took nine days to go from Tyumen to Tomsk, and forty to fifty days from Tomsk to Irkutsk. Then one took a boat on the Angara River, after that a road to Sryetensk, and then once more by boat on the Amur and the Usuri Rivers. Some emigrants even spent two years *en route*, so the only really feasible way to reach the Pacific Coast was by sea.

The Trans-Siberian Railway was planned in 1891, and completed between 1902 and 1904. It linked Moscow with Vladivostok, 5390 miles away. As this compares with 11,120 miles from London to Yokohama via the Suez Canal, the distance was cut in half. After the Russo-Japanese War travellers usually took the Trans-Siberian route if they were pressed for time in reaching Japan or Peking. They required about two weeks from Western Europe, taking about ten days from Chelyabinsk to the terminus on the Pacific. On the eve of the present conflict one took ten days from Moscow to Vladivostok, and the ticket cost £35 or 6215 francs first class, as against 26 days by P. & O. from Marseilles to Hong Kong, which costs £97 to £99 or about 17,500 francs first class.[1]

No doubt about the advantage of the Siberian route in both time and money, but since the Great War there have been the disadvantages of insecurity, political complications and discomfort. As all this has discouraged the creation of a regular clientele, the competition of the Trans-Siberian Railway has had practically no effect on the passenger traffic through Suez. The same applies to commercial transport. Shipments of soya beans from Manchuria to Germany have occasionally passed via Siberia, but in the other direction few exports are ever made overland to the China Seas. Even if the Trans-Siberian route should recover its normal activity, it would not endanger the canal.

A new road towards India is just being opened up. One can then go from Paris to Basra, crossing the Bosporus in a train ferry, and making the six-day journey of about 3700 miles in the same sleeping coach. If one adds four days at sea, one gets to India in ten days at a cost of £103 first class. This compares with twelve days from Marseilles to Bombay by sea, the first class fare being £50 to 75. Travellers who suffer from sea-sickness and who can make favourable connections will prefer this route, and so will those going overland to Beirut instead of using the Mediterranean. However, even this competition will probably not be much more serious than that of the Trans-Siberian Railway.

[1] All travel fares quoted at 1939 rates.

As it is so unsuitable for heavy merchandise we really
should not look upon this new Paris-Basra line as a transit
route, but rather as the path of political and economic penetration stretching out towards India and Asia. It has reopened the route used by the Ancients almost without
alteration, and has also joined up with and prolonged the new

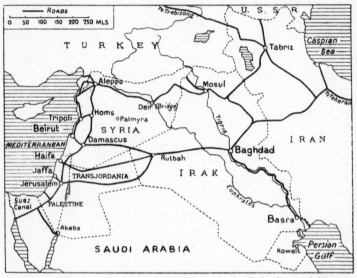

The network of roads linking up Turkey, Syria, Palestine and Trans-
jordania with Irak and Iran. (Reproduced from *L'Evolution au cours
des siécles des grandes voies de communication de l'Asie antèrieure*, by
Charles Godard)

direct line of expansion from Central Europe. This European extension did not exist at the time of Alexander the
Great, but in our time it has become quite historic as the
route of the famous *drang nach osten* leading from Prague
and Vienna, those gateways of eastern Europe, towards
Belgrade, Salonika, Bucharest, and Constantinople. After
passing Constantinople it stretches towards Persia and

Central Asia by way of Baghdad, and so reaches India through Basra. Its attraction lies in the fact that it is both economic and political, and that it goes through countries that are capable of rational exploitation and which lie adjacent to the continent of Europe. Germany excels in exploitation and colonization of this type. She uses land routes,

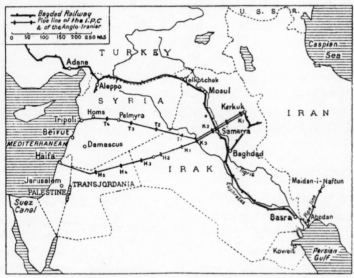

The Baghdad Railway and the oil pipe lines

in contrast to Britain who, being more commercial, prefers to expand by sea. Thus we have two points of view, which can hardly exist peacefully side by side.

To these overland routes through western Asia we should add another going across the Syrian Desert towards the Euphrates. This classic road of Antiquity and of the Middle Ages was still used as lately as 1869, and carried an important inter-continental traffic until the cutting of the isthmus dealt it a fatal blow. The autobus has now rejuvenated this old road which until yesterday was monopolized by the camel. Along its tracks, which are excellent so long as they are dry, the motor lorry can travel easily and quickly, particularly as it can cover long stretches without filling up with petrol. Furthermore, for the first time after many centuries it is now enjoying a new Pax Romana, which though precarious is quite real. The Nairne autobus service, stopping at the wells of Rhube, has joined up the Syrian coast with Baghdad. The victim of this innovation is the Bedouin, who drifts in from the edge of the desert to become the proletariat of the slums in the big cities. As a competitor of the canal this itinerary scarcely counts, and yet it should be mentioned, for in these regions it is keeping alive the age-old idea of the overland route to India.

III

Two maritime routes compete seriously with the Suez Canal, and these are Panama and the Cape.

Let us not dwell on the former for we have already defined its zone with precision. There is really very little rivalry between the two canals, for the regions they serve are too different. Certain non-geographic factors do, however, divert some of the traffic, at any rate temporarily. For example, the Panama Canal tolls are about 40 per cent lower than those of Suez, and this is apt to modify the line of cleavage between the respective zones. A tramp steamer leaving Japanese waters may hesitate between the two routes if only distance is considered, but may prefer Panama owing to its facilities for replenishing fuel oil, especially as to-day long trips without intermediate stops no longer present any difficulty. Hence the commercial zone of the American canal may slightly exceed the zone that would accrue to it for strictly geographical reasons. However, except for these rather secondary reservations, we find little or no competition. The important traffic that uses the Panama Canal has not been taken away from Suez, for the two enterprises in point of fact assist mutually, each other by creating wealth which leads to trade.

Yet, we must not be too exclusively optimistic, particularly where Europe is concerned. Cutting through the Isthmus of Panama was part of the development of an autonomous economic domain, and though Suez has not actually suffered, it does mean that something more has escaped from the grip of the Old World. It may be that the year 1914, when the second interoceanic canal was opened, will mark the end of world trade unity such as it used to exist under the aegis of Europe.

The competition of the Cape route on the contrary is direct. The only ports that are definitely closer by this route are those situated along the East African coast as far north as Beira, for even Australian ships gain slightly by passing through the Red Sea. However, other items enter into the account in dictating the choice of itinerary and create in the last analysis a borderland much wider than appears at first sight, and which varies considerably according to circumstances.

In the first place the level of prosperity exercises an effect which it is easy to recognize and even to measure. In a depression the lower the freight rates decline, the more heavily the Suez tolls weigh on the half-empty vessels, and the greater the temptation to go by the Cape where there is nothing to pay. When trade is slack and no one is in a hurry, it is easier to put up with the longer voyage. On the contrary, during a period of rising prices, rising freight rates, and general activity, the shipper tries to use his vessels to the utmost, especially if they are making good profits. So he does not hesitate to choose the shorter route and pay the high tolls which then seem of little consequence. One finds the same reasoning in industry, for an expensive machine often pays only if it can work full-time. So we come to the conclusion that prosperity favours Suez and depression favours the Cape, though relatively less.

The possibility of picking up cargoes along the route is another factor that comes into play. Half-empty tramps will naturally adopt a course where intermediate ports may help them in this, while others that are fully laden will make for harbours where they can get rid of some of their freight. In 1936 many ships coming from Indo-China preferred the Cape route in order to sell part of their rice at Dakar. As in the old days of the sailing ships, the use of fuel oil now permits long unbroken voyages, so if there is no hurry distance hardly counts at all. In a way oil has restored the conditions existing before the time of de Lesseps.

Re-routing traffic owing to political insecurity is quite another story. During the forty-five years from 1869 to 1914, no one even dreamed of such a thing, for the nineteenth century had naively persuaded itself that the future would be an era of peace, and that progress was our natural birthright. Optimism was the normal attitude of a reasonable human being. Alas, since 1914 such inborn confidence has been relegated to the past. The risk of war though veiled remains latent, and, once admitted, this danger makes itself felt by an abrupt tension in marine insurance rates.

Now the danger is not the same for all routes under all circumstances. If the centre of the storm is in the Mediterranean, and if any Mediterranean Power must be considered as an enemy, or even suspected, then the Suez route immediately becomes insecure for English and French shipping, especially as this sea is narrow and very suitable for ambushes. During the whole period which preceded the war of 1939, Italy was looked upon as a direct adversary, and the degree of Mediterranean insecurity could be measured by its repercussion on the rates charged for marine insurance.

Before 1935 the accepted rate was 6d. per £100 of insured merchandise, and was the same for both routes. But since October 23rd of that year, or since the Abyssinian War, the figure has risen to 1s. 6d. for the Cape route, and to 5s. through the canal. On August 27th, 1937, at the time of the Spanish Civil War, the rate remained fixed at 6d. for the Atlantic, but for the Mediterranean between Gibraltar and Malta it rose as high as 7s. 6d. for regular services, 10s. for tramps, and even 20s. for tankers. At the beginning of 1938 the tension eased up considerably, but in September came the Munich Crisis and the graph then shot up in a vertical line. On the 27th of that month marine insurance reached 100s. via Suez, and 20s. to 50s. via the Cape. The Mediterranean route became prohibitive, a circumstance which had never before occurred in time of peace. State aid for marine insurance, the solution adopted by England and France, has managed to avert catastrophe, but it has not removed the underlying dangers.

It is not surprising that whenever war clouds gathered before 1939 the percentage of traffic going by the Cape increased. This is strikingly so in the case of Australia. Before 1931 the proportion of Australian traffic passing that way was under 40 per cent. It rose to 45 per cent during the following year, and then in 1936, 1937 and 1938 shot up to above 60 per cent. It actually reached 64.7 per cent in 1938. Though less accentuated one finds re-routing in the traffic between Europe and Siam, the

Straits Settlements, Indo-China, and the Dutch East Indies. The traffic diverted around the Cape used to amount to about 10 per cent, but it rose to 18.3 per cent in 1932, and 17.1 per cent in 1936. Though it does not seem very probable that these tendencies will be consolidated in the Far East, it does seem possible in the case of Australian trade. This might mean an important change in equilibrium between the rival routes of the Red Sea and South Africa.

The situation is quite different when the centre of the storm is not situated in the Mediterranean, as was the case at the beginning of the present war. We can in fact foresee circumstances in which the Atlantic may be as dangerous or even more dangerous than the zone stretching from Gibraltar to Port Said. The Cape route then would not be preferable, and the rates of Atlantic insurance would stiffen. A graph of these rates, if it were obtainable, would be rather like one of those meteorological charts showing barometric pressure which are used by sailors. In the present tragic and uncertain circumstances, it is impossible for us to be more precise, but at least we can determine under what conditions equilibrium will be established between the traffic going through Suez and that via South Africa.

IV

The aeroplane has brought an entirely new form of competition, but it is still too early to decide how important it will become. It is not much use for freight, but for passengers flying offers incomparable advantages. The sea trip from Marseilles to Bombay requires, as we know, twelve days and costs from £50 to £75, or about 10,000 to 13,000 francs.[1] But to fly from Paris to Calcutta by Air-

---

[1] All fares quoted are previous to September 1939.

France takes only 5½ days and costs 15,000 francs, or about £85. Marseilles to Saigon by the Messageries Maritimes lasts 22 days and costs 13,500 to 15,000 francs, or from £80 to £85. On the other hand by Air-France, Paris to Saigon requires only 6½ days and costs 19,500 francs, or about £110. Thus the rate by air is a little greater, but the economy in time is enormous.

It is evident from this that the canal will lose a certain amount of its rich clientele, notably people who are pressed for time, as has, for example, already occurred in the London to Paris crossing. Going by air is found to be more fatiguing for some people, and it has the added inconvenience of limiting the traveller to only about 40 lbs. of luggage. It is also probable that the canal will lose part of its postal traffic, since nearly half the mails to Indo-China already go by air.

We should not exaggerate such competition, however, for when we examine the actual figures we find that the total volume of air travel in any one year has not yet reached anything at all serious. In 1937 Air-France carried to the Far East a total of only 212 passengers, and the Dutch lines 3912. This is a mere nothing alongside the 300,000 civilian passengers who annually go through Suez. Undoubtedly the number of air travellers will rapidly increase, but even then the quantitative repercussions on the canal's passenger traffic will still be small. From the point of view of quality it may well be quite otherwise, for it is the wealthy travellers who will be lost.

If the mails finally go entirely by air, and the Government shipping subsidies therefore cease, it is possible that the traditional type of 'mail boat' may disappear — that is an eventual menace, but still only eventual. Commercial letters sent by air are generally duplicated by others sent through the ordinary post, and furthermore the aeroplane can carry only a feeble tonnage, particularly for long distances. When I looked at one of the three-decker flying boats belonging to Imperial Airways as it rode at anchor in Alexandria harbour, I seemed to see before me one of Columbus's caravels; all that was needed was to replace the wings by masts and sails! After all, in matters of transport competition creates traffic, and in the end the air may be capable of bringing the canal more passengers than it steals from it.

It is possible that by becoming an airport of first rank, Egypt may present the canal with a new stream of travellers. Technically there is of course no limit to the way in which the length of non-stop flights can be extended. To-day 3000 miles is by no means extraordinary, an aeroplane can fly very high and straight and can cut across peninsulas which ships have to circumnavigate so laboriously. Thus we can conceive of two or three thousand miles as a normal hop. This reasoning is largely theoretical, for like merchant ships commercial aeroplanes are a business proposition, and depend on the freight and passengers which they pick up. This consideration has a decisive influence on the choice of intermediate airports.

It seems that Egypt is especially well suited for air travel. Its atmosphere affords maximum visibility; it is situated at an important junction where the routes to India and the Cape bifurcate; also, thanks to the presence of the British Army, it enjoys real security. There are of course other direct air routes to various destinations, as for example the one across Siberia, or the one which goes to the Far East by following the Great Circle as it passes over the Arctic. There is the route towards Mesopotamia and India via the Dodecanese and Syria, and another through Algeria and Lake Chad towards the Cape, without passing near the Nile.

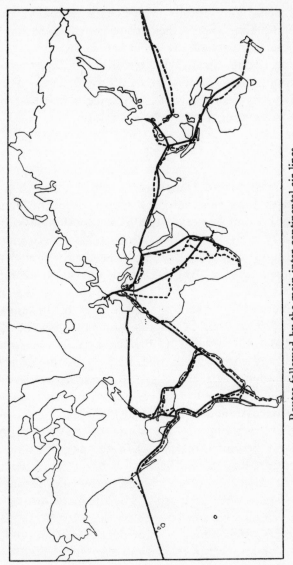

Routes followed by the main inter-continental air lines

Nevertheless, the reasons which have attracted the airways to the Delta are sufficiently compelling to have convinced the majority of the great international lines. As a
matter of fact the eastern Mediterranean is almost an obligatory stopping point for anyone flying to India, the Far East,
Australia, or South Africa. So once again Egypt has
become interesting to the whole world.

v

The underground transport of petrol through a pipe-
line is something relatively new for the Levant. The Suez
Canal cannot but be seriously affected by this development
now that Western Asia plays so important a role in supplying
the oil requirements of Europe. The Anglo-Iranian Company (formerly the Anglo-Persian Oil Co.), which has
developed the Abadan field, is controlled by the British
Government and furnishes a large part of Britain's consumption. The Irak Petroleum Company has the Kirkuk
field. It is jointly owned by British, French and American
interests, and through the intermediary of the Compagnie
Française des Pétroles it serves French needs. What
directly concerns the isthmus is how the oil is transported.

The Anglo-Iranian Oil Company employs tankers, which
use the canal route. In 1938 out of 5,220,000 tons of
mineral oil flowing northwards, 4,327,000 tons or about
83 per cent came from Abadan. This oil company is thus
one of the canal's important clients, and would be lost either
if the oil should be taken around by the Cape, or if a direct
pipe-line should be constructed to the Mediterranean. In
the first case the detour is enormous since it doubles the
distance at least, and in the second case the capital expenditure would be considerable. As the statutes of the canal

do not permit differential tariffs, the directors must make up their minds as to how much sacrifice they should consent in order to retain this traffic.

The Irak Petroleum Company on the other hand sends its oil to the Mediterranean by a pipe-line about 600 miles long; it divides at the Euphrates into two branches, one ending at Tripoli and the other at Haifa, and annually transports some four million tons. The canal never actually lost this business for it did not exist until 1935 when the pipe-lines were built, but the mere fact that Europe is partially getting supplies from Kirkuk diminishes the amount it requires from the Persian Gulf, which of course passes through Suez. This fact can be observed in the annual returns, for in 1935, after the pipe-lines were opened, the total movement of tankers in both directions shows a nett reduction of a million tons as compared with 1934. Shortly afterwards, however, the previous figures were regained, and have since even been exceeded. The position which the tankers occupy in the total traffic of the canal shows an increase from 15.8 per cent in 1929 to 17.3 per cent in 1938.

v i

Only two out of all these competitors can be regarded as serious: the Cape for merchandise, and the aeroplane and certain railways for passengers. We must not forget that even in 1929, a record year, the receipts from passenger traffic accounted for only 1.2 per cent of the total gross income of the Canal Company. So in the last analysis there is only one real menace, the recovery of the Cape route as a reaction against the potential insecurity of the Mediterranean. This threat, therefore, is less commercial than political, but this does not minimize its gravity. Apart from war, the traffic through the Suez Canal is therefore not in danger, indeed, one can even say that it has practically no competition. The effect of the opening of new routes has been to stimulate general activity, so that what the canal loses on the swings it gains on the roundabouts.

The important thing is that the world should become richer, that intercontinental trade should grow, and that a complementary exchange of goods should be maintained between different parts of the world. Unfortunately, we can hardly say that the twentieth century is in any way striving to realize this programme.

Nevertheless, the general pattern of maritime trade routes, as they were established in the nineteenth century after the opening of the Suez Canal, was founded on the interplay of these essential factors. In January 1939, *The Times* published an interesting map of the world which showed the position at a given moment of all British ships sailing the high seas. It gave a marvellous idea of the whole network of trade routes. Each unit was represented by a black dot — or more exactly by a small oval like an insect, and their density showed up the busiest thoroughfares. It looked like a procession of ants, converging on a central ant-heap, namely England — or western Europe, if you prefer. The map proved that the latter area remains the main centre of international trade, with the United States still only in second place.

It is relatively easy to discern the voyages which chiefly interest the Suez Canal. If we start at the circumference and work towards the centre, we first meet with two unusually dense processions. One comes from the Far East, India and the Persian Gulf and makes for the Red Sea; then passing through the canal and the Mediterranean it

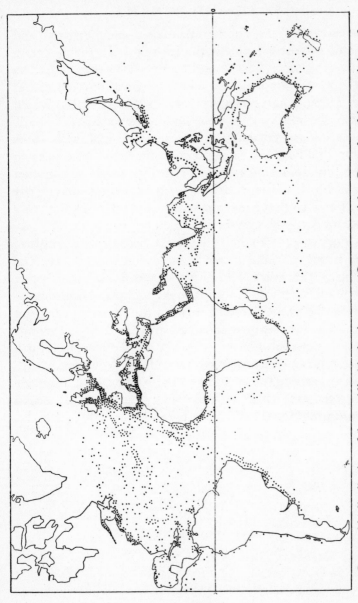

Geographic distribution of the world's shipping in 1937. (Crown copyright. Reproduced by permission of the Controller of H.M. Stationery Office)

circumnavigates the Iberian Peninsula and Brittany, and ends either in the Channel or the Irish Sea. This is the cream of the Suez traffic. The second current flows from Australia and the west coast of Africa, and after rounding the Cape of Good Hope points straight towards Dakar, after which it rejoins the first current near the south-west coast of Spain. Two secondary currents unite Australia, first with India and the Red Sea, and secondly with the China Seas passing by the Philippines. Lastly one can distinguish still another current which is less clearly defined. Its ships start partly in the Far East, but some also come from India, and all pass round the Cape in a westerly direction.

In this we have a complete arterial system with England as the heart. Perhaps it would be more correct to say that Europe is the heart, for England serves as her shipper, commission agent and international broker. According to this map the Old Continent remains the principal centre of world trade, but it is no longer the only centre. New currents have now been set in motion beyond its confines, for North America has already become an independent centre. All this is rather like the twilight of the Roman Empire, when a vast structure, which yesterday had been universal, began to break up. However, the present structure still exists. . . .

CHAPTER XIII

THE ROLE OF THE SUEZ CANAL IN THE SANITARY DEFENCES OF THE WEST

I

MARSEILLES is the gateway to the East, they say, but it would be more accurate to apply the phrase to the Suez Canal. 'When we reach Suez', wrote Gobineau, 'we are not far from the realm of the unknown, for it is here that we first become aware of the atmosphere of Asia.' Now Asia may be the continent of mystery and enchantment, but it is also the source of contamination, filth, and corruption. The West must defend itself unremittingly against its contagion, for widespread epidemic diseases would quickly sweep over Europe, were it not for the constant vigilance and perfect organization of the sanitary cordon. Just as the Roman Empire sheltered itself from barbaric invasions behind its famous walls, so, by its policy of filtration, has Europe succeeded in keeping the scourges of Asia at a safe distance. On the frontier between East and West we find in a new form the equivalent of Rome's great system of self-preservation, and it is at the canal — that narrow gateway to the Mediterranean — that the principal functions are carried out.

The worst centres from which diseases emanate lie in the north-west of India. Like everything else, the microbes take the two historic routes in their journey westward, going either overland or by sea. By land they follow the traditional road through the Khyber Pass towards Afghanistan, Persia, and Mesopotamia. An important diffusion point is the little half-ruined city of Meshed, through which countless travellers pass on foot, all potential germ carriers. A second centre is at Kermanshah, near the boundary between Iran and Mesopotamia. Here the current divides into three: one infected stream flowing northward into Turkey along the Baghdad Railway; the second crossing the Syrian Desert to Damascus, and the third going towards Basra, whence it can reach Egypt by sea. Nevertheless, the principal trail of contamination has generally been the direct sea passage from the Indian Ocean via the Red Sea, calling *en route* at Aden and Suez. As we have already seen an enormous traffic of passengers and merchandise moves along this highway.

One is tempted to liken the sanitary defence built up in these regions to a barrier behind which we are entrenched, so comparison with the Roman walls comes naturally to mind. The modern defence is more complex, and in any case the Roman walls were effective only when reinforced by a clever policy of political intervention carried far beyond their limits. The West has adopted similar methods to ward off the microbe invasion, for it also has built up a system of successive defences, of which Suez is the last. The object is to track down the diseases as they travel towards Europe, and to combat them at their farthest point of departure, as well as at every intervening port of call along the route. When a ship that is suspected proceeds westwards, it is more and more closely supervised, and more and more frequently denounced as dangerous: in many cases the barriers close down on it long before the disease actually reaches the last sanitary frontier at the southern entrance of the canal.

Viewed from this angle the defence system proves to be

much more complex than it seemed at first sight. The canal is more than a simple wicket-gate opening on to the Western world, through which disease is forbidden to pass, or where quarantine is imposed. Actually the efficiency of the defence is the result of an ingenious international organization with its network extending over the whole world, and particularly along all the routes from India and the Far East. The chief plan is to fight disease at its source, and wherever possible to dry up centres of infection. Next they try to prevent the diseases from spreading. The rat plays his well-known part as a common carrier for germs, and therefore efforts are made to destroy him by de-ratting the ships. Whenever these methods prove incomplete the diseases creep up towards the barrier, so the next step is to be well informed of their progress, and to know, for example, that there is cholera in Shanghai, and which ships are suspected of carrying it as they pass from Bombay towards Aden, or from Jibuti towards Suez.

The principal collecting points for such medical information are Washington, Singapore, Alexandria, and the League of Nations headquarters at Geneva. Egypt, as a potential centre of disease dissemination, has required exceptionally delicate supervision, especially as it lies on the principal route to the East. Until 1938 a Marine Quarantine Board was responsible for the sanitary defence of the country. Its outlook was international, not Egyptian. It was set up in the nineteenth century, and confirmed by several treaties, and so belongs to the capitulations period in Mediterranean history. Both its executive and medical men employed Western methods in an international spirit. Most of its technical personnel were foreigners, but there were also a few Egyptians. This regime has been a complete success, for the epidemic diseases which used to spread terror at the end of the last century are to-day, if not conquered, at least held in check. It is many years since plague, cholera, smallpox or typhus have been an immediate danger for Europe. Except for the special case of pilgrims to Mecca, the necessity for quarantine has thus become rare. Under these conditions and by these methods, the defence walls of the Occident have been entirely efficient.

II

Sanitary defence is one of the most interesting aspects of the world-wide civilization which Europe has everywhere imposed. The reason why the West has so fully succeeded with its sanitary cordon is not merely because of her medical science, but almost as much due to those methods of international organization which the white races have conceived and carried out. By the nineteenth century Europe exercised a general supervision over the world. This still exists, but we have to admit that her dictation is being challenged more and more every day. A host of countries that were previously in a state of tutelage are now becoming emancipated, and who can blame them for demanding all the rights that go with independence? They tolerate international control with growing impatience, declaring that they themselves will take over the functions which the West has hitherto assumed.

Such is precisely the case in Egypt, which on the morrow of the Treaty of Lausanne negotiated for the suppression of the Quarantine Board. From now on, at Suez, Port Said, and Alexandria, a corps of technically capable Egyptian doctors will administer the posts that yesterday were filled by their European colleagues. The West has thus confided the defence of the gateway to guards who are not Westerners. I doubt if Europe would have consented a few years earlier, but now her authority is in full retreat. We shall see whether the system will maintain its efficiency under non-European control. The Egyptian personnel will no doubt possess medical competence, but will the new regime have either sufficient inherited general culture or administrative experience? That is the crux of the question, and on it depends the safety of the civilization of the whole world as created by Europe in the nineteenth century.

CHAPTER XIV

THE CANAL AND MEDITERRANEAN MILITARY PROBLEMS

I

THE military problem connected with the route to India may be divided into two main parts: the defence of the canal, the isthmus, and Egypt itself on the one hand, and on the other the maintenance of the freedom of communications on the high seas and through the narrow straits along this route. Since the Great War (1914-1918) the hypotheses of this problem have altered completely, for though it can be said that Britain controls this vital artery, it is also no exaggeration to add that her control is precarious. Politically the outlook in the Mediterranean has radically changed from what it was at the end of the nineteenth and in the early years of the twentieth centuries. After all, the situation in this region is completely different according to whether the war rages or does not rage in the Mediterranean. With Italy neutral, with Russia unable to emerge from the Black Sea, and with Turkey favourable to the democracies, the route to the Indies can still be used. It is difficult at the present moment (November 1939) to discuss this question except in the form of an hypothesis. Yet certain fundamental observations stand out clearly, and these at any rate allow us to sketch out the problem to be studied.

The International Conference at Constantinople entrusted Egypt with the defence of the canal, and this was reaffirmed by the Treaty of Versailles. But in point of fact Great Britain has made herself responsible for this task. In 1888 she acted as the Power in occupation and in 1919 as the protector, but since Egypt became independent in 1936 she is only an ally. In reality there has been little change, although the conditions under which the canal and the delta could be defended are by no means what they were yesterday.

Since the Great War and especially since Djemal's attack in 1915, England has learnt the lesson that the canal cannot be defended in the zone itself. Furthermore, the desert, far from constituting a protection by its very emptiness as had been supposed, is on the contrary a source from which dangerous surprise attacks may come, and so must be carefully watched. British policy accordingly has relied on the Palestine mandate and has aimed at indirect but effective control of the Arab countries. The time is passed when the canal could be considered as a front line defence system behind which to take shelter. However, the problem is still unsolved, for though an attack on the isthmus used to be expected from the east, one must now also prepare for an offensive coming from the west. Should the latter hypothesis materialize, the defence of the canal would be closely linked up with that of Egypt, which would virtually have become its shield.

A new circumstance which has altered the main factors in the problem is that, since the Abyssinian War and the Treaty of 1936, the co-operation of the Egyptians has been assured. Their sincerity in respect of a defence of this nature has been so evident that by common agreement many points, which only a few years ago gave rise to the bitterest controversies, now attract no attention at all, nor are they likely to in the future. The construction of new barracks, which were to have been built in the isthmus at the expense of the Egyptian Government, has now been postponed, and the British Army remains at present at Cairo with the tacit consent of the Egyptian Government. The military occupation of the capital is no longer humiliating now that it is part of an agreed policy of collaboration. Thus the venom which poisoned Anglo-Egyptian relations ever since 1882 has been eliminated, and this situation will continue at least as long as Egypt continues seriously to fear Italian aggression.

In the event of an attack coming from Africa and not from Asia, we find that the defence of the canal has been turned about, and now faces the west, where it benefits from the protection afforded by the Nile which is a more effective barrier than that of the canal itself. However, beyond the western frontier there lies another desert, no less dangerous than the one in Arabia. An invading expedition, sweeping across the vast empty spaces of the Libyan frontier would be formidable, particularly if it possessed modern equipment and sufficient personnel. It might well be able to penetrate Egyptian territory, though that would depend on the efficiency of the defence put up by the British and Egyptian forces, not to mention a counter attack from Tunis.

After the desert comes the river, and the delta with its countless canals and areas that can be easily flooded. These will constitute an exceedingly formidable barrier, especially against an invading army whose lines of communication are precarious and which is in danger of being cut off from its base, as was the case with the French expedition under Napoleon. To conquer Egypt would not be sufficient, for it would be necessary to hold it, and as at the time of Aboukir, the answer would be given at sea. Thus the question ceases to be local; the real decision would be taken elsewhere.

If on the contrary the attack on the canal should come

from the north under conditions which it is impossible to foresee at this moment then the defence would present problems quite different from those of 1915. England is now covered by her occupation of Palestine and Irak, and also by the French occupation of Syria and the friendly support of Turkey. Further, the Suez Canal Company would collaborate with the British Army with the same enthusiasm as it did in 1915.

11

The British learned another lesson during the Great War, namely that in the case of armed conflict the road to India via the canal has ceased to be safe.

It will be dangerous should the war involve the hostility or malevolent neutrality of any Mediterranean Power, even a lesser one. An enemy can poison the whole passage if he can manage to obtain a foothold anywhere along this narrow sinuous sea, which lends itself so well to ambushes and surprise attacks. It is not even essential as it was in the past for him to possess military control of the lines of communication. Even without gaining a naval victory he would virtually possess a right of veto. No one could pass, or at least if they did it would only be as the outcome of an adventurous raid . . . a great naval achievement involving casualties.

The truth of this was realized by the British Admiralty in 1916 and, during the post-war period after 1919, it was steadily confirmed as the offensive power of the submarine and the aeroplane continued to increase. Though the Treaty of Versailles at first seemed to open up vistas of security, yet judging from their debates the British experts foresaw new conditions which ten years earlier would not have occurred to anyone. As far back as 1926 I clipped from *The Times* the following report of an important speech made by Sir John Marriott, M.P., in which the problem is bluntly stated:

'Sir John was not certain, looking at the matter from a distant perspective, that the instinct of those statesmen who, from the point of view of English diplomacy and world power, opposed the cutting of the canal was not right . . . If the canal had never been made, he was not sure that our world position would not have been stronger . . . The Mediterranean was a very narrow sea, and the advent of the submarine and aircraft had made it even narrower than it was in 1914. If they reflected what that development might mean in a sea like the Mediterranean, with possible rivals on more than one shore, they would realize that we might find ourselves more embarrassed than helped by the necessity of holding the canal route. If that were true, how enormously it enhanced the necessity of keeping the Cape route to Great Britain, and the importance of keeping both sides of Africa free from hostile powers! It was an essential part of the German plans to have Central Africa, with very important posts both on the east and west coasts. That action would have hit Great Britain, whether we retained the canal route or stuck to the Cape route.'

At the time when this opinion was expressed, Britain had no enemies in the Mediterranean, for Italy was regarded as a friend. In the 1935 crisis, when the British fleet was bottled up in the narrow harbour of Alexandria, it felt that it was at the mercy of a surprise attack. In any event its mere presence was incapable of imposing Britain's will, as had been the case in the past. This decisively brought her face to face with problems, which several experts who were capable of looking well into the future had already foretold. It was now a question of weighing up the effective value of the Suez route in case of war.

Should a war occur in which the Powers bordering on the Mediterranean remained neutral or even could be considered friendly to Britain and France, then the link with India through the Suez Canal could be maintained. Indeed, this actually occurred during the first months of the 1939 war. But if Italy were included among the adversaries, then the Mediterranean obviously is liable to become impracticable as a commercial highway, at least at the outset. Military communications might be maintained, or more precisely might be re-established after a naval encounter. It would be difficult to organize convoys as was done in 1917-1918. Therefore, if one got through, it would be only after incurring dangerous risks.

The disadvantages arising from such a situation would be serious but not fatal. The British Empire existed and was powerful long before the Suez Canal was opened. Even to-day it is estimated that only 11 per cent of British imports have been passing through the Red Sea, though another 9 per cent actually have been coming from countries on the Mediterranean itself. (France similarly has been drawing 11 per cent of her total from countries beyond Suez.) At any rate only about one-fifth of the foodstuffs and other supplies destined for Britain would have to be re-routed.

One can always fall back on the Cape route, which should serve quite well for commercial transport, as regularity is more important during a crisis than speed. One must not lose sight of the fact that as the distance is much longer, the return obtained from the merchant fleet would be seriously diminished. The most conservative estimates mention 30, 40, and even 50 per cent, as the increase in tonnage which would be necessary for both France and England should they be forced to abandon the Red Sea route. Nevertheless, even if the Mediterranean were to be blocked, nothing absolutely vital to the system of Franco-British supplies would be lost.

One must admit, however, that from a military point of view the route around the Cape alone is not enough to assure the defence of India, for there would be too much delay in transporting troops. Delay indeed would be serious if the enemy succeeded in reaching Basra, and even more so if he controlled Suez, for then the Cape route itself would be short-circuited and imperilled. England was fully alive to this danger at the time of Napoleon's expedition to Egypt, and again later when Ferdinand de Lesseps obtained his concession. So even if the worst came to the worst there can be no question of giving up the Mediterranean, even though it may not be used, for this solution would be equivalent to abandoning the whole of the Near East. It also would indirectly expose the alternative lines of communication around the Cape. The security of the latter route after all is not automatic, but is a by-product of general policy.

However, no matter what happens, and even if the Mediterranean does remain open, we see that owing to these circumstances Vasco da Gama's route has recovered the first class importance that it certainly lost after 1869. Ever since the centre of military interest shifted to the rival route, its equipment had been more or less neglected. However, during the past few years this matter has become urgent. Long before the Suez Canal was constructed, when the Atlantic and Indian Oceans were essential parts of the main maritime artery of international trade, England fairly sprinkled this route with bases and naval stations. Doubtless she is now delighted to hunt them up again and refurbish such ports as Durban, for example, or Simons Town at the Cape, Lagos, Freetown, Bathurst, St. Helena, Ascension, etc.

France's strategic points are as valuable to England as they are to France herself. Madagascar lies at the cross-roads between India and Australia; Dakar is even more important, being situated on one side of what may yet prove to be the most important oceanic narrows in the world, as this is the junction of the maritime routes coming from the Indian Ocean and from South America. We can easily understand how extremely important it is for Britain that the Union of South Africa should remain loyal to the Empire, as was proved by the Dominion's attitude at the beginning of the 1939 War.

We can also appreciate how serious it would be to admit a possible adversary along these lines of communication by ceding colonies or mandates. It would mean ruining the security of an artery which is more vital than ever before to the safety of the Western Powers whose fate is bound up with Britain.

No matter what strategy Britain may adopt in a war concerning the Mediterranean itself, one thing is certain, and that is her ability to control both its outlets. An enemy may be able to prevent her from passing through, but she in her turn can maintain a complete and hermetically sealed blockade. As Italy draws 70 per cent of her imports from the trade routes which emerge from Gibraltar and Suez, she will find herself directly affected. This accounts for the anxiety expressed in Mussolini's speech at Milan on November 1st, 1936, when he said, 'The Mediterranean is simply a highway for others, but for us Italians it is life itself'. In conclusion he declared, 'I will not allow us to be hemmed in'. Their preoccupation is easily understood as it is a decisive matter for them, and it is not astonishing therefore that their traditional policy, at any rate until 1935, was based on friendship with Britain.

For France and Great Britain the Mediterranean problem is quite different. It consists chiefly in assuring freedom of passage if possible, and if not, then the safety of the alternate route, particularly along the nearest and most vulnerable section between Dakar and Brest. In addition to the ships coming from the Indian Ocean and the South Atlantic there might also be considerable maritime traffic starting along this section of the route itself, for it is here that one would find the sea terminus of the overland traffic which France eventually might have to divert across the desert from Algeria and Tunis towards Casablanca, should it be found impossible to cross the Mediterranean. She might of course succeed in sending out maritime convoys from Oran or even Algiers towards the Straits of Gibraltar and the Atlantic Ocean.

If the Mediterranean is not considered simply as a thoroughfare, but rather as a decisive objective in political strategy, then the role played by Egypt and the Levant is entirely different. It is no longer a question of keeping open a passage way, but of creating a fortress, an advanced outpost, in the defence of India. Except for Alexandria the English and French bases along the eastern Mediterranean shores are decidedly mediocre, neither Port Said, Haifa, Famagusta in Cyprus, nor Beirut can shelter more than a few ships, whereas the Italian bases at Tobrouk in Tripolitania and Laros in the Dodecanese are dangerously close should there be a rupture with Italy.

Greece and Turkey, however, possess several magnificent

harbours such as Smyrna, Ismid, Mudros and Salamis . . . hence the necessity for an *entente* with both these Powers. Turkish support is, in fact, essential, for without her the entire defence system is threatened in the flank. One need only to look at a map to understand how with a hostile Turkey the overland route to the Persian Gulf loses all security, and even the isthmus itself is indirectly exposed. Since her remarkable recuperation, Turkey has become the leading Power of the Near East. She is capable of giving solid military support, and so has become a political attraction for her neighbours. This applies as much to the Balkans as to Persia and Afghanistan, and even to the Arab countries and Egypt. With the Anglo-Turkish *Entente*, now reinforced by the Franco-Turkish *Entente*, the Near East is protected.

The equilibrium of the routes linking up Europe with the Indian Ocean and the Far East can be likened to a scales in which de Lesseps is balanced against Vasco da Gama. The route to India via Suez is the more vulnerable, and it would be threatened, commercially at any rate, in the event of a war in which the Mediterranean were involved. On the contrary if the Mediterranean remains free, as at the beginning of the 1939 War, then the importance of this route is doubled. However, in all circumstances the Cape is still almost indispensable as an alternative. Having said this we may conclude that on the day when peace triumphs, de Lesseps will win.

The nineteenth century, imbued with the outlook of St. Simon and his followers, could scarcely have foreseen the problems which now confront us. There is reason to doubt whether humanity has made any real progress for a long time now.

CHAPTER XV

THE FUTURE OF THE SUEZ CANAL

I

THE concession granted in 1854 to Ferdinand de Lesseps, and which he conveyed to the 'Universal Company of the Maritime Canal of Suez', is destined to end in 1968, when the canal reverts to Egypt. The future of this great enterprise is therefore uncertain, for it is hardly likely that the present regime will be maintained once the concession has expired.

In 1910, at a time when the company was about to undertake certain costly capital improvements, it tried to negotiate in advance for a renewal. The plan then discussed was to prolong the period for an additional forty years, or up to the year 2008. In exchange the Egyptian Government was to receive the following compensation: after 1969 it was to be allocated 50 per cent of the profits provided they exceeded 100 million francs, but if on the contrary they did not reach this figure then its share was to be limited to any excess over 50 million. In addition it was to receive at once an indemnity of four million pounds, and was to participate in the dividends, its proportion starting at 4 per cent in 1922 and reaching 12 per cent by 1961. Finally, one-half of the sum which would have resulted from the liquidation of The Company in 1969 was to be paid over to Egypt at that time, when three Egyptian directors were also to be appointed. The Company in turn was to be freed from any obligation to maintain the port of Suez, and also from the necessity of pensioning its personnel at the end of the concession.

These negotiations were carried out with Mr. P. H. Harvey, one of the British financial experts in Cairo. Sir Edward Grey, the British Foreign Minister, gave his approval, and was content merely to advise the Egyptian Government, which at that period was docile enough to act on any suggestion coming from London. Matters seemed to have reached a satisfactory conclusion when, unexpectedly, the whole question of renewing the concession was submitted to the Egyptian General Assembly, which ordinarily was convened only every two years. The Egyptian Prime Minister at the time was a Copt named Butros Gali. He was violently attacked when he submitted the plan, was accused of alienating the future, and of betraying his country's interests. One fanatic even wanted to make him pay for it with his life! This explosion of nationalism expressed itself in a negative vote that was almost unanimous.

The British Government did not intervene in order to support the Bill, though it would have been easy for it to have pulverized such opposition. The truth is that England at heart was also hostile, either for fear of tying up the future too far in advance, or because she disliked the idea of having France in the isthmus for ever. Since then there has been no further talk of prolonging the concession, although the question of renewal undoubtedly exists. What then is the present attitude of the various interested parties, Egypt, the Great Powers, and The Company?

II

When one discusses the canal with Egyptians, a certain amount of bitterness is apparent. What share have they had in this great enterprise on Egyptian soil? The administration is French; the shares are owned by the French and the English; the large profits all flow immediately out of the country, particularly since Egypt has never become an entrepôt for the Orient. The traffic scornfully passes through the isthmus, leaving nothing in its wake. The crowning grievance is that it was on account of the canal that Egypt lost part of her independence, for it has made of her one of those nerve centres which the Powers can never leave alone. Sometimes influential Egyptians are overheard to say that it would have been better for their country if the isthmus had never been cut. I remember one of them standing in front of de Lesseps' statue at Port Said, crying, 'There is the man who is the cause of all our troubles!'

One wonders if such exclamations are quite sincere, for they leave out of account the undeniable advantages which the canal has brought to Egypt. Before de Lesseps' time the region surrounding the isthmus was absolute desert, and now all along the fresh water canal it is green with vegetation. The canal zone itself is teeming with activity, with three flourishing towns — even more if we count separately Port Fuad and Port Tewfik — and two of these cities, Port Said and Ismailiya, did not even exist before. After all, if the Egyptian State had wished to develop the town of Suez they could have made it into a flourishing harbour for foreign trade. Finally, if we wish to draw up a complete balance sheet, we must also put down to The Company's credit the large sums which it has spent within the country, not to mention what is constantly being spent by its employees. We must not forget that this money comes in the first instance from tolls which are levied on traffic that is essentially international in character.

When de Lesseps founded the canal, he wished to associate the Egyptian Government in the profits of his enterprise, both by persuading it to become a shareholder and by reserving 15 per cent of the profits. As these advantages were alienated as the result of imprudent finance, Egypt has only her own Government to blame. Still, that does not make the present situation seem any less unjust to-day to the Egyptian people, and naturally their desire to obtain control of the canal will grow steadily as the end of the concession approaches. Like the Khedive Ismail they will unhesitatingly say, 'We want the canal to belong to Egypt'.

Yet, to tell the truth, public opinion scarcely bothers about the matter at all. We Westerners are ready to calculate thirty years ahead, but for an Oriental thirty years means never. Though very few people are thinking about it, those who do have laid down the principle that in no circumstances should Egypt allow herself to be robbed of this magnificent undertaking which is eventually to be returned to her. Meanwhile they also say that even to-day many of the executive posts should be redistributed. Why should they not share them with the foreigners?

The proportion of Egyptians who have been employed up to the present in the canal's administration has been relatively low. By a very wise agreement concluded with the Government in 1936-1937, The Company promised to recruit part of its personnel from among young Egyptians so that in 1938 they accounted for one-third. At the same time two Egyptian directors were welcomed to the Board, and a third seat was reserved for them should the number of directors ever be increased. The Company also took into account the desire of the present Government to be again associated, even in a small way, with the financial success of the canal, so each year the State is to receive a fixed sum of 300,000 Egyptian pounds. Further, the Suez

Canal shareholders are to be subject to Egyptian income tax at the rate of 10 per cent on their dividends. This tax became possible only when the Capitulations were abolished. However, as a result of this agreement we can now say that the country which originally granted the concession is once more participating in the profits of the canal.

These various arrangements and the fact that the end of the concession is drawing near, have to some extent modified Egypt's position. She feels that at last she has become an associate, and is now beginning to look upon herself as the coming heir. It is obviously in her interest to preserve intact this enterprise which will be hers to-morrow, and in the meanwhile prevent anything happening which might impair its status. That, too, is the attitude of France, whose shareholders had the courage and even the idealism to furnish the bulk of the capital needed. We should also add that the company which represents them has carried out its duty by providing an efficient management for this essential international service. Such has been the basis of France's claim to administer this enterprise, and this claim will remain genuinely valid until the very end of the concession.

As for England, who at first was hostile to the canal, her share in its control arises from the fact that she has been the principal user — actually at one time providing about four-fifths of the traffic — and also because she was wise enough to acquire a large proportion of the issued capital. Ferdinand de Lesseps had hoped to enlist British support in the beginning, and when later it was imposed instead of being offered, he nevertheless welcomed it graciously. How wise was the policy pursued by this great Frenchman! He also wished the concessionary State to participate, and would certainly have approved of the spirit of the 1936-1937 Agreement, which again associated Egypt in the success of the canal. So France, England, and Egypt will henceforth be interested in maintaining a regime which all three in their several ways have helped to establish and consolidate.

There are, however, certain malcontents, Italy in particular; she for some years now has been carrying on a noisy opposition campaign. Her part in the nett tonnage passing through the canal was 6.5 per cent in 1934, but it increased to 18.5 per cent in 1935 and 20.2 per cent in 1936. In 1937 it fell again to 16 per cent, and in 1938 to 13.4 per cent. The Italian mercantile marine is active as we know, both in the Mediterranean and out in the Far East, but the sudden swelling of the figures after 1935 obviously represented the Abyssinian War. Reinforcements and supplies for the new colony all have to pass through Suez, and pay tolls which seem all the higher since the trip is so short. Relying on her percentage in the total traffic, Italy has declared her impatience with the established regime, particularly as it admits of no discrimination whatever, and because she has no voice in its control. Hence a whole series of recriminations, expressed with more noise than accuracy, but which have not yet been made the subject of any official demands.

Though the canal may be run by France, England and Egypt, yet, they contend, Italy's claims for a share in its administration are well founded. It appears that an Italian named Negrelli was the real initiator. This Negrelli, however, actually was a well-known Austrian engineer, and a member of the exploratory syndicate set up by Enfantin. Negrelli died in 1858, a year before the first shovelful of sand was even dug. Then they claim that Italy answered de Lesseps' appeal in 1858. True, the Italians did subscribe, but only for 2719 shares out of a total of 400,000.

More convincing are their arguments based on their use

of the canal, for their percentage as we have seen is relatively important. Italy has the same right as any other client to take a commercial interest in the level at which the tolls are fixed, but she cannot expect discrimination in her favour, as this would infringe the terms of the concession. As both France and England also have possessions in the Indian Ocean, Italy's case is in no way exceptional.

The admission of an Italian to the Board of Directors would be the most natural thing in the world, provided he were to join as a collaborator and not adopt a threatening attitude. In any case Italy cannot demand it as a right. In agreement with Article 24 of the statutes, the Board is chosen 'from among the nationalities most interested in the enterprise', but what Ferdinand de Lesseps had in mind was those who had contributed to the realization of his scheme. Actually the users are represented, for British shipping interests have seven directors. Italy would un-doubtedly be welcomed if her demands were not purely political and if the way they have been presented could be overlooked.

What she really wishes is to participate in the political and military control of the isthmus. Now this control is based on the concession of 1854 and on the International Convention of 1888, that is to say on definite legal documents, and there can be no question of upsetting them. Neither France nor England, nor above all Egypt, is likely to alter a regime which is based on equal treatment for all, and from which the world has profited during three-quarters of a century without ever having had reason to complain. Any discussion outside these limitations becomes purely political, and implies the overthrow of an entire system born in the nineteenth century under British guidance. It is quite evident that, should Britain and her allies suffer a severe military defeat, the present regime in the isthmus and also in Egypt would be terminated. The question thus resolves itself into a struggle between forces far exceeding either the technical or the local aspects of the canal.

III

In the West we like to plan a long time ahead, so we are already wondering what will be the fate of the canal after 1968. To prophesy is futile, for we cannot know at all how the question will be put at that date . . . What will Egypt be, and what will England be? What will be the equilibrium between the oceans and the continents? And the United States, what will they have to say? or Japan? or any other new star in the political firmament? Obviously we cannot know, but the future regime of the canal will depend on the answer to all these questions.

One thing is certain, and that is that there will be a struggle between Egypt and the clients of the canal. The latter will be anxious to see a satisfactory service maintained, whereas Egypt will try to remain mistress of her new possession and draw from it the highest profits she can. It would be rather naive on the part of the Egyptian Government to imagine that they can own an undertaking which is essentially international in its functions, without also assuming serious obligations. In the Orient people dream about jobs but do not worry much about their own competence to fill them. The canal users will have a very different point of view. Also, whoever may be mistress of the seas to-morrow will certainly wish to intervene in fixing the tolls, organizing the transit, and in the military defence of the isthmus. She will certainly insist that the administration shall be adequate, so Egypt will not enjoy complete liberty of action.

One may suppose that the Egyptian Government itself hopes to undertake the management of the canal. If when the time comes it is not in a position to do so, then recourse to a concessionary company might be possible — but how can we imagine what a concessionary company would be like in 1968? Meanwhile, is the present company likely to try to make another attempt, similar to that of 1910? This is scarcely probable, for it would hesitate to risk a second snub and consequent loss of face, although it naturally would not refuse to listen to any proposals.

If no other suitable solution has been found by 1968, Egypt would probably itself fall back on the alternative of trying to prolong the concession, but it is certain that such negotiations would be carried on in very difficult circumstances. The Egyptians, hungry after their long fast, will be jealous of the advantages which have eluded them for so many years. It is certain that they will be very exacting, both as to their share in the profits and regarding employment. Thus any prolongation of the present concession would be dearly bought. It is also possible that the shareholders might refuse to pay a price which to them might appear excessive, in exchange for advantages amounting to only a fraction of those to which they have become accustomed. This would apply more especially if the concessionary Power should refuse to tie itself down for a long period.

Furthermore, what will England's attitude be — providing of course that she still has a deciding voice in the affair? Perhaps she would wish to form an exclusively British company, or would she be faithful to her traditions —

supreme argument! — and content herself with the Franco-British group to which she is already accustomed? Doubtless, also, other nations will give their opinions, though unasked.

The truth is that the only workable solution will be one which is satisfactory at once to Egypt and to Europe — again supposing that thirty years from now Europe still is able to impose her will in a matter which at that time will not be looked upon as exclusively Egyptian, Mediterranean, nor even European, but world-wide.

PART TWO

THE PANAMA CANAL

CHAPTER I

THE ISTHMUS COUNTRIES AND THE AMERICAN CONTINENT

I

Suez is at a cross-roads between three continents, and it has always been bound up with the history of our civilization. Panama, on the other hand, is strictly American, which means that in this study we must adopt a mental outlook which is entirely foreign to us. America in the fullest sense of the word is a New World, and I must be pardoned if I emphasize this somewhat hackneyed expression. It is a new world possessing its own colouring, its own special tone, and its own unique and new problems. From the preliminary observation that we cannot understand South America without having visited North America and vice versa, I come to my second, which is that to judge American affairs with any sense of proportion, we must not commit the mistake common amongst Europeans, of keeping to the Atlantic coast and neglecting the Pacific.

There is a strong continental unity in America, and many things become clear only when we realize that the adjective 'American' should be applied to the whole of both continents, which I consider as one. The two Americas may be contrasted from the cultural point of view, but they resemble each other geographically. When one has visited North America, South America does not seem so completely new. If one folds the map over against itself, one gets an astonishing amount of correlation. The Andes correspond to the Rocky Mountains, the pampas to the prairies, Brazil to the Antilles, and even to Louisiana. Similar resemblances can be found in the economic, social and political life of both continents. They have the same conditions of exploitation, the same racial problems, the same conceptions of republican government of a kind that is foreign to the French and British parliamentary spirit. Their governmental systems rely basically on plebiscites, and on the president, a purely American inspiration though somewhat resembling the First Consul as created by Napoleon. Finally, we have the same underlying optimism, an optimism which can only be found in this new world, and which is common to all Americans.

Geography, the basis of Pan-Americanism, has tended to unite the two continents, whereas history separates them. The inhabitants have sprung from different origins, Catholic and Latin on the one hand, and Protestant and Anglo-Saxon on the other. How are we to know which of these two factors, history or geography, will carry the day? If it is to be history, then their link with Europe will hold, and the axis of their communications will remain horizontal. If on the contrary it is to be geography, then the axis will be vertical, and the Pan-American spirit will gradually dominate in this part of the world. The best analogy that I can think of for this problem is the weather-vane. We must keep this struggle of the axes constantly in mind, for we shall run across it everywhere, in Canada and in the Argentine, and also in Panama.

II

Central America is a region of isthmuses. The unity of the two continental masses of North and South America is broken, for about 30 degrees of latitude, by two deep submarine depressions, the Gulf of Mexico and the Gulf of

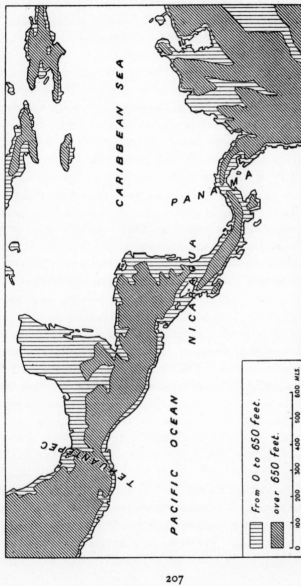

Mountain ranges and low country in Central America. (Reproduced from 'Mexico and Central America', by Max Sorre, Volume XIV in the *Géographia Universelle*, published under the direction of P. Vodal de la Blache and L. Gallois, Librairie Armand Colin, 1928)

Antilles. This sunken zone is continued by a trough running under the Pacific Ocean, and it is interesting to note how in these features an east-to-west direction predominates. Actually they are the outcome of great medial faults which are oriented in this direction, and which have profoundly modified the configuration of this area. We have Bartlett's Trough stretching from the Gulf of Honduras to Santiago, Cuba. It is about 1000 miles long, 100 miles wide, and 20,000 feet deep. Again we have Brownson's Trough lying to the north of Haiti and Puerto Rico, which is over 26,000 feet deep. Then there is the Trough of Anegada, 13,000 feet deep, between the Virgin Islands and the Lesser Antilles. As late as the Oligocene Age communication is supposed to have existed between the Atlantic and Pacific Oceans, which seems reasonable as the instability of the earth's crust is most pronounced in this area, and even to-day the Lesser Antilles, Mexico, and Central America are among the most volcanic regions of the world.

Philip II vetoed the plan for a canal at Panama. 'God has shown His will,' he said, 'by creating a continuous isthmus.' The engineers have learned by experience the truth of this observation, although geologians may contest it. The latter draw attention to the curious shape of Central America, and especially to the numerous waist-lines running across it. At some points these waists are exceedingly narrow, only 122 miles at Tehuantepec, 163 at Nicaragua, and 44 at Panama. Central America is simply a series of lands that have emerged from the sea, and its continuity is an illusion.

The isthmus countries stretch for 1800 miles from Tehuantepec to the Gulf of Uraba, but their unity is more apparent than real. They are just two groups of islands that have joined up: the southern extremity of Mexico,

Guatemala and Honduras form one, and Nicaragua, Costa Rica, and Panama the other. The northern group of islands has certain characteristics in common with the Rockies, but the other is purely tropical in climate. The extreme boundaries of these two 'islands' are well defined. On the north they are at Tehuantepec — how well I remember the platitude about 'its infinite sadness under a rainy sky!' At the other end is the formidable breach of the mouth of the Atrato or Gulf of Uraba which separates two distinct worlds, the axis of Panama from the axis of the Andes. So from the point of view of geology, the contention that Panama should be united with Colombia is sheer nonsense.

The Isthmus of Panama is a narrow ribbon folded like the letter S . Its territory is mountainous, being the backbone of a much larger zone now invaded by the two oceans. Geologically it is composed of sediments folded during the Middle Tertiary Period, with granite intrusions appearing in the core of the anticline. The mountains are disposed in echelon; from the west to the east we have the Sierras of Veraguas, of Azuero and of San Blas. Their summits reach from three to five thousand feet, and at the Guatemala end as much as ten thousand or more.

By reason of the peculiar shape of the isthmus, the town of Panama on the Pacific shore is actually located to the east of Colón, and looks out towards the south-east. The sun rises in the Pacific and sets over the land. At first this seems fantastic, and it takes a traveller a long time to get used to it. Because of the rainy climate the mountain peaks in the isthmus have suffered from intense erosion and disintegration. Much of the soil has been washed away, and the sea has penetrated far into the estuaries, which has given the Gulf of Panama all the characteristics of a submerged continent. From this have arisen certain consequences interesting to engineers, such as the low altitude, less than 300 feet, of the Culebra Divide, and also the wealth of rivers which resemble a network of mountain streams. The central divide is most complicated, for there is no main backbone to the isthmus, and yet in spite of their feeble altitude these hills are mountains in miniature. They must not be considered as a continuation of the Cordilleras, however, for they have a character of their own.

In its geological composition, the ground is not homogeneous. On the Atlantic side there are Tertiary sediments, and Tertiary volcanic rocks in the central part, with an anticlinal axis raised up and pierced by volcanic intrusions, which finally took the form of vertical eruptions breaking through the earth's crust. We first find marsh lands on the Colón shore, then approaching Panama a series of irregular little hills separated from one another, and shaped rather like little waves in a choppy sea, the dark green colour of the vegetation further accentuating the comparison.

It is this region near the Pacific that was subject to landslides. Sometimes the slides took place on the surface when the rocks, being penetrated with humidity, were disintegrating and gave way to the force of gravity. At other times the sliding was far underground. This happened when there was a juxtaposition of two sorts of ground with no elements capable of forming cement in between. These landslides proved fatal to the French engineers, and very serious for the Americans, particularly in the Gaillard Cut, where they had to hew through the underlying strata. The landslides have at last come to an end, or at any rate they can now be foreseen and dealt with in time.

Among the many difficulties with which the builders of the canal had to contend, the climate was almost as bad as the geology. We have here a sub-equatorial climate, actually one of the worst in the world until American medical science learned how to deal with it. First there is the dry season from December to May, with trade winds constantly blowing from the north-east. Then from June to November we have the wet season when rain-bearing winds come up from the south. The tropical deluges in these regions must be seen to be believed. The sky seems to be pouring out buckets of water without the slightest respite for hours on end. The clouds are black as ink, and one searches in vain for the faintest opening. Quickly the brooks fill up to the banks and become rivers, which in turn overflow and empty into the canal in boiling cataracts. After the storm, the green mantle of the countryside is spangled with a network of silver threads. One can imagine the effect of this on a vast piece of engineering work, and the men's discouragement when some implacable stream threatened to carry away their precarious achievements.

There is a certain difference between the two shores of the isthmus. The northern slope receives a certain amount of rain throughout the whole year, even in winter. This is the domain of the tropical forest, where the vegetation is unbelievably exuberant. The southern slope on the contrary has a dry season. Panama, for example, receives only 56 per cent of the rain that Colón does, and at times looks as parched as the Mediterranean coast at the end of summer. These, however, are trivial matters. Taken as a whole this country is more closely akin to South America, especially the Amazon Basin, than it is to Mexico. We have the same luxuriant foliage of the virgin forest and the jungle, which seems here to spill over into the canal. We have Nature in the same aggressive mood, endlessly struggling against the invader. The impression that Panama left on me is that to-day, even after thirty years of the most efficient sanitation, this constant struggle with Nature is still going on, and that here she is evil. If guard is relaxed for an instant, she will recapture all the ground previously wrested from her. In the face of such elemental and superhuman forces, one cannot but reflect on the precariousness of our civilization.

III

After having twice visited the isthmus, the dominant memory I retain is of Nature in excess, primitive, overwhelming. Man may hold her in check, but she still defies him. After a trip across the Caribbean Sea and through Colombia, I am particularly conscious of the grandiose structure of the continent which forms a base for Central America. I also realize the essentially primitive character of this isthmus as it lies isolated between two immense oceans. The life of all these regions seems to be influenced by such underlying factors as the vast proportions of the geographic framework, the difficulties of transport which the aeroplane alone has been able to overcome, and the impediments encountered in developing the boundless natural resources of the country.

The Isthmus of Panama may be narrow and broken, but the neighbouring continent is solid and massive. Colombia is huge, not merely because its area is 449,000 square miles, but because its whole structure has been conceived on what we may call the American plan. Each region is formidable in itself. One is first confronted with the Andes, a trident of mountain chains rising over 15,000 feet high. Then there is the vast expanse of the Llanos lowlands, and lastly the enormous rivers — the Atrato, the Magdalena, the Cauca, the Meta, the Orinoco, the Putumayo and the Amazon.

Both the Atlantic and Pacific coasts extend on so vast a scale that even to-day they have never been completely surveyed. Here man is not the measure of things, as the philosophers said of ancient Greece. When one speaks of America one must realize that Nature there is on quite a different scale to what she is in Europe.

One does not always fully appreciate how difficult communication is in these countries. There are really only two means of transport, the mule and the aeroplane, and yesterday there was only the mule. In less than twenty years they have passed from one extreme to the other, almost without a transition stage. Roads are only now beginning to be built, and the railways are still unfinished, and generally badly equipped. So except for some transport on the rivers, the mule used to be the only available means of getting from one place to another.

If we lose sight of this background, which is so different from our own, it may be difficult to understand the history of the canal's construction, and particularly the relationship between the isthmus and the Colombian Government. Only yesterday it required at best ten to fifteen days to go from Baranquilla on the Caribbean Sea to the capital at Bogotá. One went by boat up the Magdalena River, and then by train. I made the trip by air in three hours and a half! To go from Bogotá to Panama before the advent of the aeroplane one had to spend two additional days at sea if one went by way of Baranquilla. Another plan was to go to Buenaventura on the Pacific coast by rail in two or three days, but in the middle of the journey it was necessary to transfer to an autobus and do about sixty miles that way. After that a boat took you on to the isthmus in another forty-eight hours, so in all the trip required four or five days, provided all connections worked out exactly and no time was lost waiting. To-day one can do this trip in seven hours!

When the canal was being built, remember, neither the aeroplane nor the railway were available. When Bonaparte Wyse went to try to get a concession in 1878 it took him eleven days on horseback to reach the capital. I have met many people who in their youth left Bogotá on muleback to go to Europe. At the time of the revolution in 1903, it was quicker to go from Panama to New York than to the capital at Bogotá. Who knows whether Colombia would have lost the isthmus if the aeroplane had existed then, for it has since completely altered transport conditions. But that is forty years ago, and the isolation of the Colombian Government, on its high plateau at Bogotá, was almost inconceivable.

To develop these countries is bound to be difficult. Their natural resources are splendid, of course, for they have all the tropical products such as coffee, bananas, tobacco, cotton, and sugar cane. In the mining world they have gold, many minerals and metals, as well as oil. Like Americans and Australians one is tempted to talk of 'unlimited possibilities'. At the same time we have to admit, however, that this wealth is not only difficult to exploit, but also to reach and even to discover. The forests, the plains, and the mountains form masses which often are impenetrable. Then one must consider the distances and the climate, while the altitude is a test in itself.

In such circumstances exploitation, if it is to amount to anything, must be done in a very large way, and that necessitates great accumulations of capital which must be sought abroad, as well as an organization for production and distribution far exceeding the local means. All this needs foreign intervention in some form. Although superbly endowed by Nature, this country is evidently fated to rely on help solicited from outside. If it prefers to be left alone and independent, then it must let development slow down.

I V

It was in an environment such as I have described that the canal across the isthmus had to be built. To-day the Panama-New York axis is all important, but in the past it was the one from Panama to Bogotá that was imposed. It still must not be ignored, though politics, following the lead of geography, has since succeeded in separating Colombia from the isthmus countries.

Let me try to describe the scene as I saw it from the air. The sudden changes of altitudes and environment encountered in these air trips are the severest test that one can apply to the human frame. On the Colombian 'savane' or plateau we were at a height of nearly 9000 feet. It was cold and the air was so thin that we suffered from lack of oxygen. Until people become acclimatized they are always out of breath. Our heads ached with a vague form of mountain sickness. Even the most vigorous could not climb the stairs several steps at a time. A few hours later when we were down on the coast, the temperature was torrid in contrast with the rarefied air of the plateau, the atmosphere felt rich, dense, stifling, almost visible. Even centuries of habit cannot prepare the human constitution for such abrupt changes, which are to be found not only in the weather but also in the political and moral climates as well.

After leaving Bogotá our aeroplane flew first over the eastern branch of the Cordilleras, then over the central range, and finally over the western. In Peru the Andes,.

rising rocky and dry, form a single barrier between the Amazon and the Pacific. In Colombia, on the contrary, each of the three mountain chains is over fifty miles wide, and between them lie magnificent valleys, relatively low and filled with a sheer triumph of tropical vegetation. Here are sugar cane and bananas, and above the 3000 foot level we get coffee.

Only from an aeroplane can one realize the fundamental structure of the country. It is green almost to the summit of the mountains, apart from two or three peaks where reign the eternal snows. Everything else consists of vigorous rump-shaped mountains like the spine of some monstrous animal. The enormity of it all is what strikes us Europeans so forcibly. On the slopes, stretching interminably down towards the bottom of the valleys, one sees roads winding about on the sides of the precipices, climbing the cols, and clinging, Heaven knows how, to the edge of cliffs that rise almost vertical and sheer. Travelling in a motor car these roads are very dizzy-making, and yet looking down on them from high up in the sky one experiences a queer sense of relative security. Between the mountain chains the two great Colombian rivers, the Magdalena and the Cauca, wind their way along the bottom of the valleys. Higher up one comes to bounding forest streams and silver waterfalls.

On the Pacific slope the virgin forest stretches away to the horizon. The ridges and summits of the mountains seem as endless and indistinguishable as the waves of the sea. Here and there at great distances apart one discerns minute clearings, which indicate banana plantations. Then one descends rapidly at the landing ground of Turbo, lying in the deep narrow Gulf of Darien at the mouth of the Atrato River. At this point the Atlantic penetrates more deeply than anywhere else into the South American continent.

One cannot imagine a more exotic airport. Far away one can see the Gulf, the colour of pea-soup, and right down to the ocean stretches the forest. A narrow strip of ground has been cleared for a landing place, and in a simple log cabin the customs formalities are carried out, for this is where the Republic of Colombia ends. Facing us about six miles off are the seven mouths of the Atrato, one of the most powerful rivers in this region. After leaving Turbo we flew over the Delta country, which reminded me of the estuary of the Nile owing both to its mud and its stagnant ditches, and also because of the series of flat islands which are being formed from the silt and which will presently block up the whole of the sea floor.

Here we are at the frontier of the Republic of Panama. Then in a straight line the aeroplane cuts across the famous isthmus about sixty-five miles south of the canal. The country is prodigiously savage, jungle pure and simple, crossed by wide muddy and swiftly flowing rivers. From the heights above other streams tumble in cascades. The rivers are always full, as rain is almost continuous in these parts. Everywhere one sees storms piling up on the horizon, and sweeping across the sky.

A few minutes more, and then the thrilling sight of the Pacific! It appears astonishingly flat and peaceful, as if to justify its name. The aeroplane follows the shore. On the left towards the ocean the colouring is azure blue and limpid, like another Mediterranean. Looking inland, however, the water seems decomposed and unhealthy, tinted yellow, rose, or the green of putrefaction. It seems to creep into the interior, and one pictures these forests, with their unbelievable vitality, having their roots in some liquid element. There seems to be no solid ground anywhere on which to land. One can easily understand that here the main

obstacle to overcome is the excessive richness of the vegetable kingdom, which defends itself against man by its
unwholesomeness and density.

In the far distance a ribbon of silver! It is the canal.
A red town juts out on a promontory into the sea. That is
Panama. Behind it the sombre green mountains look like
a succession of isolated virgin hills, recalling the outlines of
a Chinese landscape. Now at last we are on the Pacific;
China is just on the other side.

CHAPTER II

CHRISTOPHER COLUMBUS TO FERDINAND DE LESSEPS

I

On October 12th, 1492, Columbus landed on the island of San Salvador. In 1502 he explored the shores of Darien, Panama, Nicaragua, and Honduras. In 1513 Vasco Nunez de Balboa reached the coast of the Pacific, and the town of Panama was founded six years later in 1519. Cortes landed in Mexico in 1520, and in the same year Magellan discovered his famous straits, and so opened up a route to the Pacific Ocean. Four years later, in 1524, Pizarro explored the western shore of the South American continent. In 1533 Pedro de Heredia founded Cartagena, and in 1538 still another new town, Bogotá, was started by Jiménez de Quesada. Thus in a few years a whole new empire was created for the white race.

Christopher Columbus had no sooner discovered America (without realizing it!) than he recommenced his search for a passage to the Indies, since, like the rest of his contemporaries, he was haunted by this quest. The natives now told him of 'a narrow land between two seas', and it was to unravel the secret of this isthmus, and if possible find a strait through it, that he made his fourth voyage. He landed in the Bay of Limon at the mouth of the Rio Chagres, still hoping that some natural waterway would lead through to India.

The first European actually to see the Pacific was Balboa, a soldier of fortune, and magistrate of Santa Maria de la

Antigua at Darien. The Indians had told him of the existence of an ocean which one could see from the mountain tops, and they also disclosed the fact that there was gold in the rivers flowing into it. An expedition was organized, and on September 25th, 1513, Balboa discovered the Pacific. Four days later he arrived at the sea, and took possession of it in the name of the King of Spain. He called it the Southern Ocean, for at this point the isthmus twists in such a way that the ocean lies to the south. Balboa was appointed governor of the province of Castilla del Oro, but he was soon replaced by Pedro Arias de Avila, who put him to death in 1519. All these men met a tragic fate.

Avila founded Panama in 1519, where the ruins of the old town still exist; it was from here that Pizarro set sail five years later. This town was destroyed by Morgan and his buccaneers in 1671, but it was reconstructed two years afterwards on the site which it still occupies to-day. After that time it became the main distributing point in the trade relations between Spain and her rich American colonies along the Pacific coast. In our day Panama is a conglomeration of Spanish origin but with a cosmopolitan atmosphere. The market gardeners and merchants are Chinese, the shop-keepers are Hindus, the hairdressers are Japanese, and the rank and file of the population is Indian, many with a tinge of negro blood. At the top are a few families of pure Spanish stock.

To conjure up the spirit of Old Spain, one should go five or six miles to the east along the sandy ocean beach, and visit the ruins of Old Panama. Here under the coco-nut and banana trees, beside the blue-green Pacific with its great white waves rolling in, are a few rose-red brick walls entirely covered with foliage, a daring camel-back bridge, a church tower, the remains of a convent — that is all.

When I arrived a few Indian fishermen alone broke the silence. It was the peace of the long dead past, heavy with memories. Why, I wondered, did Hérédia not consecrate one of the sonnets in his *Trophées* to this Old Panama?

For many years the Spaniards believed in the existence of a strait. Then, when they were finally convinced that the barrier was continuous, they thought of digging a canal. They wanted a route at all costs. The first road was constructed in 1519. It went from Panama to Nombre de Dios on the Atlantic coast, cutting through the jungle across both mountains and rivers. It was roughly paved with stones, and marked by a line of posts, and was the only transcontinental route until 1535. The Chagres River was then opened up for navigation by shallow boats. Finally, in 1597, Puerto Bello became the terminus of the road instead of Nombre de Dios. The paving was so solid that part of it exists to-day, and the section from Panama to Las Cruces is still used by the Indians.

I found the remains of this old track very moving. Here is an extract from my notes, jotted down in 1931 after I had seen it for the first time:

'Going along the modern American cement road our car ran over an enormous snake, at least eight or ten feet in length. Then at one point we penetrated into the jungle, where they showed me the tracks of the old Spanish path across the isthmus, a few flat stones placed here and there to prevent the vegetation from swallowing it up. The jungle had joined up so completely overhead that it was as dark as in a room when one has closed the green shutters. These few paving stones seemed poetic witnesses of a by-gone age.'

There were no other transit routes competing with Panama. An interoceanic road was organized across Nicaragua and also at Tehuantepec, but soon the idea of having some artificial water communication grew up. In 1529 Alvaro de Saavedra Ceron discussed the possibility of cutting through the isthmus at Tehuantepec, Nicaragua, Panama or Darien. In 1534 Charles V had a survey made on the spot, at the Isthmus of Panama between the River Chagres and the Pacific. However, the Governor of Panama decided that the plan was impracticable, so the Emperor dropped the matter.

In 1556 Philip II ordered a similar inquiry to be carried out at Nicaragua, but it reached the same negative conclusion. He too abandoned his canal policy, and it was not broached again until the nineteenth century. 'God has shown His will,' he gave as his reason. But at the back of his mind was evidently the fear of harming the trading monopoly which Spain enjoyed with Peru, and no doubt this explains why even the opening up of new roads overland between the two oceans was thenceforth forbidden on pain of death.

II

Two centuries passed and more, and then Humbold's famous voyage again attracted attention to the question of an interoceanic canal. He suggested nine possible locations between Tehuantepec and Darien. His study was superficial, but it brought the problem again to the fore. In April 1814, the Cortes decided to build a maritime canal for large sized ships, and suggested that a company be formed for the purpose. Nothing was done, however, and by 1823 the Spanish Empire in America had disintegrated.

Bolivar in 1824 chose the town of Panama as the meeting place for his Pan-American Congress. It was 'the veritable capital of the world, the centre of the globe, with one face turned towards Asia and the other towards Africa and Europe'.

About this time Goethe became lyrical over the maritime route that he wished to see opened up between the Atlantic and the Pacific. 'This work', he said, 'is reserved for posterity, and for some great creative spirit. It will be done one day, but I shall not see it, just as I shall not live to see the Suez Canal. I should have liked to have lived several centuries later, in order to see these two gigantic undertakings completed.'

Hitherto the United States had shown no signs of life in this matter, indeed it was only after the liberation of the Spanish colonies that she began to take any interest at all. The centre of gravity of her own development was now steadily shifting towards the west. California in 1846, and Oregon in 1848, became American territory, and in the latter year gold was discovered in the Sacramento Valley. There was still no transcontinental railroad, for the Union Pacific was not completed until over twenty years later, in 1870, so the gold miners had to find another way to reach the west. Also adequate communications between the east and the new states on the Pacific coast had now become a political necessity. These and many other reasons implied that the United States should intervene in the future should any canal be constructed between the two oceans.

It was obviously in the interests of the Americans that this work should be accomplished, but they were afraid that Europe might assume sole control of it, for they kept a jealous eye on any enterprises she undertook in the New World. President Monroe in his Message to Congress on December 2nd, 1823, decisively expressed the unanimous conviction of his fellow citizens in this respect: 'The

American continents, by the free and independent condition which they have assumed and maintained, are henceforth not to be considered as subjects for future colonization by any European Powers . . . It is impossible for the European governments to interfere in their (South America's) concerns without affecting us . . .'

For the first time a definite canal policy was now created, in which the United States, without claiming exclusive control, insisted that it should be 'free to all nations on equal terms'. It was in the same sense that Henry Clay in 1825 declared that in his opinion it should be 'effected by common means' and 'not left to the separate and unassisted effort of any one Power'. This principle was confirmed by a resolution in the Senate in 1835, and in the House of Representatives in 1839.

At this time numerous American plans for canals saw the light of day. Aaron H. Palmer put forth one in 1825 that was incomplete; then there was another in 1839 sponsored by John L. Stephens, who favoured the Nicaraguan route, but subsequently admitted that the moment was not favourable. There were many others, but all vague. The European schemes were equally numerous, and among them were several advanced by the French. In 1838 a syndicate, organized by Salomon, obtained from New Granada a concession to build a railway terminating at Panama. In 1843 Guizot sent a mission there, headed by Napoleon Garella, who established that the ridge was 375 feet above the sea, and proposed a canal of 34 locks and trenches or tunnels 158 feet above sea level. From his prison in Ham the future Napoleon III in 1846 also planned a Nicaraguan canal, and he even offered to give up politics if the French Government would authorize him to undertake the work.

But all this was most unsubstantial. The first serious work was when the United States began to take diplomatic precautions as their territory gradually approached the Pacific. They began by concluding a treaty with New Granada in 1846 relative to the Isthmus of Panama, and this was ratified in 1848. It conceded free right of transit to the American Government for all present and eventual forms of transportation. In exchange the American Government guaranteed both the complete neutrality of the isthmus, and the sovereign and proprietary rights of the New Granada Government over the territory in question. The wording was decisive, and we will meet with it again in 1903 at the time of the secession of Panama.

Apparently the French Minister at Bogotá was not far wrong when he wrote at this time, 'Should New Granada summon the aid of the United States to suppress any threat of secession on the part of Panama or Veraguas she will deliver to the Americans a position of military and commercial importance which will mean more to them than Gibraltar does to England. Should we not take the liberty of warning the New Granada Government of the folly of compromising themselves without considering the effect that their action may have on the future? The road which the United States is trying to construct at its own expense across the isthmus will so modify the present state of things that, when the day comes that public opinion in the Union abandons its present indifference and takes an active interest in the matter, it will be irresistible'.[1]

In 1849 shortly after this was written, another treaty was signed which reserved to the United States the exclusive right of constructing an interoceanic canal in Nicaraguan

[1] Correspondence of the French Minister at Bogotá, August 10th, and December 7th, 1848.

territory; in the following year the Vanderbilt Syndicate was formed to carry it out. This was the beginning of a sentimental preference among the American people for the Nicaraguan route, a preference which continued until they were forced to adopt the rival course in 1902.

Meanwhile the urgent need of a transit route was making itself felt more every day because of the gold mining rush. The 'forty-niners' were numerous and in a hurry. Shipping lines were started between New York and Colón, and between Panama and San Francisco, but that did not do away with the journey over the old Spanish trail. No other route was practicable, for the trek across the American continent was long, difficult and unorganized — an aeroplane now does it in a night! — and the voyage around South America and through the Straits of Magellan was interminable.

About 1847 Mateo Klein obtained a railroad concession on behalf of a French company, but it did not succeed in raising the necessary capital.

In 1848 the New Granada Government gave a Mr. Aspinwall from New York a railroad concession similar to the one they had given to M. Salomon ten years before. The Panama Railroad Company this time received a monopoly for overland transport, and in 1867 a further law was passed stipulating that no canal concession should be granted near the railway without its consent. The duration of the concession had originally been for forty-nine years, but in 1867 it was prolonged to ninety-nine, which meant that it would be in force until 1966 when the entire property would revert to Colombia. This statute is still in force, and as we shall see presently, it proved to be a stumbling block for Ferdinand de Lesseps. In spite of the terrible death roll due to malaria — yellow fever is not mentioned —

the railway actually was built.. The line lay along what was later to be the projected course of the French canal. It started at Colón — then renamed Aspinwall — and ended at Panama. It was opened for traffic in 1855, and was the first and only workable interoceanic route since the Spanish trail until the canal eventually was completed in 1914.

III

As a result of this the United States encountered British hostility. On January 1st, 1849, a warship took possession of San Juan de Nicaragua, and Britain intimated that she was not disinterested in what was taking place in this part of the world. This worried Clayton, the American Secretary of State, who suggested negotiating, but Palmerston accepted only with condescension. At this period the United States, although emphasizing that they were 'specially interested', also admitted in principle that the proposed maritime route should be open to all. They were not seeking special privileges for themselves, but they were opposed to the idea of any other Power doing so, and England in particular.

The Bulwer-Clayton Treaty of 1850 applied to all canal projects, both at Panama and Nicaragua, and laid down that, should any enterprise be carried out, it would be placed under the joint patronage of the two Governments. The canal was also to be neutral, no fortifications were to be allowed, and the principle of equality of treatment was to be respected. Neither England nor the United States was to try to dominate Central America nor obtain new colonies there. Though the signatories promised to carry out any plan on 'fair and equal terms', it is clear from the text that they were very suspicious, and that each of the two partners was mainly concerned lest the other should get some exclusive advantage. In point of fact the effect of the Bulwer-Clayton Treaty was to retard rather than stimulate marine communication between the two oceans.

One wonders if this joint control really was in conformity with the Monroe Doctrine, and at any rate the public accepted it with growing impatience. After the War of Secession the contrary policy tended to gain ground; it aimed at exclusive American control of any canal, and has been expressed very frankly in many official documents. In 1869, Hamilton Fish, the Secretary of State, wrote to the American Minister at Bogotá, 'The President is disinclined to enter into any entanglement in participation of control over the work with other Powers; he regards it as an American enterprise, which he desires to be carried out under American auspices, to the benefit of which the whole commercial world should be fully admitted'.

On March 8th, 1880, shortly after de Lesseps had called on him, President Hayes addressed a special message to Congress in which he said, 'The policy of this country is a canal under American control: the United States cannot consent to the surrender of this control to any European country'.

Blaine, President Garfield's Secretary of State, tried in 1881 to get England to revise the Bulwer-Clayton Treaty. He wanted the United States to have exclusive strategic control, and to substitute a single trusteeship for the joint partnership agreed to in 1850. There naturally was no question of their having a monopoly in the use of the canal, and the official declaration renewed all the guarantees about equal treatment for all nations, etc., but the desire for exclusive political control contrasted with the former conciliatory attitude.

Since the victory of the North in the American Civil War, the American people felt more confidence in themselves. It was an American canal on American soil that Grant foresaw in his first Message. The success of the Suez Canal in 1869 also played its part in bringing interoceanic communications into the limelight. In 1871 the Navy Department made a special survey of the Isthmus of Tehuantepec, it being situated nearest to the United States. In 1872 Congress appointed a technical commission, and it pronounced in favour of the Nicaraguan course in 1876. Meanwhile the western states were developing rapidly, as the first transcontinental railway had been running since 1870. The country was about to acquire its present economic balance with two façades, one looking out on to the Atlantic and the other on the Pacific. Thus it was less likely than ever to be indifferent to a canal across the isthmus.

Then France intervened, and gave a decisive impulse from which, in the last analysis, America was to draw the profits.

CHAPTER III

DE LESSEPS AND THE INCEPTION
OF THE FRENCH COMPANY

I

FROM 1854 to 1869 no one in France could think of anything except the Suez Canal. Then, as was to be expected, the sheer triumph of this enterprise attracted attention to the possibility of building other interoceanic canals, particularly one in Central America. It was the scientific circles that took the initiative, for at two geographical congresses, Antwerp in 1871 and Paris in 1875, the question of an American canal was discussed.

When the Paris Geographical Society realized that the topography of the isthmus was totally unknown, they decided that a survey of the territory would have to be made, and they turned the matter over to their Committee of Commercial Geography, later to become the Society of Commercial Geography. On March 24th, 1876, this committee, being anxious to enlist useful support, enlarged itself into the French Committee for Cutting the Interoceanic Canal. The executive consisted of Ferdinand de Lesseps as president; and two vice-presidents, Admiral de la Roncière Le Nourry, and M. Meurand, president of the Society of Commercial Geography. There was also a secretary named Bionne, and among its members were Levasseur, Malte Brun, Foucher de Careil, and Cornélius Hertz.

Money was needed, however, before anything could be accomplished, so contact was soon established between geography and finance. The geographers were avid for knowledge, and the financiers thought that it might be interesting to exploit a concession, or even merely to negotiate for one. A limited company was formed, the Société Civile International du Canal Interocéanique de Darien, in order to defray the cost of the preliminary work. The driving force came from three men: first, General Türr, an Italian friend of de Lesseps and a Hungarian by birth; secondly, Bonaparte Wyse, the General's brother-in-law who was a naval lieutenant and also a grandson of Lucien Bonaparte; and lastly, the Baron de Reinach. Türr actually was in possession of a Colombian concession dated May 28th, 1876.

Bonaparte Wyse, together with another naval lieutenant named Armand Reclus, and several French and foreign engineers, embarked immediately on a first voyage of exploration. Although three of the eight members of the expedition died *en route*, the others brought back a plan for a canal across the isthmus at Darien. As it was to have locks and tunnels, de Lesseps refused to agree to it, for at that time he was still in favour of a sea level canal. Wyse started out again in the following year, and after inspecting the region of San Blas and Panama he decided on a new course. Then, after having got into contact with the railway company, he travelled to Bogotá in eleven days on horseback, and there obtained a confirmation of the concession on March 20th, 1878. The concession was to be for ninety-nine years, but was conditional on the agreement of the Panama Railroad Company being obtained should the Panama route be adopted. This point was to be submitted to the decision of an international committee of experts.

During this initial phase, the prime movers as we see were drawn from widely different spheres. First came the geographers, who had no ulterior motives, but they did not leave Paris. Then we have the financiers, who owned the concession, and who of course wanted to build the canal but who were possibly even more anxious to make their securities saleable. Then finally there were a few daring explorers who were ready to risk their lives, for it was a real danger to penetrate the jungle at either Darien or Panama. These first steps were important but, let us be under no illusion, the matter would probably have ended there had it not been for Ferdinand de Lesseps. His name alone could galvanize the public and attract capital. Geographers, bankers, explorers — they all needed him and him alone.

An International Congress to study interoceanic canals met at Paris from May 15th to 29th, 1879, under the chairmanship of the hero of Suez. Its purpose was to choose the route of the canal, to prepare exact estimates, and to calculate eventual costs and profits — in short, to prepare the way for the bankers and engineers. The meetings were held in the Boulevard St. Germain, in the Geographical Society's hall which Parisians know so well. The Congress consisted of 138 members, of whom 98 took an active and enthusiastic part. They had come from all over the world. De Lesseps' role needs explanation. He was one of the chief enthusiasts for this 'new Bosporus', but he was there only as chairman of a committee appointed by the Geographical Society. Presiding over the meetings he was active and authoritative, but he felt that he had simply been asked to give the matter a send off, so in the beginning at any rate he limited himself to this.

The Congress divided itself into five sub-committees: statistics, economics, navigation, engineering, and ways and means. The delegates took their work seriously for, as their number was limited, each felt morally responsible for the way he voted. When it came to settling on the course of the

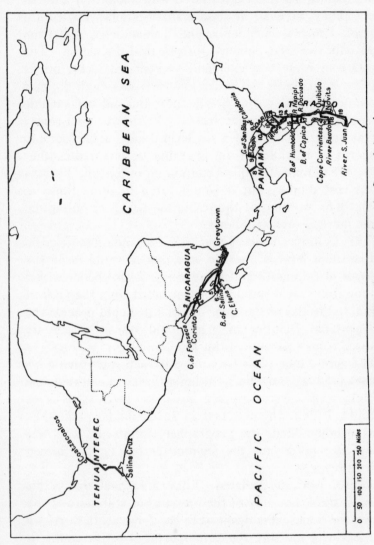

Locations of nineteen different canal projects in Central America
(From the Isthmian Canal Commission, 1901)

233

canal, they found themselves faced with about fifty alternatives. They were all at four main locations, Darien (or Atrato), Panama, Nicaragua, and Tehuantepec, and from them only two were retained for practical discussion. The Nicaraguan route was long and necessitated locks, but it might eventually be the easier. Panama was more difficult and more expensive, but it was short and did not exclude the possibility of a sea level canal. Ferdinand de Lesseps was at heart in favour of a sea level canal for his 'oceanic Bosporus' as he called it, for in reality he pictured another Suez. He did not attempt to restrain his optimism. Panama might cost double, but it would bring in three times as much. The wording of the resolution which he submitted to the meeting was as follows:

'This Congress believes that to cut an interoceanic canal at a constant level is possible, and that it would be in the interests of commerce and navigation. It also believes that this maritime canal should be constructed from the Gulf of Limon to the Bay of Panama, and that it should provide the indispensable facilities of access and transit which are required from a passage of this kind.'

The voting took place by a roll-call, each voter giving his reasons. Many members, although they advocated the Panama route, were opposed to a sea level canal — for example, Eiffel, who felt that locks would be preferable. On the other hand, the geographer, Levasseur, who was acting as reporter for the Committee on Traffic, agreed with de Lesseps.

'I vote "Yes",' he declared. 'I have always felt that in this we must think not only of the present but still more of the future, for the canal is destined to last for centuries. As we cannot to-day measure the development of future traffic, it is important that the conditions of passage through the canal should resemble as far as possible what they would be in a natural strait. Consequently a sea level maritime canal is preferable to any other system. The Technical Commission has decided that it is possible to keep to sea level and that the best route is Panama. The resolution presented to the vote of the Congress is definite on this point. I therefore give it my entire support.'

One should try to picture the assembly at the time of this historic vote. The atmosphere was most exceptional. It was with a certain solemnity that the chairman inaugurated the voting.

'Now that this Congress has completed its deliberations,' he said, 'it is my duty to state clearly that it has carried out its task conscientiously. Others who will profit from this interoceanic canal will one day say that we have merited well of humanity.'

There was great excitement. The 'noes' were received with jeers, and it was in a scene of intense emotion that the result was declared. Out of 98 voters, there were 78 in favour, 12 against, and 8 abstentions.

What exactly had the Congress approved? The principle of a canal at sea level across the isthmus at Panama, at an estimated cost of about a thousand million francs, which would take twelve years to construct, though possibly only eight if adequate equipment could be obtained.

11

While they were taking this vote which was to be so pregnant in its consequences, pressure was being exercised on Ferdinand de Lesseps to induce him to accept the management of the enterprise. Instead of being merely chairman of the Congress, they wished him to become chairman of a limited company. Without him the promoters well knew that their concession might remain a valueless piece of paper. The truth was, however, that pressure came spontaneously and irresistibly from all quarters.

The popularity of this man, 'The Great Frenchman', as Gambetta called him, was immense. He was one of those rare figures who was known to everyone in Paris; everyone had seen him — as a child even I had seen him — riding through the Bois followed by a squad of his children. The Suez Canal shareholders were numerous, and all were well satisfied.

'The other day I was going to my office in a cab,' he himself recounted. 'The coachman shook me by the hand, and said, "M. de Lesseps, I am one of your shareholders".'

He was the man who had made Suez, and in him the patriotic saw the man who would make Panama, and obtain a peaceful revenge for France's military defeat. From all sides came appeals of this nature. Victor Hugo said to him, 'Astonish the world by the great deeds that can be won without a war!' The rumblings of the Congress reached his ears.

'There is only one man who can accomplish this new piece of work, the man from Suez.'

De Lesseps was tempted. He loved popularity. Thinking of the coachman shareholder, he may have said to himself, 'It was these little people who made Suez, and the same little people will make Panama'.

His family and intimate friends were fully alive to this atmosphere, and they were rather dubious. After all he was seventy-four years old, and anyone else at such an age would be considered an old man; but he was still young. He carried out his duties as chairman of the Suez Canal

Company in sprightly style. His life had been one of the magnificent successes of the century, and his old age was an apotheosis. But in such circumstances should one embark upon new ventures?

So said his family, and particularly his son Charles, with due respect. Charles, then thirty-eight years of age, had been one of his most faithful collaborators at Suez. 'What do you wish to find at Panama? Money? You will not bother any more about money at Panama than you did at Suez. Is it glory? You have had enough glory. Why not leave that to someone else? And as for us who have worked at your side, are we to have no repose? The task of Panama is certainly grandiose, and I believe that it can be carried through, but think of the risk that will be run by those who put themselves at its head. You succeeded at Suez by a miracle. Be content with accomplishing one miracle in your lifetime, and do not hope for a second.'

Ferdinand de Lesseps appreciated the weight of these arguments, but in face of requests which poured in from all sides he felt himself weakening little by little.

'I have committed two follies in my life. At Rome and at Suez. I am about to commit a third. I hope to live long enough to see those who to-day are attacking the Panama scheme recognize that there was some spark of reason in this folly.'

I cannot imagine anything nobler than the attitude of this son, who, having said all he could, devotedly promised to follow his father.

'Should you decide to take this step,' he said, 'and should you wish me to join you, I shall do so with the best will in the world. I shall not complain no matter what happens. All that I am I owe to you. What you have given me you have the right to take away.' One may surely compare

Charles de Lesseps with some of the most pathetic figures in the ancient Greek tragedies.

The hour of decision arrived with the closing of the Congress. After the voting on the resolution, the chairman arose at the end of the session.

'Before we separate,' he said, 'I must admit to you that I have been going through a most perplexing time while the Congress has been meeting. Two weeks ago I little dreamed that I should be obliged to put myself at the head of a new enterprise. My best friends have tried to dissuade me, telling me that after Suez I should take a rest. Well, if one asks a General who has just won a first victory whether he wishes to win a second, would he refuse?'

After several minutes of applause, Admiral de la Roncière, to whom de Lesseps had relinquished the chair, replied:

'Gentlemen, May 29th, 1879, will mark the beginning of one of the greatest undertakings of modern times. Permit me, as we depart, to close this meeting by a wish which is already in your hearts. May that illustrious man, who has been the heart and soul of our deliberations, who has captivated us by his charm, and who is the personification of these great enterprises, may he live long enough to see the end of this work which will bear his name for ever. He has not been able to refuse to assume its command, and in so doing he continues to carry out the mission which has made him a citizen of the whole world.'

So we find Ferdinand de Lesseps engaged in the new business. One can understand his state of mind: the call to action is irresistible to a man of his nature and he could not disregard it. Also his optimism was increased by a certain light-heartedness which had served him so often and so well, as for example when he had inaugurated the Suez

Canal Company without having the concession in order, and when he walked out on Rothschild. Not only had he confidence in his own star, but he was encouraged by the conviction of his many friends that he was fully equal to any task. I cannot help comparing the responsibilities of a scientist or a professor who signs a resolution, with those of the president of a board of directors who has to conduct the business. They are really worlds apart. And as we turn away from the acclamations of this Congress, may I remind you of the proverb that counsellors do not pay the bills?

III

Before proceeding further let us analyse the atmosphere existing in France at this time. One can still discern indications, dim but persistent, of the spirit of St. Simon, who had preached the doctrine of social regeneration through work, and universal peace through great public undertakings, and particularly by developing communications between the peoples of the world. St. Simon had included interoceanic canals in his programme, but with him it was not a question of imperialism but of service to humanity. The finest spirit of the nineteenth century is expressed in this doctrine and served by this technique. De Lesseps was the perfect representative of the idea of peaceful progress.

As the French public were imbued with these traditions, they were tempted to seek fresh laurels for their country in the Panama affair, which they hoped would be as magnificent a work of humanity and as profitable a business venture as the Suez Canal. Personally I do not believe that we should suspect any imperialistic motives, but rather that we should look for an obscure but instinctive desire for revenge for the great defeat of 1870. This revenge was to be won on the battlefields of peace and progress rather than in war.

Nothing is ever quite so honest and straightforward as all this. The 'complex' from which Panama was to emerge was indeed far from simple. 'The heroic age is over,' Gambetta had said. The Republican Government wanted to show that it was in earnest and capable of carrying out its tasks. Furthermore it wished to add some material accomplishment to its theoretical policies. Had not its Exhibition in 1878 been as great as the one in 1867 under the Empire? The Suez Canal had been built under Napoleon III, but could not Panama now be done during the Presidency of M. Grévy? As we look back on it, the tone of this period seems to have been a prolongation of the imperialistic regime in some ways, particularly as the keynote was the prestige of material progress under liberalism and capitalism. This is explained in M. Daniel Halévy's book, *République des Ducs*, in which he writes:

'At that time they realized the poetry of capitalism, a poetry which is forgotten to-day. The laying of the first submarine cable from Europe to America, and that more recent marvel, the building of the Suez Canal . . . This is private enterprise, this is the shareholders' democracy which is gradually changing the face of the world and setting humanity free. At the same time scientists like Berthelot are making available all manner of unknown forces, and explorers like Stanley are steadily pushing back the frontiers of the world. The spirit of St. Simon has penetrated deeply beneath the otherwise calm surface of politics.'

Such influences undeniably swayed the opinions of the Republican statesmen of that epoch. Many of them believed that from the point of view of the material progress being achieved by democracy, the Republic could win very real victories, which would be almost the equivalent of the longed-for 'revenge'. Gambetta had been converted to this policy of great public works, which enlisted the support of the country's economic forces for the Government, and also led to the apotheosis of labour. All this may sound a bit like speeches made at an agricultural fair or a prize distribution, yet among the leading statesmen this inspiration was sincere. They hoped for a union between politics and the nation which would serve France and also help the republican cause.

Let us beware, however, of being too idealistic in this. The business promoters were associated with this movement, for after all they were needed, but unfortunately they wished to grab everything. Scurrying about alongside de Lesseps, who was magnificently disinterested and unselfish, were not merely sound business men, but also a band of speculators, profiteers and sharks. On the upper level, when the statesmen of the day called in high finance to their aid, they were simply carrying out a perfectly legitimate Government operation; but in the lower levels we find politicians who were in the pay of financiers, and who perhaps believed that they were putting finance at the service of the Republic. Let us give them this slender excuse.

In his symbolic figure, Bouteiller, Barrès has described this type of politician to the life: 'For reasons hidden even from himself and which yet were more powerful than his need of money and his political scheming, he directed his steps towards financial and industrial circles, where at that time his intelligence, or better still his instinct, told him he would find the nourishment he required. At the beginning of his political career, Bouteiller had been greatly attracted by Gambetta, as a man who could sway the crowd at will. In the same way he was now fascinated by budgets and loved to study them. He was particularly influenced by "The Great Frenchman" who could command money and who, by the force of his persuasion, could obtain vast sums, comparable to the budgets of a State.'[1]

This conception of government, with its curious mixture of materialism and idealism, was undoubtedly that of the 'Opportunists'. Under this influence they pass unconsciously from a platform of principles to one of public works . . . 'You are wrong, gentlemen, not to appreciate how times have changed. The day is gone when a public man could have a literary or a legal bent. Nowadays he must be imbued with the spirit of commercialism, industrialism and finance.'

Barrès puts these words into the mouth of his character, Bouteiller, and I myself heard them repeated hundreds of times about 1885. In my memory they recall with striking clarity the atmosphere of this period. In them the idealism of the nineteenth century was still intact, with its unshaken confidence in perpetual material progress. But after the heroic period opportunism was coming into power, and lofty principles had to be acclimatized to the conditions necessary to government. Finally, though still a child, even I sensed the presence of gluttonous sharks, rogues and cynics. They may not have been there in person perhaps, but as in *Hamlet* I guessed that they were behind the arras.

If we substitute hypocrisy for cynicism, we shall now find these three personifications of this epoch gathered around de Lesseps when he embarked on the Panama undertaking. He represented and expressed the splendid optimism of the century. At first he was supported, but later was coldly

[1] Maurice Barrès, *L'Appel au Soldat*, pp. 79-80.

dropped by the Government; but the sharks were to pursue him, heedless of the nobility of his aims. His defeat was to be complete and resounding. Yet the enterprise still has an element of grandeur owing to the disinterestedness of its leader, the fine technical collaboration of his subordinates, and the tragic fate of his son who had foreseen it all. We are about to recount a sad, but not a disgraceful story.

CHAPTER IV

THE FRENCH COMPANY AT WORK

I

THE total cost of constructing the canal was estimated by the Geographical Congress at 1174 million francs. Out of this total the actual engineering work was expected to account for 612 million, unforeseen expenses 153, banking and administrative expenses 38, interest over a period of twelve years 241, and lastly maintenance 130 million. At the end of ten years they figured that the traffic would amount to $7\frac{1}{4}$ million tons, which at 10 francs per ton would bring in gross receipts of $72\frac{1}{2}$ million francs. From the business man's point of view, this income was barely sufficient. Yet the Congress had considered these estimates, and voted for them with enthusiasm. We must add, however, that out of the seventy-eight members who were in favour only twenty were engineers, and only one of them had ever been to Panama.

Nevertheless, Ferdinand de Lesseps immediately set to work organizing the new company. The Congress vote had been taken on May 29th, 1879, and by June 21st he had procured 2 million francs for initial expenses by applying to 'people interested in the creation of great enterprises'. These founders purchased 400 shares at 5000 francs each, and were given an additional 100 shares free. In the name of the international company which had still to be created, de Lesseps bought the Türr-Wyse concession on July 5th, promising to pay 10 million francs, one half in cash. Experience was soon to prove that this document was of doubtful value, for the exclusive right to construct a canal really belonged to the Panama Railway. One had to pass through Caudine Forks in this matter.

Once the Compagnie Universelle du Canal Interocéanique was formed, the next task was to find the money. Recalling his experience with Suez, de Lesseps thought he could approach the subscribers direct as he had done in 1858. He contented himself with advertising in Europe and America the text of the resolution that had been passed by the Geographical Congress. Unfortunately both high finance and the Press, whose support he despised, were hostile to him in spite of an affected indifference.

The subscription took place on August 6th and 7th, and was a failure. The Company was asking for 400 million francs, divided into 800,000 shares of 500 francs each. It obtained only about 30 million.

De Lesseps then realized that it was impossible to proceed further until he had seriously educated public opinion, and had shown that the business was likely to be profitable. A new phase then commenced, and from this moment to the very end Panama was to be a vast publicity scheme. The president, who was no novice in these matters, began by publishing *The Bulletin of the Interoceanic Canal*. This was a fortnightly sheet, the first number appearing on September 1st, 1879. His object was to keep the public interested and optimistic, so in it he put out circulars which were like war-time *communiqués*.

Then this wonderful old man undertook a lecture tour of France, and in October or November he set off in person for Panama. He reasoned that not merely was it necessary for him to study the difficulties on the spot, but also that a spectacular gesture would be sure to impress the general public. In order to prove that the isthmus was not dangerous and that there was nothing to fear from the climate, he took his wife with him, and three of his young children. An international committee of nine technical experts also accompanied him. He was full of confidence and the joy of life. If there were any obstacles he preferred not to see them. To all objections he replied, 'The Canal will be built'. There was something rather forced about all this optimistic publicity. Bishop, the author of a book called *The Panama Gateway*, compared him to an American booster.

De Lesseps arrived at Colón on December 30th, and his six weeks' stay in the isthmus was an uninterrupted pro-gramme of fêtes. 'The reception which they gave us at Colón', he wrote to his son Charles, 'and then all down the railway line has been a series of indescribable ovations. Here in Panama we have now been celebrating for three days with illuminations, decorated windows, fireworks, troop reviews, and excursions out into the beautiful Bay of Panama. This bay is at the mouth of the Rio Grande where the exit of the maritime canal will be.'

As he decided to pursue a policy of symbolic gestures, he had the bishop bless the spot where the canal was to emerge into the Pacific. Then, the first stroke of the pick was solemnly made by his daughter, the charming Mademoiselle Ferdinande. A rock was blown up at Culebra to amuse the crowd, *coram publico*. On all occasions both public and private, the great leader expressed his astonishing optimism which was obviously sincere.

'Now that I have gone over the various localities in the isthmus with our engineers', he wrote to his son on January 20th, 'I cannot understand why they hesitated so long in declaring that it would be practicable to build a maritime canal between the two oceans at sea level, for the distance is as short as between Paris and Fontainebleau.'

He went on to discuss the climate, which they 'insist is deadly', but that is only the 'invention of our adversaries'. He even went so far as to write in the *Bulletin*, 'This canal will be easier to begin, to complete, and to maintain than was the case with the one at Suez'.

His return journey took place in February and March by way of the United States. He was cordially welcomed in New York, Boston, Chicago, San Francisco, and Washington. Again there were many receptions and banquets — but then that is normal in the New World where they love to lionize people. Nevertheless, America remained reticent, and at heart hostile. The bankers did not lend their support. President Hayes addressed a special Message to Congress after he had received his illustrious visitor, in which he categorically declared, 'The policy of this country is to advocate a canal under American control'.

When one has studied the United States, and particularly the part they have since played in this matter, one can easily understand their attitude. Yet apparently Ferdinand de Lesseps either could not or would not appreciate it. He telegraphed to the *Bulletin*, 'The Message of the President has assured the security of the canal,' and he described his reception there as 'an enthusiastic and unanimous adherence to our cause'. England, Belgium and Holland were the last stages of his great pilgrimage, after which the situation seemed ripe to attempt a second share offering.

On its return from Panama the technical commission estimated the cost of the engineering work as 843 million francs, which was 78 million higher than the figure arrived at by the Congress; however, they did not include the 409 million for interest, miscellaneous expenses, etc., which the latter had provided for. On the ship on his way from

Panama to New York, de Lesseps also revised his calculations. He too passed over the non-engineering expenses in silence, and after making several economies and halving the reserve for unforeseen items, he succeeded in compressing his total estimate: his budget was for 658 million francs only, or in round figures for about 600.

According to a new by-law passed in Paris on October 20th, 1880, the capital of the company was fixed at 300 million francs. The original idea had been to create an international company, which was to have been mainly Franco-American. In view of the lack of enthusiasm which de Lesseps had encountered in New York, he had to fall back on a mere committee in the United States. It was composed of three bankers, who incidentally were very well paid for their trouble. Ex-President Grant was asked to be chairman, but he declined. The subscription therefore had to be, and actually was, carried out in France alone.

We must note that this time de Lesseps prepared for the issue according to the rules of the game. He staged a round of conferences and banquets, which the Press, henceforth well remunerated, magnified by a blast of publicity. Further, an underwriting syndicate was organized by Lévy-Crémieux. All this cost no less than 32 million francs, but it was completely successful. By the end of October 1880, the public subscriptions amounted to 600 million francs, or twice what was asked. The first general meeting took place on January 31st of the following year and on March 3rd the company was finally constituted, naturally under the presidency of Ferdinand de Lesseps.

The Congress of the Geographical Society had figured on $72\frac{1}{2}$ million francs of future gross receipts against a total expenditure of 1174 million. The Company on the other hand estimated the costs at only 600 million, and the receipts at 90 million. Nevertheless to embark with only 300 million in the till on an enterprise which in any event would cost about a thousand million, and with no provision for interest, incidentals and various unforeseen expenses, surely was giving an excessive credit to the future!

I I

Ferdinand de Lesseps did not like engineers. He preferred what people call practical men. 'At Suez', writes M. Bunau-Varilla who later was closely associated with the Panama undertaking, 'he acted as umpire in settling differences of opinion between the experts. Sometimes he used common sense, and sometimes he relied on intuition, but his decisions showed a dangerous amount of courage although they generally proved to be right. However, they might have turned out wrong. At Panama he believed that he could use the same methods as before.'

His first inclination was to turn again to Couvreux and Hersent, the large contractors who had collaborated with him in Egypt. They specialized in great civil engineering works, and as they had proved their ability not only at Suez but also in Belgium and on the Danube, they enjoyed a world-wide reputation. Couvreux had been one of the party that went to Panama, and he had come back full of optimism. According to him the total excavations would not exceed 80 million cubic yards, and the cost would be not 843 million francs, nor even 600, but only about 512. Instead of acting as a brake upon the president, who already was inclined to be overconfident, he was even more exuberant. The speech which he delivered at Ghent in June seemed deliberately to ignore both the dangers of the climate and the chance of unpleasant surprises when the work was being carried out. It is certain that at this time, even after the first inquiry had been made, no one knew anything about the practical conditions under which the isthmus would have to be cut through.

What we may call the contractors' period began on March 12th, 1881. Couvreux and Hersent then undertook to construct the canal, either at their own risk or on a cost-plus basis, whichever was preferred, for the total sum of 512 million francs. But the agreement was conditional, and was to become binding only after two years' experience. Actually before this time had elapsed, on December 31st, 1882, they decided to withdraw from doing the work at their own risk although they declared they were still willing to continue at the expense and risk of The Company. Their engineer, M. Blanchet, had died on the isthmus of yellow fever, and they were thoroughly discouraged by this time by the unexpected difficulties they had encountered. From then on The Company could not count on getting one general contract for the whole work. This was the first setback.

The second setback was still more serious. It occurred when The Company realized that its concesson had no value, since it became valid only after agreement had been reached with the Panama Railroad Company. According to a law passed by the Republic of Colombia in 1867, no canal could be constructed near the railway without its consent. As it thus possessed a monopoly of all transport, it was quite evident that the canal company would have to purchase the railway itself at whatever price the shareholders wished to name. The railroad had 70,000 shares of a nominal value of $100 each, and they were scarcely quoted at par. The Company bought them all at $250 a share! It was a real Stock Exchange hold up, of the type that was fairly frequent in

Wall Street at that time. What with commissions and additional negotiations for overdue coupons and also the cost of the bonds, the sum spent on the railway exceeded 100 million francs.

III

After 1883 came the engineers' period. As The Company now had to give up the idea of securing a general contractor to take on the whole job, they had to reorganize their own administration completely. First they had to build up a technical staff of their own on the spot, and then find new sub-contractors. The first general manager was a M. Dingler, a senior engineer obtained from the French Government Department of Highways and Bridges. Dingler's duty was to subdivide the work among various sub-contractors, and to designate to each their particular task. At the same time a consultative committee of international experts was functioning in Paris. Dingler was a thoroughly competent man, and quite equal to his task, but his difficulties were immense.

First of all he had to get the enterprise started afresh under a new regime. As none of the leading firms of contractors had applied he had to fall back on people of lesser standing, and whose financial means were mediocre. The Company had to furnish them with both material and provisions at prices advantageous to them. This method was bound to prove expensive, particularly as the contractors were protected by Colombian law, according to which tenants could not be evicted without interminable judicial proceedings, and then only at the price of heavy indemnities.

The labour problem was no less delicate. There could be no question of employing white labour except in senior

251

positions. The Indians simply were no use, and the yellow race, who would have proved excellent, would not stay on the job but soon became shop-keepers or sub-contractors on their own account. Only the blacks remained, but they had the immense advantage of being immune from yellow fever. The negroes from the French West Indies were very poor workers, pretentious, and always complaining, for they had been ruined by the political customs in vogue in the old French colonies. Finally The Company resorted to Jamaican negroes, whose output is just passable, and it was these who in the end accounted for most of the recruits. In the autumn of 1886 it was estimated that out of a total force of 40,000 negroes, The Company was getting an average of daily work from only 15,000.

The French technical staff included a series of distinguished engineers. From 1883 to 1885 Dingler was in charge; then Léon Boyer, who had previously built the viaduct at Garabit. He died of yellow fever three months after his arrival. His successor was Jacquier, who was to remain to the end of the work. In the interval between Boyer and Dingler the task was carried on by Philippe Bunau-Varilla, a young engineer of only twenty-six years of age. His name was to be closely associated with the history of the canal. When he was still a pupil at the Ecole Polytechnique in Paris, he had attended a lecture given by de Lesseps. From that moment he had become obsessed with the thought of Panama. It is not too much to say that without him the Panama Canal might never have been constructed by the Americans! This engineering staff does credit to France, and deserves no reproach. Dingler in particular should be praised for his driving force and organizing ability. The amount of machinery that he got into action was enormous for that period.

Soon it became obvious that the promoters had chosen to ignore one terrible obstacle. De Lesseps had sarcastically referred to the 'supposed deadliness' of the climate, but the epithet, bandied so lightly, now proved to be more than true. The mortality that occurred among the white race was frightful. Seven months of torrential rains produced a most depressing humidity. Both yellow fever and malaria were raging, each claiming about the same number of victims. Together they produced a ghastly and sensational hecatomb. M. Dingler, the director general, lost his wife, his son, his daughter and her fiancé, all in a few weeks. The engineers, Blanchet and Boyer, died at their posts; 30 other engineers disembarked at the isthmus in October, 1886; in the following month 13 were dead. Out of 27 students from the Ecole Centrale de Paris who arrived in 1885 and 1886, only 16 were left in 1887. The Mother Superior of the Sisters of Ancon arrived with 24 collaborators; 21 disappeared.

Sir Claude Coventry Mallet, the British Consul at Panama, tells of going with an engineer into the upper valley of the Chagres. They were accompanied by a group of 22 men; of these 20 fell ill and 10 eventually died. The Consul and the engineer returned alone. Next morning Sir Claude waited in vain for his friend, whom he had invited to lunch. He eventually went over to his hotel to inquire, only to find that he was already dead. Such tragedies can be continued *ad infinitum.*

It is impossible to enumerate all the victims and even to make an approximate guess at their number. We know only that there were at times forty deaths a day, and that the white members of the administration had constantly to be replaced. And yet the French took the question of sanitation very seriously. The workmen's quarters were first class, and the hospital at Ancon excellent. Unfortunately medical

knowledge of tropical diseases at that time was still rudimentary. The world was still ignorant of the fact that the
'carrier' for yellow fever was the stegomiya mosquito, and
for malaria was the anopheles mosquito. At Panama no one
worried much about mosquito screens. Windows were not
covered with either glass or netting, and to prevent ants from
invading their beds, people generally stood the feet of their
bedsteads in little dishes of water. In this way they provided
a breeding ground for mosquitoes right in their own bed-
rooms! It was not until about twenty years later, towards
the end of the century, that an efficient means of defence
was discovered, which was to make the isthmus habitable.

Meanwhile the French struggled on, fighting against the
impossible, as the judgment of posterity has already admitted. Bishop, later secretary of the Isthmian Canal Commission, has written in his book, *The Panama Gateway*,
'France can well be proud of the fact that for eight years
sufficient of her men were always available and ready to fill
up the ranks which disease was steadily depleting'.

After the reorganization at headquarters in 1883, the
plan adopted was to construct a canal at sea level, 50 miles
long, 30 feet deep, and 73 feet across the bottom. It was
to utilize the bed of the Chagres, a dam at Gamboa being
constructed to control this river's erratic course. After that
the valley of the Obispo was to be used, and the Cordillera
Range was to be traversed by the Culebra Cut. Finally,
the channel of the Rio Grande would lead the canal on to the
Pacific, where there was to be a sea gate.

Taken as a whole there were no insurmountable difficulties; but at two points serious obstacles did arise, namely
the floods of the River Chagres and the landslides at Culebra.
The Chagres is a fairly large river, although not very long;
ordinarily it appears calm, but sudden floods transform it

into a devastating torrent. As the canal was to utilize its bed, at any rate as far as Gamboa, these floods periodically threatened all the work that had been accomplished.

Much more serious, however, was the problem at Culebra where the ridge was nearly 300 feet above sea level. It was a question of opening up a trench eight miles long across the Cordillera Range, and particularly for a mile and a half through the main height of land. There was nothing impossible about this task even in 1883, had it not been for the peculiar composition of the ground which presented an almost insuperable difficulty. Owing to the juxtaposition of two kinds of soil without any cementing material, the clay strata when penetrated with moisture would slide apart, and dislodge enormous masses of ground. These landslides were constantly destroying all the finished work, and carrying away all the equipment and even the railway itself. Excavating this trench was like digging in wet soap, and became an enterprise without end. A whole series of allied problems were thus added to the original one. As the poor quality of the soil necessitated very gentle talus slopes, the cubic capacity to be excavated was thereby enormously increased. Even the sidings where the soil was dumped were extremely unstable. They were difficult to build and still harder to maintain, because like everything else they kept sliding down.

As a result of these unfortunate occurrences, the estimates of the total mass of ground to be excavated had to be multiplied to such an extent that any attempt at reckoning the final amount seemed hopeless. Bonaparte Wyse originally had estimated that for the whole canal about 50 million cubic metres[1] would have to be dug. Ferdinand de Lesseps after his first voyage raised the figure to 54 million, and the

[1] About 45 million cubic yards. One cubic meter = 1·13 cubic yards.

technical commission which accompanied him set it at 75.
By 1883 The Company had been forced to increase it to 120
million. By the end of their attempt the French had excavated over 55 million, and the Americans, before they had
finished the canal, had extracted no less than 259 million
cubic metres, of which some 116 came from the Culebra
Cut alone. No less than 56 million were the result of landslides. If we compare these figures with the 75 million cubic
metres excavated at Suez, we can appreciate the extraordinary
difficulty of the task.

It is only fair to say that the technical direction of the
work was good. The staff was competent and the equipment
excellent for the period. The French engineers, true to their
type, were most ingenious, and the creative ability of such
men as Bunau-Varilla helped them to solve some of their
most baffling problems. Nevertheless it was a work of
Sisyphus. In the Culebra Cut they had only reached by the
end of 1888 a point still 240 feet above sea level, and that
at only a few places. Obviously if they were to stick stub-
bornly to the idea of a sea level canal, their attack had failed.
But if they had fallen back on a canal with locks — a method
which had already been tried out elsewhere — they could
have succeeded. In due course they could have extracted
the remaining 36 million cubic metres. Thus we may conclude that it would have been possible, even at that time, to
finish the canal, though I do not say that it would have been
a paying proposition.

Such was the situation in 1886. The original conception
of a sea level canal had received a definite setback, but there
still was the possibility of one with locks. Ferdinand de
Lesseps resisted. For him the sea level canal he had proposed at the beginning was a question of honour. His hands
were no longer free, however, for The Company's financial

resources were rapidly becoming exhausted. From then on the problems, which previously had been connected with engineering, now became political and financial. So the centre of interest shifts from the New World to the Old. It was at Paris that the fate of the enterprise was to be decided. This will not be the finest part of the tragedy. The contribution of the technical and engineering side does not merit serious criticism, indeed it had in it elements of great heroism.

CHAPTER V

FINANCIAL DISASTER

I

THERE were a certain number of initial errors in the financial conception of the Panama enterprise from which it was never able to recover. The cubic measurements of the excavations were never calculated at their true figure, and as the amount grew steadily, more and more money had to be sought from the public. The estimates of the total expenses showed the same lack of realism. The Congress of 1879 had talked of 1174 million francs, of which 409 million were allocated to non-engineering expenses and 153 million for unforeseen contingencies. Yet Ferdinand de Lesseps had contented himself with 600 million, and had dared to start off with a capital of only 300 million, although at least a thousand million would certainly be necessary. It was the unforeseen — the duration of the work, the low angle of the talus slopes at Culebra, the supplementary tasks, the floods, etc. — which gave rise to the fantastic variations in actual costs. The Geographical Society had provided in its estimates for a reserve of 25 per cent against such eventualities, but the technical commission which visited Panama in 1880 had reduced this figure to 10 per cent, and the president then cut even that in two, and went so far as to suggest the possibility of 'unforeseen savings'.

We have here placed our finger on the vital weakness in the psychology of this great promoter. In his systematic optimism he thought he could achieve success simply by believing in it. He was determined to underestimate the difficulties, even refused to see them, for he was convinced that his lucky star would once again lead him to victory. In this new task the memory of his experience at Suez became a dangerous source of encouragement. Doubtless he recalled his former troubles, such as the way estimates had been exceeded, his financial embarrassments, the hostile campaign against The Company and its numerous narrow escapes from bankruptcy. But he also reminded himself that certain of these difficulties would not recur. He was not now contending with the opposition of the British Government, nor the sudden injunction against the use of forced labour. He may also have derived satisfaction from the knowledge that at least on ten occasions in the past he had been right and the engineers had been wrong, as for example the decision to build the sea wall at Suez, and revet the dykes where the canal entered the Red Sea. 'As we did at Suez' was an ever-recurring refrain. He hoped to cut the Gordian Knot many times yet!

In *L'Appel au Soldat* Barrès makes his character, the Deputy Bouteiller, study the Panama project and then adopt a line of reasoning that could be applied to the letter to The Great Frenchman:

'He knew the history of Suez, and so whenever an incident occurred that worried him he dismissed it from his mind, because he could find that de Lesseps had triumphed over identical difficulties and hostilities when he had united the Red Sea and the Mediterranean. Every week from 1854 to 1869 it had been said, and in fact printed, that Suez was the greatest swindle of the century. All the Panama troubles would similarly become mere trifles, and would be swamped in the grandeur of the final achievement.'

Is it surprising, therefore, if under such conditions, de Lesseps should have counted in all good faith on 'unforeseen savings'? One can accuse him of light-heartedness, even of recklessness. One may say that he had grown old although this was not apparent in his actions, but any reproach against his integrity is unjustified. It would be more accurate to observe that he soared too high in this, the last phase of his meteoric career. To his technical staff, who saw him only from afar, he was already a semi-legendary figure, a deity who sent down the final decisions from on high. The effective direction of The Company belonged to the vice-president, Charles de Lesseps. He was a man of undisputed ability, and above all a devoted son. Be that as it may, it is on the shoulders of the Grand Old Man that the entire responsibility rested, as he was so tragically to realize.

The financial history of The Company can be divided into four periods: normal finance from 1880 to 1885, difficulties from 1885 to 1887, crisis from 1887 to the end of 1888, and ruin in 1888 and 1889.

II

The capital of 300 million had all been subscribed by the end of 1880, although only two of the four instalments were called up at first. This naturally was insufficient to carry on for long, so by issuing bonds which suited the well-known preferences of the French public more money was procured as required. Now the condition of the financial market was not favourable, for the failure of the Union General in 1882 had been followed by a fall in Stock Exchange prices which caused losses to investors amounting to some five thousand million francs. We must not lose sight of this fact when we study the financial difficulties of this Company, which itself was destined to seek at least a thousand million francs.

Not much was spent in the years 1881 and 1882, but in

1883 when Dingler became Director-General expenses grew rapidly. Up to the end of 1883 The Company obtained without difficulty annual amounts of from 100 to 150 million francs. They sold 500 franc bonds at par, the interest rate being first 3 per cent and then 4 per cent. Soon the savings to which these repeated appeals were addressed began to show signs of fatigue, and bonuses had to be offered to attract the half-exhausted public. The 4 per cent issue of 1884 was made at 333 francs per 500 franc bond, that is to say at 6 per cent interest, and it took 18 months to be all absorbed. While this issue was dragging on, The Company began to run short of cash. After the third instalment of the share issue had been called for and paid in, various expedients were tried but without success. This marked the beginning of chronic embarrassments from which The Company was never to free itself. The outstanding bonds began to fall in prices, sometimes declining to as low as 160 francs per 500 franc bond. At about this time the Culebra Cut began to look like a bottomless pit into which money could be poured for ever.

III

The troubles which had been whispered about for some time by the well informed, now finally began to reach the general public. The Mastersingers, the sharks, the hyenas, and all the rest of the fauna saw no reason to keep silent. Now that the period of normal finance was over, The Company realized that henceforth it would be obliged to resort to exceptional methods. In casting about for help it naturally turned to the State, that is to say to politics. Intrigue now became a virtual necessity.

The Company became the victim of attacks in the Press.

During these years France was going through a nasty period
of cynicism, both ostentatious and affected, a relic of the
Second Empire magnified by the bitterness of the recent
military defeat. What people feared most was to be considered simpletons. I still shudder when I think of the
damning formula, 'You are not much of a Parisian!' and how
one was transfixed at the thought of what 'to be a Parisian'
really might mean. It is all extremely well told in *Les
Déracinés*, another book by Maurice Barrès; the chapter
entitled, 'Bouteiller is Presented to the Parliamentarians',
is hardly an exaggeration.

A low, dishonest Press kept hounding The Company, and
a little rag called *The Panama* followed it like a wolf. Charles
de Lesseps soon gave way, too quickly perhaps. He got into
the habit of paying for favourable publicity, and his monthly
cheques were sometimes even the price of silence. 'The
whole world battened on Panama,' wrote Drumont in *La
Dernière Bataille*.

'The top hats arrived first with enormous demands. Then
came smaller hats, and then the little ones ... mere children's
caps. Finally some vague reporter would appear, and he
would get a little cheque for having inserted a single line in a
review, mentioning The Great Frenchman, or "Tototte", or
"Ismael", or other members of de Lesseps's family. Some
didn't contribute anything, but they got their cheques just
the same. This was just hush-money from The Company
which was thankful to be left alone.' Soon The Company
was to busy itself with members of parliament as well.

Leaks are bound to occur when enterprises are spending
a lot of money, and any way Ferdinand de Lesseps had always had a weakness for display. He had furthermore the
unfortunate habit of buying assistance in order to ward off
eventual opposition. In this way great sums vanish with

nothing to show for them, particularly in squaring finance and politics. Otherwise one can say that the administration of the business itself was reasonable on the whole, and that most of the money was not diverted from its true purpose, namely the construction of the canal.

The famous 'Dingler's Folly' which proved such a weapon of attack, was nothing more than a large bungalow as photographs of it prove. The Director-General also came to grief over his 'wagon-palace', but this was simply an office on wheels and modesty itself in comparison with the private cars of the American railroad magnates of the day. If the atmosphere of the isthmus somewhat resembled that of a gold mining boom-town with roulette, champagne and women, surely that was not The Company's fault, for a sudden influx of money produces the same result anywhere. It was in Paris itself that the air was the most unwholesome, but unfortunately there are no exact medical terms to diagnose the diseases of the Press, finance, and politics.

Among the various expedients suggested to raise money, a lottery loan came most naturally to mind. As a matter of fact it had been suggested by both Germain and Mazerat of the Crédit Lyonnais in 1883. In May 1885, after calling up the third instalment of the shares, de Lesseps himself turned to the lottery idea, for this was how he had rescued the Suez Canal when it was on the point of failure. But in order to have a lottery loan a law had to be passed, and it was through this door that The Company entered the political world, or perhaps we should say the political world entered The Company.

At all events the Government sent to the isthmus a M. Rousseau, one of the engineers of the Department of Roads and Bridges. He was a Councillor of State, a former Under-Secretary of State for Public Works, and obviously a man of standing and integrity. After his trip to Panama, which he made in December and January 1885-1886, he reported that it was in the national interests that the canal should be completed, and that it was possible to do so, if not at sea level then with locks.

'I believe that it is quite possible to cut through the isthmus, and that the undertaking has reached a stage to-day where it should not be abandoned. To stop now would be a real disaster, not merely for the shareholders of The Company who are practically all French, but also for the prestige of the French nation throughout the whole of America . . . In my opinion the Government can and should use the diplomatic and administrative powers at its disposal to assist this great French enterprise. After all The Company is aiming at an eminently useful goal, and it is being directed by men worthy of respect.'

Thus the report was favourable, but it contained certain reservations which the adversaries of the canal did not fail to use.

M. Rousseau had scarcely returned when Ferdinand de Lesseps felt that he also should visit the isthmus again. He left in February 1886, accompanied by the representatives of several Chambers of Commerce, and an American delegation met them at Panama. The moral and physical energy of this old man of 81 was astounding! As he wanted to inspire everyone with fresh courage, he gave this visit the same spectacular character as the one he had made six years earlier.

'His tour of inspection along the canal', writes Bishop again, 'was a veritable triumphant procession. De Lesseps led the way mounted on a prancing steed. According to one of the members of his entourage, he was never tired and always at the head of the cavalcade. In the midst of a storm of applause from both the blacks and the whites, he galloped

up the hillside at Culebra. Everyone present was thunder-
struck by his ardour and youthfulness. A legend is still told
in the isthmus that he travelled about in a flowing robe of
gorgeous colours, like an oriental monarch.'

Truly, there is something tragic about this dance on the
volcano!

In June 1886, when de Freycinet's cabinet received the
request for a lottery loan, it drafted a favourable law under
the signature of M. Baïhaut, the Minister of Public Works.
The Company was thus assured of the Minister's support,
and at the same time it canvassed the lobbies. Nevertheless
the committee which had been appointed to study the project adjourned by 6 votes to 5, thus delaying everything
until the autumn. Meanwhile the need for money was
pressing. It was then that the president attempted alone to
launch a new issue. In this pathetic appeal the old warrior
tried once more to go direct to the public.

'They have adjourned on me. I will not accept this postponement. True to my past, when they try to stop me, I go
on. Not alone, it is true, but with the 350,000 Frenchmen
who share my patriotic confidence in the future. The Parliamentary Committee have decided not to give their permission
before the end of the year, but happily a lottery loan is not
the only type that exists. Although by their attitude six
deputies are trying to prevent me from marching forward
with you to victory in this peaceful work undertaken by
France in the Isthmus of Panama, we will overcome every
obstacle yet. You will march with me to a second victory by
providing the 600 million francs I need!'

The audacious president was not afraid to ask for the
whole 600 million at one fell swoop. He proposed putting
out bonds repayable by lot at exactly double the subscription
price. This was in reality an attenuated lottery loan. The

public furnished only 300 million, but even this is proof of the immense influence that de Lesseps still could wield. Out of this enormous sum, however, The Company actually netted only about 200 million, and that was not enough. Once again in June 1887, it had to stretch out its palm, but this time with only partial success, for the amount obtained was frankly insufficient.

IV

The crisis came to a head at the end of 1887. By this time The Company had already obtained from French savings the vast total of 935 million francs, of which 225[1] were in shares and 710 in bonds. The nett receipts naturally were far below these figures. At that moment there was less than 100 million left in the treasury, and the credit of The Company had evaporated. They then had to admit that they could not succeed with a canal at sea level, though they still could have fallen back on one with locks, if in their desperate straits they could find the means to carry it out.

At the time of the Geographical Society's Congress, a scheme of this sort had been worked out by an engineer named Godin de Lepinay. He had proposed creating an artificial lake in the centre of the isthmus by building two dams, one on the Chagres and the other on the Rio Grande, with locks at both ends. The mouth of each river was to be diverted into the completed parts of the sea level canal.

Recourse to some such solution was now essential, and had already been considered by Boyer before he died on the isthmus; such also was the advice of Rousseau. Ferdinand de Lesseps, however, made the sea level canal a question of

---

[1] Three instalments, each being one-quarter of 300 million francs.

honour as we have said, although his son Charles fully realized that they must give way. Bunau-Varilla, whose experience at Panama itself had enabled him to obtain the latest technical ideas, believed that they could make a canal with locks immediately, and so reduce to a minimum the cost of the excavations and revetments. Then, at their leisure, they could steadily reduce the level of the upper portion by dredging under water. The locks could thus be progressively done away with. Already in 1886 the experts had recognized that the sea level canal was an impossibility, and in the autumn of 1887 Ferdinand de Lesseps finally allowed himself to be persuaded. They suggested to him that the canal with locks could be looked upon as an initial step which was not binding on the future. On the strength of this he gave way, assuring himself that he was still sticking to his principles. 'I shall never consent', he declared, 'to the final substitution', but few of his associates shared his illusion.

The plan they fell back on was no longer the 'Oceanic Bosporus' proposed at the beginning, but at least it allowed them to make some calculations, and it could be completed within a time-limit that it was possible to foresee. If instead of having the bottom of the canal 32 feet below sea level it was to be 130 feet above, then the total cubic volume to be dug would be only about 80 million cubic metres. Now by the end of 1888 some 55 million had already been excavated and as a result of their years of experience, they knew that they could excavate some 12 million a year. The canal could thus be finished in three years.

One would be quite justified in saying that after five years of work the period of fumbling was over. Technical methods had been worked out, results could be accurately predicted, and the limitations were known. Delays would no longer be the result of incalculable hazards. This was the point of view of the technical engineers, who still believed that they could succeed. But even for this reduced type of canal, which it would be hard to make profitable, The Company would need still another 500 million francs, and where was that to be found?

Once again the lottery loan came into the picture. They needed 400 million francs for engineering works, 200 for general expenses, and 120 for the legal guarantee required for the lottery. The request was made to the Government of November 15th, 1887. At first it refused, but Parliament on its own initiative reconsidered the project on March 2nd, 1888, and appointed a Parliamentary Committee of eleven members to examine it. The committee started off by adopting a hostile attitude, and voted 6 to 5 against the plan. Then a deputy, Sans-Leroy, by a complete *volte face*, reversed the majority. Finally Parliament gave its consent, and the law was promulgated on June 9th.

The political atmosphere was troubled. In the lobbies one could feel the pressure exerted by The Company as well as that of the shareholders and bondholders whose petitions were piling up. Should the savings of the French people be abandoned? Members of Parliament were afraid of compromising themselves by voting for a company which was distributing money in handfuls. Also one could distinguish a real hatred against it. Some people took an unholy joy in pursuing it and trying to destroy it.

'The ruin is getting on fine!' announced Deputy Goirand, from the tribune. 'Scarcely more than fifty per cent remains to be lost'.

As for the Government, they especially were terrified of being suspected, so they slunk off and left de Lesseps to fend for himself. After all, wasn't he reactionary at heart? And yet in clerical circles they had never quite forgiven him for his attitude in Rome in 1849. So The Great Frenchman became the butt of hatred from all sides.

Baron de Reinach, who was a shrewd adviser, proposed bringing out the lottery issue in successive blocs, but the Crédit Lyonnais made them proceed with the whole amount at once. This was a serious mistake, for the effort asked from the market was obviously too great. Two million bonds of 400 francs each were accordingly issued at a price of 360 francs. Some of the lottery prizes went as high as 500,000 francs. The entire issue should have been spread out over at least a year, for just then French savings were hardly in a position to respond to the appeal. The public was all the less willing, because a violent Press campaign against The Company had been set on foot, and a bear raid brought down the market price of its outstanding securities on the eve of the subscription. Deputy Goirand's speech in the Chamber had a deplorable effect, and to make matters worse on June 26th, the day of the issue, a rumour was spread about, both in the provinces and in Paris, that Ferdinand de Lesseps had died. Defeat was inevitable. Out of the two million bonds offered, only 800,000 were subscribed. It was the end — no, not quite the end, but the beginning of the death agony.

v

De Lesseps' friends now lost all hope, but he would not give way. Once more, accompanied by his son Charles, he toured the country, going from town to town. No fewer than 500,000 Frenchmen, he said, were interested in Panama. If each of them would only subscribe for two bonds the enterprise would be saved! Security-holders' committees were set up all along his path, and one last issue was attempted in December. This time it was agreed that if a minimum of 200,000 bonds were not taken up, the money would be returned, and this was done. It was an agonizing affair. A three months' moratorium was proposed by the Government, but the Chamber rejected it. The Grand Old Man had more fight left in him yet! He tried to create a new company designed to refloat the previous one, but it was too late. By the end of the year he had to admit that he was defeated at last, and he telegraphed to Panama to stop all work. Liquidation was now necessary. On February 5th, 1889, the Tribunal de la Seine announced the dissolution of the Compagnie Universelle du Canal Interocéanique.

Ferdinand de Lesseps was 83, but so far old age had not taken its toll. However, when he was forced to order all work to cease on the isthmus, it was as if he had had a stroke. The long life of The Great Frenchman ended on that day. Though destined to survive another five years, it was only to figure as a shadow in the bitterest of tragedies.

CHAPTER VI

THE SCANDAL OF PANAMA

I

THE Panama scandal did not break out immediately. For about a year and a half the liquidation of The Company proceeded calmly enough. Then political spite, the howlings of a scurrilous Press, the bitterness of certain security holders, and the obsession of the public, now completely unnerved, began to give to this great enterprise its lamentable epilogue. To the man-in-the-street, the very name of Panama became a term of abuse. To call anyone a 'Panamiste' was another way of saying he was a thief.

The *débâcle* of General Boulanger's movement coincided to a certain extent with the failure of the canal. After their defeat in the elections of September 1889, the Boulangists and the members of the extreme Right wing were still sore and longing for revenge. At the same time a new generation of young Republicans were hoping to replace Gambetta and his 'Opportunists', who had now been in power for fifteen years. The newcomers were more than ready to declare themselves pure, and to oppose the grafters of yesterday. The result was something like a double auction, in which both sides were acting from selfish motives.

'A scandal on such an enormous scale could only happen under a republic,' shouted the Right.

'On the contrary,' replied the young men of the Left, 'we shall show you that a republic is the only regime capable of dealing out justice. Any way de Lesseps always was a reactionary.'

In Government circles they would have preferred to

whitewash the whole business, but they were thoroughly frightened, so in the end they howled with the rest of the wolves. To their shame be it said, no one rose up to remind them that to have completed the canal would have redounded to the honour of the nation, and that any government worthy of the name should not have allowed it to fail at any price.

Meanwhile a rumour was being circulated, confused at first and then growing clearer and clearer. The Company was accused of having squandered and dissipated the vast sums which French savings had entrusted to it. There was talk of money spent on luxuries, of payments for work which had never been done, and of the scandalous profits pocketed by certain contractors and middlemen. There were mutterings about the exorbitant cost of publicity, about underwriting syndicates which were purely fictitious, and lastly about the bribes that had been scattered right and left among members of the Chamber. Well-informed people, and particularly the crafty folk who had managed to get out in time, stirred up the shorn lambs.

'You were a simpleton, weren't you?' they jibed, and to be called a simpleton at that time was the worst insult of all. 'The Company has stolen your money, and you need expect no help from the Government.'

For a while the shareholders and bondholders maintained their faith in de Lesseps, and he personally was still acclaimed. Above all they hoped that the Government would at least try to save what still could be saved. Then they too became disillusioned, and resentful. Everything was ripe for a scandal.

At first numerous petitions were sent to the Government, requesting that it should try to refloat the business. After that there were a certain number of security holders, now bitter in the extreme, who were ready to demand that the directors of The Company should be prosecuted. In the

Chamber the opposition tried to make the most of these developments. The Ministers were very embarrassed, for if they prosecuted they ran the risk of slinging mud at their own supporters, and of losing their majority. If on the other hand they did nothing, they might be accused of being accomplices. Above all they were not eager to stir up mud from which embarrassing odours would arise. Meanwhile pressure from the general public was growing stronger and stronger. Finally in June 1891, the Chamber demanded a Government inquiry, and on January 5th, 1892, by a unanimous vote, it asked for the 'energetic and rapid suppression of all those who had incurred responsibility in the Panama Affair'. From that moment Parliament dared not retreat. Public opinion was on the alert.

On June 11th, 1891, M. Quesnay de Beaurepaire, the Attorney-General, acknowledged the receipt of four complaints lodged against the directors of the Panama Company. He then ordered a judicial investigation. Councillor Prinet was appointed as reporter, and he instructed M. Flory, a chartered accountant, to carry out an expert examination. In the early days of September the findings were submitted to the Attorney-General, and on the 18th of that month the latter proposed to the Minister of Justice that proceedings should commence.

In the meantime a virulent Press campaign against parliamentary corruption had broken out in *La Libre Parole*. Those in high places still hesitated. Both President Carnot and Premier Loubet would have preferred to do nothing. Even the Attorney-General himself was wondering whether he would be able to prove fraudulent intentions. Finally on November 19th M. Ricard, the Minister of Justice, ordered the trial to begin without having consulted his colleagues, and on November 21st the summonses were sent

out. Ferdinand and Charles de Lesseps, Cottu who was one
of the directors, Fontanes the general secretary, and Eiffel
the contractor, were all accused. As Ferdinand de Lesseps
was a Grand Officer of the Legion of Honour, they were all
to appear before the Court of Appeal.

Two trials took place, and they should not be confused.
The one before the Court of Appeal was for fraud; the other
before a jury was for corruption. There was also the Parliamentary scandal, which resulted in the appointment of a
Committee of Inquiry by the Chamber itself. This committee
sat at the same time as the trials in the Courts, and hoped
eventually to replace them. So the Law Courts, Parliament,
the Press, the police, banking, and the general public were
all involved, and, to quote Shakespeare, were 'full of sound
and fury'.

The real impulse came not from the Government, nor
from the Law Courts, nor from the police, nor even from
Parliament, but from an anti-parliamentary blackmail campaign carried on outside of Parliament itself, and using as
its mouthpiece newspapers such as *La Cocarde* and *La Libre
Parole*. A handful of deputies like Delahaye and Déroulède
were responsible for a good deal of it. In the last analysis
fear was the dominating factor.

'Every one was on the defensive,' says Barrès in *Leurs
Figures*. 'They all believed that if they appeared to dread
exposure, they would get on their own backs the whole
murderous gang of crooks. It was diabolically harsh, but
most satisfying to see all those cunning fellows marching
along, with blank faces and hunched shoulders, and to hear
the guilty as well as the innocent who had been dragged down
with them, repeating in chorus, "We must see this thing
through, and, if there have been any grafters they must be
executed".'

The trial for fraud commenced on January 10th, 1893, before the Court of Appeal, acting as a Criminal Court. Charles de Lesseps, who had been arrested on December 17th, bore the whole weight of the defence, for his father was absent. By a vestige of decency they had not dared lay hands on the old man, who only yesterday had been hailed as The Great Frenchman. The charges against the accused were of having committed fraud, in that they had deceived the subscribers by fraudulent manœuvres, and so had awakened hopes of quite impossible achievements, namely the completion of the canal. They were also accused of having dissipated through bad management monies which had been given to them in trust or on deposit.

The only one among the accused who mattered was Charles de Lesseps. His intelligence, his ability, his dignified bearing, all made a marked impression on the public. They began to realize that the man with whom they were dealing was not a swindler. He appeared chiefly as someone who had been struggling against a gang. He had undertaken an impossible task, and had done so against his own better judgment, and yet he had tried to fight on to the bitter end. But the sharpers had got the better of him, they had been too numerous. His mistake had been in not disregarding them completely. He explained it quite simply:

'They seemed to rise up from the pavement. We had to deal with their threats, their libels, and their broken promises.'

Not one of the witnesses questioned his good faith. M. Rousseau, the Government engineer, dismissed all thought of intention to defraud. In the opinion of M. Monchicourt, the liquidator, The Company could in all sincerity have hoped to succeed. That, however, was not the view of the Advocate General, who talked of 'the greatest fraud of modern times'. His severity astonishes everyone to-day.

'You will not hesitate to punish these great criminals, who in order to attract millions have had recourse to every manœuvre, every fraud . . . I demand the most stringent application of the law.'

The speech of M. Barboux, the counsel for the defence, is famous. His eloquence was magnificent of its kind, but became somewhat pompous and tiresome by being too thorough. For a while it seemed as if he would succeed in getting his clients acquitted, yet the verdict was pitiless. The preamble found the accused guilty of wilful errors in estimating costs, of having wrongly forecast the traffic at 7 million tons (although the figures have since then exceeded 30 million), of fraudulent manœuvres, and of bad faith, for how could they have believed in 1888 that the canal could be finished by 1891?[1]

As a result Ferdinand and Charles de Lesseps were both condemned to the maximum punishment, namely five years imprisonment and 3000 francs fine. Cottu and Fontanes were condemned to two years and 2000 francs, Eiffel to two years and 20,000 francs. The severity of these sentences seems inexcusable to-day. Owing to pressure from the public, now thoroughly enraged, the Court evidently had made scapegoats of the accused, and so would not accept the slightest excuse. This demagogic judgment was never carried out, however. It was quashed on June 18th, 1893, as having violated the laws of limitation. Mercy, therefore, was to be found only in blind red tape.

---

[1] The volume now remaining to be excavated amounted to some 39 million cubic metres. The average annual amount excavated between 1886 and 1888 had been 12 millions.

The Panama scandal gradually evolved into an anti-parliamentary campaign. When the mud was stirred up, one began to find politicians mixed up with the request for parliamentary authority to issue the lottery loan. Insinuations about parliamentary corruption were made, and although obviously exaggerated they became more and more aggressive. In September 1892, Micros in *La Libre Parole* had denounced the deputies without mincing matters. Furthermore Charles de Lesseps, in an interview which he gave to *La Cocarde* a few weeks later, let it be understood that these attacks were not without some foundation. On his side, Ducret, the owner of this paper, did not hesitate to declare that according to confidential information obtained from a director of The Company, over 150 deputies were mixed up in the business. Arton, de Reinach's principal scout, was supposed to have bought 104 deputies; the proofs still existed, they said, for the cancelled cheques had not been destroyed.

After the autumn of 1892, parliamentary corruption became the talk of the town. People were always discussing cheques and bribes, and no one seemed to remember that Panama had had anything to do with a canal! In the end one almost believed that The Company had hardly done anything at all in the isthmus, quite a contemptuous amount of work in fact, and that all the money had been spent in commissions, bribes, and buying deputies. It became almost an obsession, and if anyone mentioned exaggeration, he was at once accused of complicity. So Parliament, posing as the guardians of morality, also became aggressive at this point in order to defend itself. A Committee of Inquiry, consisting of thirty-three members, was nominated by the Chamber on November

21st. It created plenty of excitement every day. It never obtained judicial powers, but functioned nevertheless alongside the Courts of Justice. The Government, although they were sick of the whole business, felt obliged to proceed with a corruption trial against Charles de Lesseps, Cottu, Fontanes, and ten members of the Chamber, including Rouvier, Baïhaut and Sans-Leroy. They could not find sufficient grounds to proceed against Rouvier and three other deputies, but Charles de Lesseps, Cottu, Fontanes and Sans-Leroy were arrested on December 17th, and Baïhaut on January 9th. They and four other deputies appeared before the Court of Assizes from March 7th to 21st, 1893.

What did it all amount to any way? When The Company had asked for authority to issue a lottery loan, it was necessary to persuade the deputies to vote for it, and regrettable confusion had occurred between publicity and corruption. For all matters connected with publicity, Charles de Lesseps had employed two intermediaries, Baron de Reinach and Cornélius Hertz, and had given them large sums amounting to almost 10 million francs. He had avoided asking for a detailed account of how the money was used. De Reinach was chiefly in contact with the Rouvier group, and Hertz frequented the Clemenceau entourage. The scout, Arton, was given the job of working the lobbies. The influence that such adventurers can acquire is one of the vices of the Third Republic — and we have had recent examples. Cornélius Hertz was a Grand Officer of the Legion of Honour, and naturally all doors were open to him.

The only proof that was decisively established was against Baïhaut, who confessed. Let us quote from the record of the trial:

Charles de Lesseps: The Minister of Public Works,

M. Baïhaut, requested us through an intermediary to put a million francs at his disposal. A first sum of 375,000 francs was paid over on account.

The Advocate General: This money was then paid for a criminal purpose?

Charles de Lesseps: No, it was like a purse or a watch which a man hands over in a corner of the wood, when a knife has been placed at his throat.

The President: You could have called the police.

Charles de Lesseps: But what happens if the gendarme himself is the person who is holding you up to ransom?

On March 21st Baïhaut was condemned, without attenuating circumstances, to five' years imprisonment, and two fines of 375,000 francs each. Blondin, who had acted as tempter and intermediary, was given two years. Charles de Lesseps was given one year, with alternating circumstances and was declared jointly responsible with Baïhaut for the fines. The other deputies were acquitted through lack of proof. As an appeal was refused, the sentence on Charles de Lesseps was upheld, but as he had already been in preventive custody he was liberated on September 12th, 1893. His name was deleted from the Legion of Honour in the following year.

His calvary was not yet over, however, for in 1896 the taxation authorities demanded the payment of the fines for which he was jointly responsible, a total in all of 900,000 francs. As he did not possess this sum, he was ruined. All compromise being refused, he immediately left the country for three years. Finally the authorities agreed to accept 300,000 francs, and the exile was able to return. His friends had not ceased to admire him. They saw in him a touching example of filial devotion, and posterity has confirmed their judgment.

Meanwhile on November 19th, 1892, de Reinach had

committed suicide. Hertz and Arton fled across the border, the French police showing no anxiety to go and fetch them. On July 4th, 1893, the Chamber adopted the report of the Committee of Inquiry, stigmatizing in general all grafters and swindlers. The affair was still to come to life once more, but by now it had become past history.

IV

The public was persuaded that the greater part of the money which had been deposited with The Company had passed into the lobbies or had been used in graft and dishonest publicity, and that only insignificant sums had actually been spent on engineering works. These accusations are quite incorrect, or at any rate very grossly exaggerated. From March 3rd, 1881, to December 14th, 1888, the total sum received from French savings amounted to 1271 million francs. It had been employed as follows:

	Francs	Percentage of total
Expenses of making the various issues	83,000,000	6.5
Purchase of the Panama Railroad	93,000,000	7.3
Interest and sinking fund	238,000,000	18.7
Cost of administration at Panama	83,000,000	6.5
Cost of Administration in Paris	74,000,000	5.8
Engineering expenses	700,000,000	55.2
	1,271,000,000	100.0

The truth is that the work had been well carried out, under good conditions, with material which was left in excellent shape, and also that the general management of The Company was conscientious. What certainly could be critized, however, were all the incidental costs—the underwriting syndicates,

money spent on the bond and share issues, the publicity
and the graft. It all added up to a heavy total which looked
most suspicious. From the very beginning, after the setback of the first share issue, The Company had got into bad
habits which continued to grow worse. Believing that they
must succeed at all costs, they had adopted the dangerous
principle that what must be, must be.

Charles de Lesseps was personally a man of scrupulous
integrity, but he gave way too quickly to such methods
of procedure. Alluding to money spent on publicity,
the President of the Court exclaimed during the trial for
corruption:

'But that is enormous! What on earth could you be
remunerating with such sums'?

'Do not forget, Mr. President,' de Lesseps replied, 'that
we are now in the world of finance, dealing with financial
customs and usages which to-day are common practice.
When you wish to make an issue and have created an underwriting syndicate and organized the publicity, you are not
finished. Then you see arriving from the gutter a crowd of
people whom you have never heard of before. When you
are ignorant of such matters as we were, you are forced to
turn to those who are on intimate terms with these people,
and who know how to deal with them. So what do you
expect? We first had recourse to M. Lévy-Crémieux, and
after him to Baron de Reinach. We paid them handsomely
for the services they gave us, and gave them enough not only
for themselves but for the others as well.'

When the situation had finally become desperate, it was
no longer The Company who offered, but the sharks who
demanded. In this connection an illuminating dialogue
took place about M. Baïhaut between the President of the
Court and the vice-president of The Company.

The President (alluding to the bribing of the Minister): Here then are the facts, which according to the accusation constitute corruption.

Charles de Lesseps: I call it extortion.

The President: Yes, but where was the violence?

Charles de Lesseps: Is violence necessary when a Minister of the State makes demands in such conditions?

The total cost of the various issues amounted in all to 83 million francs, 32 for the issue of 1881, and 31 for that of 1888. This undoubtedly was high, but one knows of other cases in which the commissions were even heavier, and yet no indignation was aroused. The Company had fallen too easily into corrupt practices, which it had looked upon as normal. The expenses which it incurred in this way were not in themselves great enough to have caused the failure. One can truthfully say that the scandal was out of all proportion to the crimes committed.

As for Ferdinand de Lesseps, neither his good faith nor his disinterestedness are questioned at the present time, and the sentence which laid him low seems after half a century both incomprehensible and iniquitous. If it is a question of his wisdom, then that is quite another matter. For after all this superb fighter had more faith in his destiny than in his own judgment. His firm belief in the task which he had set out to accomplish was due partly to his energy, but also to his recklessness. Possibly he had grown old in this second phase of his career. And yet there were no signs of old age, for his methods were the same at both Suez and Panama. The faults which caused failure in the second Company were the very ones that had brought success in the first. Here the dividing line between merit and luck is impossible to draw.

Could he have succeeded, one wonders. It certainly was impossible to make a second Suez at Panama, but at any rate he might have succeeded in building a canal with locks and then handed it over to navigation. This would have avoided the catastrophe. The yellow fever was an obstacle which he could not overcome, but from the engineering point of view, he was certainly on the road to success. If de Lesseps failed, it was because French savings, from which he eventually demanded too great an effort, ceased to follow him once a series of belittling campaigns had ruined the credit of his Company. It was also because the Government, after hesitating whether or not they should frankly come to his aid, abandoned him in a cowardly way, and then shamefully trampled on him. Posterity has been more just, for he still remains, in spite of everything, The Great Frenchman.

CHAPTER VII

AMERICAN INTERVENTION AND THE PANAMA REVOLUTION

I

THE Panama concession owned by the French Company was valid only until 1893. If work were then stopped the Republic of Colombia would have the right to cancel the contract, and take possession of everything so far accomplished and all materials and plant found on the spot. The security holders were naturally worried about the danger of losing the concession in this way, and so they kept up an agitation in the hope of refloating the business, and getting the work started again. The liquidator was as anxious to do so as they were, but he had no financial means at his disposal, nor any great names to replace that of de Lesseps. Then also, it must be admitted, the public was sick of the very word, Panama.

The liquidator's one hope was to take all possible measures to prevent the concession from lapsing. He therefore began by appointing a technical committee, and they stated that the equipment was in good condition. This committee adopted the final plan of the Old Company, more or less, and estimated that eight years and about 900 million francs would be needed to complete the canal. The liquidator further obtained from the Colombian Government various prolongations of the concession period. The first was till 1903, and was on condition that a new company should be incorporated, and that the work should be restarted before February 28th, 1893. A second postponement pushed the final date to October 31st, 1904, and stipulated that work should start by October 31st, 1894. The third extension put the final

date on to October 31st, 1910. The latter was granted on
April 26th, 1900, but the legality of the document was
doubtful as it was issued by a revolutionary government.
None of these expedients led to any solution, however.

On October 24th, 1894, or eight days before the first
period expired, the New Company was incorporated to meet
the emergency. It was entitled the Compagnie Nouvelle du
Canal de Panama, and had 60 million francs capital. The
chief subscribers were directors and others who had collaborated in the work of the original company, as well as a few
banks; but the public abstained entirely. With such limited
means there obviously could be no question of completing
the canal. The sole object was not to allow the concession to
lapse, and to keep the title deeds in order in the hope of
selling them should opportunity occur. The directors were
honourable men, but were devoid of conviction and only
trying to gain time. It is not surprising therefore to find
them shunning publicity, and confining themselves to the
appointment of a second technical committee. This committee met ninety-seven times, but it did not submit its
report for four years, actually not until November 16th,
1898. The moment it was issued an offer of sale was sent
to the President of the United States.

The Americans received this French proposal rather
coolly, although the canal had become for them a matter of
immediate concern. The war with Spain had just been concluded, and as the U.S.A. now included Puerto Rico, Cuba
and the Philippines among its possessions, it would rank
henceforth as a first class Power, not merely in the Caribbean
zone but also in the Pacific. Interoceanic communications
therefore were a pressing problem. The cruiser *Oregon*,
which had been lying in San Francisco harbour, had been
obliged to spend ninety days rounding the Horn in order to

take part in the Battle of Santiago de Cuba. This exploit had aroused the enthusiasm of the public, but it had also revealed the extreme weakness of the communications between the two oceans. The necessity of constructing a canal across the isthmus now became an urgent matter.

II

Ever since the American Civil War, the United States had become increasingly taken with the idea of an American canal, on American territory, built and managed by the American Government. The French attempt had been viewed with suspicion, and without a vestige of goodwill. When the question came up again in 1898, the Republican leaders who were in power at the time still held to this point of view. It is no exaggeration to describe both President McKinley and Vice-President Theodore Roosevelt as imperialistic in their outlook.

The first question to be settled was whether the Panama or the Nicaraguan route was preferable. Technically Panama was the easier, all the more so as the work had been begun, but it meant double negotiations, first with the French Company and then with the Republic of Colombia. Nicaragua necessitated a longer route, sharper curves, and more excavation. On the other hand it had the advantage of needing no negotiations whatever, since the Treaty of 1849 with the Nicaraguan State was still in force.

We must also add that the public had a sentimental preference for this second route. Nicaragua seemed more like a real American canal, in comparison with Panama which they considered to be French, and if a plebiscite could have been held it would have given a crushing majority in favour of Nicaragua.

If this solution had prevailed, it would have wiped out all the French interests. All the work that had been accomplished under the impulse of de Lesseps, would have been lost, especially as the Americans in future were not likely to tolerate a European-owned canal alongside their own. Thus the New Company was not in a happy position to begin negotiations, for they were faced with only one possible buyer, and their concession was not indispensable even to him.

In 1898 it looked as if the Nicaragua route were sure to be chosen. An American Government commission was about to report favourably on it (report actually issued on May, 9th, 1899), and apparently the French offer of sale had produced no impression. The New Company's affairs were represented in the United States by a lawyer, Mr. Nelson Cromwell, who displayed great activity both with the administration itself and in the lobbies of Congress. It was at this moment that the former chief engineer, M. Bunau-Varilla who still was a passionate enthusiast of the Panama route, succeeded in interesting two influential Americans, Mr. Bigelow and Commander Asher Baker. They were able to persuade McKinley that a committee should be appointed to choose between the two routes, and this was done in the month of June 1899. So the future was still open.

A sub-committee was sent to France to get into contact with the New Company. The latter asked $109,141,500, and received a provisional offer of $40,000,000. This was confirmed by the Senate at the end of 1901, and accepted by the New Company at the beginning of 1902. All this was the result of a series of conferences which Bunau-Varilla had arranged on his own initiative in the United States. This persuasive and indefatigable man succeeded in convincing Myron Herrick, General Dawes, and above all the influential Senator, Mark Hanna, who was one of the confidential advisers of the President. However, the question was far from being settled, for though the Senate Committee showed a preference for Panama on January 18th, 1902, the House of Representatives nine days earlier had given an almost unanimous vote in favour of Nicaragua.

In the month of June the Senate itself was to be called upon for its vote, but in the interval an event had occurred which our brilliant impressario was to use so cleverly that it finally tipped the scales in his favour. On May 6th the terrible eruption of Mount Pelée had taken place on the Island of Martinique. Now the State of Nicaragua had been rash enough to issue a postage stamp with a picture of a volcano with a feathery plume of smoke emerging from its crest.

'I will obtain ninety of these precious documents, one for each Senator!' cried Bunau-Varilla. 'Meanwhile my secretary will type on ninety little slips of paper, underneath where the stamps will go, the following appropriate wording: *"Postage stamp from the Republic of Nicaragua. An official witness of volcanic activity on the Isthmus of Nicaragua."* I will fire this broadside, loaded with explosive truth, on June 16th, three days before the vote is to take place.'

The effect was instantaneous. There is no doubt whatever that this propaganda was largely responsible for the victory of the Panama route. The so-called Spooner Law giving preference to the French canal was passed by the Senate on June 19th, and on the 26th by the House of Representatives, now completely won over.

III

When it once more took up the question of interoceanic communications in 1898, the American Government did not have an entirely free hand, at any rate from the diplomatic point of view, for the Bulwer-Clayton Treaty permitted the construction of a canal only under the joint patronage of England and the United States. This limitation seemed extremely humiliating to this young and victorious people, who wished to build the canal alone and administer it alone. Though they were ready to concede both neutrality and equality of tolls, they were determined to reserve the right to close the isthmus in case of war, and look after it themselves.

However, England, their partner in the Treaty of 1850, was in a friendly mood, and she agreed to recognize the dominant position of the United States in Central America. In consequence she was quite disposed to give up joint control, but she still held firm on the question of neutrality and above all on equality of treatment. This attitude covered an orderly retreat, for at that time she was very busy indeed in the Transvaal. It also acknowledged that henceforth British foreign policy, outside of Europe, would be based on the effective co-operation of the two great English-speaking nations. This was a turning point in the history of Anglo-American relations, and the substitution of the Hay-Pauncefote Treaty for the Bulwer-Clayton Treaty on November 18th, 1901, was a milestone marking the end of a period.

According to the new document it was agreed that the United States alone should construct and administer the canal, which nevertheless was to be available on equal terms to the merchant vessels and warships of all nations. The canal was to be neutral, or at least was to be governed according to the general principles laid down for the Suez Canal by the International Convention of 1888. There were two significant omissions, however, and these were to limit considerably the importance of this treaty later on. The words 'in case of war' did not appear anywhere in the text; this literally meant that in case of war the Americans could close the isthmus. Further, fortifications were not specifically forbidden, hence the conclusion that the builders of the canal could fortify it and maintain there a force of military police. Thus the United States were to be the sole guarantors of this new maritime route, and were to receive the equivalent of a mandate from Britain. The Panama Canal in truth was to be American, more American than the Suez Canal was British.

I V

Having settled with England, the Americans had now to come to terms with Colombia, for the transfer of the French concession had to be approved by the State that had originally granted it. In 1902 Colombia had scarcely emerged from the exhausting internal disturbance known as the 'War of a Thousand Days'. Its government was weak and of doubtful legality. In 1898 the President, Señor San-Clemente, had been imprisoned by his Vice-President, Señor Marroquin. After that the latter had contended that San-Clemente was 'absent' and had seized power on July 31st, 1900. Since then he had governed as a dictator without recourse to Congress. When he was obliged to convene it to discuss the treaty with the United States in 1903, it was the first time that he had appealed to its aid.

The negotiations began at Washington between Mr. Hay, the American Secretary of State, and Señor Martinez Silva, the special envoy from the Republic of Colombia. It was President Roosevelt, however, who effectively directed the business. He discussed it with Mr. Hay, his Secretary of State, nearly every day, whereas the late President McKinley had hardly considered it more than once a month. Martinez

Silva did not stay long in Washington, for he was presently replaced by a Minister Plenipotentiary, Señor Concha. As the latter was at heart opposed to the project, he ceded his place to Señor Herran, secretary of the Colombian Legation, and it was he who finally signed the Treaty on January 22nd, 1903, under the ill-disguised pressure of the American negotiators.

The New Company was authorized to transfer all its rights, privileges, properties and concessions, as well as the Panama Railroad, to the United States; Colombia, the concessionary country, was not to interfere. Colombia in turn was to cede in the isthmus a strip of land six miles wide, and although maintaining theoretical sovereignty the concessionaire was to have the right to administer and police this zone, as well as set up special law courts. By way of indemnity the Colombian Government was to receive $10,000,000 at once, and nine years after ratification an annual sum of $250,000.

The Hay-Herran Treaty as it was called was ratified by the American Senate on March 17th, but was not discussed by the Colombian Congress until June 20th. Its reception at Bogotá was chilly to say the least. The Colombians were highly indignant over the suggestion that their sovereignty over the canal zone was to be limited, and more particularly over the establishment of special courts. The fact that they were not to be allowed to negotiate direct with the New Company closed the door on possible interesting combinations; also the indemnity seemed insufficient. Why could they not have received $15,000,000 from the United States? And $10,000,000 from the New Company for permitting the transfer of the concession?

This ill will was not merely a question of self-interest. It also reflected the old Latin-American hostility towards the Anglo-Saxon race, more especially at this time when they felt that the isthmus was passing into the hands of the latter.

'A shameful contract,' shouted the Press. 'Herran's insult to the good name of Colombia can never be wiped out. The gallows would not be punishment enough for such a criminal.'

'This is a violation of our fundamental institutions, a violation of our sovereignty,' wrote the President of the Senate himself on October 13th in the *Nuevo Tiempo*. 'I should like to see a Colombian canal set up for all eternity. So, there is not going to be a Colombian canal! Very well then, there will be no canal at all.'

Here again was the old argument brought up by Khedive Ismail, when he hoped that the Suez Canal would belong to Egypt. But the Colombian Congressmen were under a grave illusion, for the position of their country had all Egypt's disadvantages without any of her advantages. Suez was only a few hours from Cairo, but Panama — at any rate in 1903 — was quite fifteen days from Bogotá. The discussions went on in this sullen atmosphere, with a feeble president who scarcely dared take part.

The American attitude embittered everything, for it was clumsy and inconsiderate. In their private correspondence and in conversation they were anything but polite. Hay talked of 'those dagoes'. Roosevelt was even more insulting. He called them 'Contemptible little creatures! Jack Rabbits! Foolish and homicidal corruptionists! Greedy little anthropoids!' etc. Of course the Colombians did not hear these epithets at the time. Mr. Beaupré, the American Minister at Bogotá, refused to compromise in the slightest, and even tried his hand at intimidation. Finally on August 12th the Colombian Senate rejected the Treaty by a unanimous vote. In reality Colombia was hoping to reopen the whole affair on another basis, for someone had pointed out that the delay granted to the French Company lasted only until October 31st,

1910. As this prolongation was of more than doubtful legality, the concession actually would lapse on October 31st, 1904.

In this case why not simply wait until the concession had matured and then take possession of the canal and all the work done on it? They could then either entrust the enterprise to other concessionaires, Germans for example, or possibly get more than $10,000,000 out of the Americans, as well as the $40,000,000 which the Americans were ready to pay to the French. On October 31st the Colombian Congress adjourned without having reached a decision.

The blindness of the Colombians in this matter passes all understanding. They failed to see that if they refused to come to terms there was always the chance that Panama might secede. People who visited the isthmus at that time heard this project discussed on every side. At Bogotá, where even telegrams sometimes took two weeks to arrive, the Ministers reassured themselves by saying that the Treaty of 1846, guaranteeing the sovereignty of Colombia over the isthmus, was still in force. 'We have nothing to fear', they thought, 'and perhaps a great deal to gain.' As things turned out they had everything to fear, for the counter-attacks which could be directed against them were almost too tempting.

V

When he learned of Bogotá's refusal, Roosevelt responded not as a diplomat but as a man of action — he was 'pure act' according to Henry Adams. If Panama did not revolt, he planned to occupy the isthmus, and undertake to finish the canal himself. He argued that he could do this in virtue of the Treaty of 1846 which stipulated that 'the free transit from one ocean to the other was never to be either interrupted or restricted, no matter what means of communication might exist or be about to be created'. Quite apart from international law, the weakness of this thesis, which had been evolved by John Bassett Moore, the well-known lawyer, was that it overlooked the alternative route in Nicaragua, and that this alternative had been retained as a second string to the Spooner Bill. Moreover it was a dangerous time, for it was now the year before the 1904 Presidential Elections, and in the United States Presidential Elections, first, last, and all the time, are more important than anything else.

Now the temptation for the Province of Panama to secede was so natural that it needed no prompting, for should the Americans return to the idea of the Nicaraguan route, all would be lost. The ruling class in Panama doubtless were Colombian, but the link was weak, and in the past countless revolutions had taken place. Even Señor Obaldia, the Governor, though a nominee of President Marroquin, was himself a secessionist.

At the end of September 1903, the conspirators decided to send an official agent to New York to feel out the ground. Their choice fell on a Dr. Amador who had previously been the physician attached to the Panama Railroad. He first got into touch with Nelson Cromwell, the energetic lawyer employed by both the New Company and the railroad. But Nelson Cromwell, after having first encouraged him to disclose everything, left for Europe, fearing that if he took part in the intrigue, it might lead to the total loss of the concession. At that moment the disheartened delegate from Panama happened by the purest luck to meet in the Waldorf-Astoria Hotel Mr. Bunau-Varilla, who had just arrived in New York on September 22nd. Bunau-Varilla at once took the affair in hand, and from then on he conducted it with incomparable *brio*. Everything he did received the tacit approval of the

White House, where he had been *persona grata* ever since his lecture tour.

Dr. Amador and Bunau-Varilla then sketched out the details of the revolution together. They were certain of the support of the local garrison of about five hundred men, who had been stationed for some time in the isthmus under the command of General Huertas. Colombia would of course send other troops, but they could only arrive by boat and must not be allowed to land. This would have to be undertaken by the United States, but the Treaty of 1846 gave them the right to do so. After all it was something that they had done more than once before. The revolution certainly would succeed if American warships could be in the locality and ready to intervene. It was therefore merely a question of a discreet warning to Washington, and this the Frenchman took upon himself.

One difficulty remained. Amador had no money to give to General Huertas' soldiers, whose pay was long in arrears. Bunau-Varilla, therefore, promised him an advance of $100,000, and made himself personally responsible. It was agreed that the revolution should break out on November 3rd at the latest, and that the new State should nominate Bunau-Varilla as Minister Plenipotentiary at Washington where he would serve as liaison agent.

Officially the American Government knew nothing whatever, but everything transpired as though according to a preconceived plan. The warship *Nashville* arrived from Kingston, Jamaica, at Colón, in the evening of November 2nd, but the next morning there also arrived the Colombian General Tovar with 500 men. He notified the manager of the railroad that he wished to get to Panama immediately, but as the latter was in the plot he declared that he had no trucks available at the moment. However, he sent the

General and his staff on alone instead, and thus isolated him from his men. As soon as the General arrived at Panama on the evening of the 3rd, he was arrested, and the revolution was proclaimed.

Next day the commander of the *Nashville* forbade the transport of the Colombian troops, and finally he persuaded them to leave. His excuse was that he was protecting the liberty of transit, thus relying on the Treaty of 1846 which seems to have had a very broad back. The two gunboats which had come with General Tovar went over to the revolution. A third one which happened to be at Panama fired a single shell at the town. It killed a Chinaman, who was thus the only victim of this comic war. The fuse of this shell is on show at the little historical museum at Cali, where I have seen it myself. The revolution was over, and on November 6th the new State was recognized by the United States. On the 10th Hay, the Secretary of State, notified Bogotá that in future he would oppose any debarkation of troops.

Everything was finished, except the negotiations between Panama and Washington with regard to the canal. They presented no difficulty since Bunau-Varilla was the accredited agent to Roosevelt, with the title of Minister Plenipotentiary, and so could conduct the negotiations. The Panama Government, however, regretted that they had appointed a foreigner, so on the 11th a delegation left Colón to discuss the treaty itself. But Bunau-Varilla was already in agreement with Hay and in any case his credentials were in perfect order. The treaty was hastily concluded, and was signed on November 18th. The document has come down to history as the Hay-Bunau-Varilla Treaty.

Later on the day that it was signed, Amador arrived in Washington but only to learn at the railway station, where his Plenipotentiary met him, that everything was settled.

At first he was aghast, as one can well imagine. But soon the doctor in him won the day over the conspirator, and he shouted out, 'Well, at any rate, yellow fever will disappear from Panama!' General Reyes, who had been sent from Colombia, arrived in his turn on the 27th, and he also discovered that it was all over, for the Treaty had been ratified on the previous day. Panama gave its consent on December 1st. Think what you will about this revolution, but from the point of view of sheer technique it was a little masterpiece!

By the Treaty the American Government received all the sovereign rights that it would have had, if in fact it had been sovereign. This extended over a strip of territory ten miles wide called the canal zone. The Treaty also authorized the Americans to requisition such ground or water surfaces as the canal might require. At both Panama and Colón it was allowed to substitute its own personnel for the Panama authorities in order to undertake any measures necessary for the maintenance of order and the preservation of public health. In exchange the United States guaranteed the independence of the Republic of Panama, which was also to receive an indemnity of $10,000,000 and at the end of nine years an annual indemnity of $250,000 was to be added.

The people of Panama protested against this Treaty, which had been drawn up by an American and a Frenchman, and which gave the Americans the lion's share. Yet one may wonder whether a delegate of their own could have got better terms.

It is very probable that without Bunau-Varilla the revolution would never have taken place. Its success certainly was assured by the marvellous fertility of his imagination, but he was acting not as is often believed merely as the agent of the New Company. In any case the French Embassy at Washington had prudently kept well out of the whole intrigue.

All credit, therefore, as well as all responsibility for his initiative, rests with him alone. In him the Panama Canal had a passionate disciple, convinced and efficient.

We must add, however, that this daring political operation would not have been possible without President Roosevelt. In his Message to Congress on January 4th, 1904, he naturally denied all complicity: 'Neither the Government in the person of any one of its members, nor any of its collaborators has taken the slightest part in the preparation, the incitement or the encouragement of this revolution. Except from reports from our military agents, we had no previous knowledge of this revolution beyond what could have been surmised by any intelligent person who reads the newspapers and is well versed in public affairs.'

Yet in spite of all this, it is obvious that when he knew what he should know and in sufficient time, he had acted with decision and without hesitating over embarrassing scruples.

'If I had kept to the routine of traditional methods', he said in an address at Berkeley University on March 11th, 1911, 'I would have submitted to Congress a solemn document of some 200 pages, and the debate would be going on yet! Instead I took the canal zone, and left Congress to discuss it afterwards. While they are talking the canal will be built.'

Finally we must note the complete absence of international spirit in this statesman, who was responsible for the status of Panama. 'Our naval force will be doubled', he said, 'provided we do not commit the folly of seeking an international guarantee, or of allowing other Powers to interfere in this purely American enterprise.' In this way President Roosevelt simply confirmed the tradition handed down by all his predecessors since the American Civil War. The canal was to be built by America and run by America on American territory.

CHAPTER VIII

THE AMERICANS BUILD THEIR CANAL

I

OUT of the 210 million francs which the American Government paid to the New Company, the latter in accordance with its statutes retained 77,400,000 francs, or 129.78 francs per 100-franc share. In other words the formation of the New Company had been a successful business venture.

The Old Company received 128,600,000 francs, which was divided among the bondholders who received 11 per cent of the face value of their securities. This was based on the liquidator's schedule of admitted liabilities, which included unpaid coupons. As for the shareholders and holders of partly paid shares, there was nothing left over for them. It was one of the greatest disasters in French financial history. The four annual drawings of the *Civil Company for the Amortization of the Lottery Bonds of the Panama Canal*, which had been incorporated on June 14th, 1888, well illustrates the extent of the ruin, for all the sums salvaged, thanks to a payment of 55 francs per bond, were enough for only one series of lottery prizes. The French share in the enterprise was thus ended; all that was left was the financial ruin and the remnants of their plant in the isthmus.

According to the Spooner Law, which was henceforth to be the charter of the canal, authority to carry out the work was concentrated in the hands of the President of the American Republic. He was to act through the intermediary of a committee of seven, whose composition required the

Senate's approval. There was no longer any question of a profitable business, to be carried out by private initiative in one form or another; that stage was over. From now on we are dealing with an undertaking which is purely political, the State being entirely responsible for its finance, administration, and technical execution. Comparison, therefore, becomes practically impossible, either with the Suez Canal or with the old Panama Canal Company.

The Americans were now faced with a momentous decision: should their canal be at sea level, or should it have locks? The first plan had many partisans, not only in the engineering fraternity, but in Congress and among the general public as well; an international committee of experts also seemed to prefer it. The President, however, who was greatly influenced by Bunau-Varilla, inclined towards the second alternative, and after taking the advice of experts and consulting with both Houses of Congress, he definitely adopted it in 1906.

This plan was almost exactly the same as the one recommended by Godin de Lépinay to the Geographical Society in 1879. 'Dam the Chagres and the Rio Grande near the sea at the first point where a barrage is possible,' he had advised. 'Raise the level of the water to 80 feet above the sea, and construct locks to allow the descent from this lake to sea level at both ends. You will then have practically nothing to do in the valleys of the Chagres and the Rio Grande. Your cuttings in the Obispo Valley and across Culebra will be eighty feet less deep, and this will enormously reduce your work.' This description corresponds in almost every detail with the Panama Canal as it exists to-day.

While the Americans were perfecting their technical plans, they hesitated for some time before setting up an efficient staff to carry them out. During the first period up to March 1905, the commission attached to the President was functioning under the direction of the Secretary of War. It received extremely wide powers. It was responsible for administration, policing, and even legislation. But they gave it three heads, a chairman in Washington, a governor, and a chief engineer in Panama, and as a result there were constant delays owing to red tape. Mr. Wallace, the chief engineer, on whom rested the technical responsibility, resigned in exasperation at the end of a year. Authority was then concentrated in a committee of three, consisting of the chairman at Washington who was in charge of contracts, a governor in Panama, and alongside him the new chief engineer, Mr. John F. Stevens, who was well known through the Western States as a great railroad builder. This administration did not manage to ward off political interference however, so the chairman resigned. The chief engineer became discouraged in his turn, and finally recommended the adoption of autocratic methods.

At about this time, in April 1907, a military regime was set up, and it eventually was to bring the affair to a successful conclusion. In the isthmus full powers were now given to Lieut.-Colonel Goethals, a senior officer in the Engineers. He was a recognized expert on canal locks, and in January 1906, he became to all intents and purposes the dictator of the canal. It was he who achieved the completion of the great work after seven years of effort, thanks to his technical ability and a moral authority, both of which soon manifested themselves. This soldier was never seen in uniform, for he relied solely upon his technical reputation. The workmen respected him. 'He's up to his job, and he's square,' they said. His methods were those of an expert playing the part of a benevolent tyrant. As he was supported in the highest quarters, he succeeded in keeping politics out of everything.

To-day Goethals has become a legend, and with the outstanding engineers of the French period who must not be
forgotten either, he was the real builder of the canal.

II

Yellow fever and malaria had contributed quite as much
to the French failure as their financial and engineering difficulties. As the Americans were well aware of this, they
realized from the start that they would have to make the
isthmus healthy to work in. Now what had been impossible
between 1880 and 1889 was quite possible in 1904. The
French knew nothing of the role that mosquitoes play in
carrying tropical diseases, and therefore they had been
chiefly concerned in struggling against 'miasmas' or mists
rising from the swamps. They really did not know against
what to protect themselves.

During the American occupation of Cuba, and especially
owing to the work accomplished by Sir Ronald Ross at
Ismailiya, it had been discovered that both yellow fever and
malaria are transmitted by mosquitoes. Thus when Colonel
Gorgas was made Director of the Department of Hygiene
at Panama in 1904, his problem was how to reduce the pernicious effect of the mosquito, and if possible to suppress
these germ carriers altogether. He had just completed a
sojourn in Havana where he had been in command of the
American Military Medical Service, and this had admirably
prepared him for the heavy task which he had now assumed.
In a later chapter we shall study the sanitary regime which
was adopted, and which had been rendered possible owing to
certain very wise clauses in the Hay-Bunau-Varilla Treaty.
It is sufficient for the moment to say that by the end of 1905

yellow fever had disappeared, and although malaria continued, it was well under control and very considerably reduced.

Labour was the next problem. The necessary skilled workers were recruited from among the whites, indeed they were almost exclusively Americans, but in addition there was a veritable army of manual labourers. These were of various types, but mainly black. The two groups corresponded to two social levels, or to two standards of life, and actually they were paid in different kinds of money. The first were called the 'gold force' because they received dollars, while the second, or 'silver force', were paid in the local currency. This curious nomenclature is still used to-day to distinguish the technical and clerical staff from the mass of labourers, although it no longer means anything.

Panama had a deplorable reputation. In the beginning at any rate one had to offer exceptional advantages in order to attract anyone belonging to the white race. Their salaries were from 25 per cent to 100 per cent above what they would have earned in the United States; also they had living quarters thrown in free, six weeks' annual holiday with pay, and canteens or company-owned stores that were extremely cheap. An excellent 'gold force' of about 5000 men was soon built up as a result.

Recruiting the 'silver force' was much more difficult, for the New Company had maintained only a skeleton staff of about 700 men, who were really employed only so that the French could show that work was still being carried on. Everything had to be started anew. The local Indians were quite useless, being utterly indifferent and shiftless, but the Jamaican negroes who had already been tried out by the French were still available. True they also were lazy and vain, and their output was low. They were ready to stop work as soon as they had earned enough for their immediate needs, but at least they could stand the climate. The Chinese were too intelligent, for they soon left the canal to start up in trade, and anyway the Americans had little liking for them. On the other hand the Spaniards from northern Spain, when they were reinforced by Italians, Greeks, and a few Frenchmen, soon created an efficient nucleus, but being unable to speak English they were kept in subordinate positions. As the Jamaican negroes did not share this drawback, in the end they became the mainstay of this army of workmen.

During the period of active construction there were about 45,000 workers in the isthmus, of whom 30,000 were blacks and 12,000 were European, the latter figure including no fewer than 8000 Spaniards. It is interesting to note that in time the output of the Europeans declined. They may have been driving themselves too hard in a climate to which they were not physically suited, or perhaps contact with the blacks sapped their energy.

Now it is a curious thing, but exactly the opposite occurred among the Jamaicans. As they spoke English they came directly under the influence of American customs, and the atmosphere of materialistic civilization in which they were now living fired them, and especially their women, with new ambitions, which could only be satisfied by regular work. For this reason, and also because the climate did not wear them out, they were able to get through in the end as much work as the men from Southern Europe. To-day it is negroes of this type who are providing an increasing proportion of the labourers in the canal zone.

The administration had to see to its equipment. The plant received from the New Company was in good condition, and it included dredges and barges which were utilized to the very end of the work, as well as many machines of other types including 104 locomotives. A careful inventory was made of all the material handed over by the French, and according to Bishop, the secretary of the Commission, a large part proved to be very valuable, particularly an extremely important collection of maps, plans, designs, and calculations. As all this work had been admirably done, it turned out to be most useful. However, as great technical progress had been made since the work had stopped fifteen years earlier, the Americans regarded many of the steam shovels and other machines as obsolete. They considered them too light for the work which had to be done, and also they did not correspond to the ideas of the New World in either design or construction. They were condemned especially because they necessitated too many labourers to work with them. The American engineers in fact were astonished that their predecessors had been able to accomplish so much with them.

'We have been very critical of the French equipment,' said John F. Stevens, before the International Commission in 1905, 'but we have hardly been fair. Their material was modern at the time it was made, but to-day it is like a baby carriage compared with an automobile. What I am about to say is not intended to offend the French in any way, for I cannot understand how they were able to succeed in doing the work they did with the equipment they had at their disposal.'

In spite of the praise which it contained, Mr. Stevens' opinion was not quite just. It is interesting however as it underlines the differences between the methods employed. The French have no megalomania for machinery. They employ tools that are lighter but quite efficient — and which in this case were more adapted to the instability of the ground since very heavy machines would have been unusable. To talk about 'baby carriages' is to misunderstand entirely the methods which after all actually had succeeded.

But the Americans love anything big. They prefer powerful machines capable of economizing labour and increasing the per capita output. What enabled them to succeed where their predecessors had halted was the possession of some very modern machines, of excellent technical methods and above all of unlimited financial resources.

III

The execution of the task falls into three periods. During the first the administration had to give the public the impression that they had got started, and unfortunately they committed the error of working without making sufficient preparations first. The consequence was a certain amount of fumbling and set-backs. The second period covers the Stevens' administration, when this great engineer was organizing the railroad and getting the equipment into action. Finally the third period, the decisive one, was that of Colonel Goethals. Being a consummate master of both his material and technique, and possessing absolute authority, he was able to bring the great undertaking to a completely successful conclusion.

In these immense workyards three splendid achievements rivet our attention: the locks, the Gatun Dam, and the Culebra Cut, the latter now renamed the Gaillard Trench. The infinitely powerful resources which the Americans had at their disposal allowed them to succeed where their predecessors had failed, although they too were confronted with staggering difficulties, especially at Culebra. There were repeated landslides, which grew more frequent the deeper they dug. This meant that the amount still to be excavated had to be calculated afresh each time, just as had been done during the French period. The International Commission had estimated it at 50 million cubic yards in 1905, but by 1908 the figure was raised to 78 million, by 1910 to 84, by 1911 to 89, by 1912 to 94, and finally in 1913 to 100 million! In 1880 de Lesseps had thought that he could dig the whole canal by removing only 45 million cubic metres, but before the enterprise was completed a total of no less than 300 million had actually been excavated. The French contribution had amounted to some 55 million cubic metres, but only a little over 40 per cent of their work eventually was utilized by the Americans.

After work was resumed in 1904, it took ten more years to finish the canal, and on August 15th, 1914, the new inter-oceanic route was officially open for navigation. On August 3rd, however, an ocean-going ship, the *Christobal*, had made the first journey from the Atlantic to the Pacific, and on the same day Europe plunged into a world war. The coincidence is symbolic, for from that moment a fundamental change took place in the equilibrium of the continents.

The American effort was entirely successful. It had been made possible by the sanitary work on the isthmus, the possession of powerful machinery, and above all by having plenty of money, which was never stinted. The French had spent 1271 million francs, and the Americans in their turn spent the equivalent of 1115 million francs, without making allowance for military credits. In other words, by the time that the canal was inaugurated it had cost the world no less than 2386 million francs. Expressed in dollars, the Americans spent $223 million, after deducting the $40 million paid to the New Company, and the $10 million given to the Republic of Panama. To bring it to completion the canal had required resources which no private company could have furnished without the greatest difficulty.

CHAPTER IX

DESCRIPTION OF THE CANAL AND ITS WORKING

I

PANAMA and Suez are both maritime canals, each uniting two seas across an isthmus, but I believe that is about all that they have in common.

The Isthmus of Suez is a completely flat sandy desert, with a climate of unexampled dryness. The Mediterranean shore is so low that one scarcely perceives it on arrival, and, like Venice, Port Said and Alexandria rise out of the sea. The Panama Canal on the contrary cuts through mountainous country of complicated geological formation. It lies in a ferocious jungle, which grows without restraint in this atmosphere of prodigious humidity. When one approaches the American shores in this area, the sky-line seems to be sketched in with bold strokes, outlining the hardy summits which are covered by this crazy vegetation. Everything is a sombre green — 'rheumatic green', Léon Daudet would have called it — and it reminded me a bit of the colouring of our valleys in Normandy between Trouville and Honfleur.

Thus, stretches of sand in the one case, and virgin forest in the other; in short, the difference between the desert East and the equatorial West. At Suez one looks out on the caravans and tents of the nomads, and all the Biblical life of the Levant that de Lesseps loved so well; but Panama is a stifling greenhouse, swarming with animal and vegetable life, with serpents and crocodiles swimming alongside the transatlantic liners in the waters of Lake Gatun, as I personally can testify. One feels that at the slightest relaxation the jungle would quickly recapture all the ground which man has won from it.

To contrast the technique in the construction of the two canals is no less striking. Suez is a sea-water canal built at sea level. Here they had no engineering difficulties to overcome, the lack of fresh water being the chief problem. Panama on the other hand is a canal with locks, and dams which create an artificial sheet of water in the interior of the isthmus. It was not lack of water but too much of it that proved to be the most formidable enemy, particularly when it streamed down the hills and formed devastating floods. Still, without this humidity how could they ever have filled the lake! We are apt to forget that had the climate been the same as at Suez, the canal as it exists to-day would never have been built.

In various respects the two enterprises bear the imprint of these circumstances. Suez is a magnificent ditch-digger's dream! Once the canal was finished, it functioned like a harbour or a port. Panama, owing to its dam and lock gates, is more like a factory. One's impression is less of navigation than of a great modern workshop, filled with splendid machinery that operates as accurately as a watch. This very fact makes it terribly vulnerable.

To tell the truth Panama does not remind me of Suez at all, and I sometimes wonder if the experience the French gained in Eygpt could have helped them in any way in Central America.

II

The Panama Canal runs from north-west to south-east, so that the town of Panama on the Pacific shore actually is located 20 miles to the east of Colón on the Atlantic side.

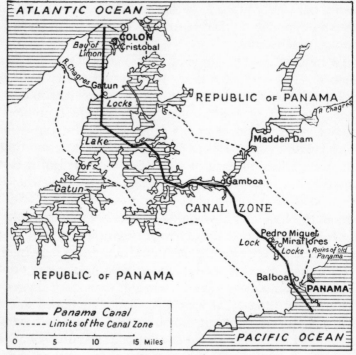

The Panama Canal

The canal is 40½ miles in length from coast to coast, or 50
if we include the maritime channels at each end. At Suez,
as we remember, the length was about 100 miles from shore
to shore. At Panama the minimum width at the bottom of
the canal is 300 feet as compared with 200 feet at Suez.
The minimum depth is 40 feet, with an allowable draught
of 37 feet as compared with 34 feet at Suez. Thus Suez is
over twice as long, but Panama is half as wide again and
slightly deeper. The size of the ships at Panama is limited
by the dimensions of the lock chambers.

Let me describe the trip through the canal from the

Atlantic to the Pacific. The first contact with Panama is somewhat disquieting because of the climate, as I noted in my diary seven years ago. At noon on July 7th, 1932, Colón was coming into view, and I wrote, 'The sea is the colour of molten lead; the shore appears to be a frenzied jungle of a dark green hue; the sky is as black as ink with white clouds piled up on the horizon above the Sierras. The heat is suffocating.'

After leaving the port of Christobal, which is a suburb of Colón, the ship crosses the Bay of Limon. It then enters the canal, which goes through the swamps of Mindi. A little way to the east lies the old French ditch, which the Americans did not utilize. Seven miles farther on we reach the Gatun Dam and locks. An artificial lake, 17½ miles long and 85 feet above sea level, is held in check by this dam. The dam itself is 8400 feet long, 105 feet high, about 2200 feet broad at its base, and 100 feet across the top. It looks like a vast earthworks covered with turf, and the Americans have laid out an 18-hole golf course on top of it.

On the Upper Chagres about seven or eight miles above Gamboa is a second or reserve dam called the Madden Dam, which is also known as the Alhajuela Dam. Since 1935 it has been used to accumulate water during the rains in order to replenish the lake during the dry season. At Gatun there are two sets of three locks each, and coming by ship from Christobal they look like three steps in some gigantic Babylonian stairway. The length of each lock chamber is 1000 feet, and the width is 110 feet.

As one steams into it, the interior lake seems like a tropical river with its numerous inlets and winding course. Nature is still unconquered here, in fact no attempt has been made to tame her. The jungle maintains its sway, to be interrupted only here and there by a tiny unkempt banana plantation.

311

Crocodiles swim in the water, and on the shore sits an Indian in silence. These are not our contemporaries. When the water was let into the lake, whole forests were drowned so completely that only the tree-tops emerged above the surface at certain places, and one still sees thousands of dry dead branches sticking up out of the inundated depths. The few plants that have survived give the impression of baskets of flowers poised on the surface of the water. Between Darien and Gamboa, where the Chagres River enters the lake, the banks close in and we enter the notorious Culebra Cut.

The Gaillard Cut, as the Americans have renamed it after one of their engineers, is 8½ miles long. It measures 300 feet across the bottom, and its width varies from 320 to 900 feet at the surface of the water. At bottom it is 40 feet above sea level, that is to say much lower than the level planned by the French, for they talked of constructing it 130 feet, or at least 100 feet, above the sea. Imagine a rugged ravine overhung by sharp reddish brown crags, with great masses of soil which seem ready to cave in. Meanwhile the water from the last downpour is emptying in rushing torrents into the canal.

We soon reach the other slope. A double lock-way at Pedro Miguel leads our ship down to little Lake Miraflores, which is 54 feet above the level of the sea. As at Gatun these locks are 1000 feet long and 110 feet wide. After crossing this lake we get to another double set of locks of the same dimensions as those at Pedro Miguel. Then we come to the canalized course of the Rio Grande, which being at sea level rises and falls with the tides. A canal of eight miles leads into the Pacific, leaving on the left the heights of Balboa and three little islands, Naos, Perico and Flamenco, joined to the mainland by a mole. In the distance one can see the Perlas Islands lying out in the ocean.

The equipment annexed to the canal includes the two ports of Christobal and Balboa. They are magnificently laid out, especially Christobal, and both possess deep-water quays for the biggest ships. Their coaling wharves to-day are usually deserted of course in favour of their oil stations.

We must also mention the railway, which continues to play a role of first importance in the life of the isthmus, for up to 1936 there had never been a highway joining the Atlantic and the Pacific. There were two branch roads, however, one going from Colón to Gatun, and the other from Panama to Gamboa. The monopoly of the Panama Railroad, inscribed in its original concession, had a tough life! Before constructing a road from one ocean to the other they had to await the ratification of the treaty of 1936 between the United States and the Republic of Panama. This ratification took place at Washington on July 27th, 1939, and now that the work has been decided upon it will be accomplished before long.

I I I

Transit is easier here than at Suez, for the Panama Canal is wider, but it has its own peculiar problem of the lock gates. Passage through Panama thus includes two distinct aspects: pilotage and general transit conditions on the one hand, and on the other the functioning of the lock gates. The pilot takes over the ship at the entrance to the canal without its having to anchor. With him three other officials come on board, the Customs agent, the toll collector, and the doctor. After that the ship proceeds into the canal without stopping.

The passage is directed from two control points at Christobal and Balboa, which are run by American naval officers. They are assisted by signals transmitted from several observation posts. The pilots have more initiative than those at Suez, because ships are allowed to pass one another under way; also navigation is quite free on the lake, which accounts for over half the total length of the trip. Going through the locks, on the other hand, requires very careful staff work in order to avoid jams. Passenger ships are given precedence, and tankers and ships carrying explosives are also sent through quickly. So far as possible heavily laden ships pass through alone, and it is arranged to have them meet other boats only on the lakes.

The pilots are all Americans. The service is hard, and requires considerable skill. It is divided into two sections, one from Balboa to Pedro Miguel, and the other from Pedro Miguel to Christobal. Except when actually in the locks, the pilots direct everything, giving orders on the ship and also to the staff on shore. I was up on the bridge when our ship went through, and I personally saw our pilot himself ringing down the signals to the engine-room.

The difficulties are not exceptional, but they must not be overlooked. There is less trouble over steering than at Suez, except that when going from fresh water to salt water and *vice versa* there are ticklish currents and eddies to watch out for. Careful manœuvring often requires the assistance of tug boats, and they are available both at the locks and in Culebra. In a general way navigation is easier than at Suez, and yet skill is needed, for the slightest error could have serious consequences, particularly as the sides of the canal are dangerously rocky, and it would be fatal to touch them. The journey through the canal requires eight hours on an average. It is only done by daylight and the ships set out at half-hour intervals, the first being dispatched at 6 a.m. and the last at 2.30 p.m. from Balboa, and 3.30 p.m. from Christobal.

The locks and their working are a magnificent sight. What surprises one at first is the almost complete absence of workmen, the silence and the calm simplicity of the operation. A ship on its arrival at the lock basin is seized by six steel cables each fixed to an electric locomotive moving on a rack-and-pinion railroad; there are two in front to tow the ship, two in the middle, and two behind to hold it back. These locomotives act as tugs, for the ship's own engines are not running, in fact the ship is entirely passive during its journey through the locks. A chain stretched across the canal protects the lock gates, and a second safety barrier is also provided, for an accident would certainly be extremely serious, and might even risk emptying the whole lake.

Few men are to be seen because the work is mechanized. When one visits the machinery chambers underneath the quay, one is shown the motivating machines, whose very size gives some idea of the prodigious technical effort carried out. In the control post a few operators move nickel-plated levers from time to time. The silence is almost religious, giving an impression of force, calm and security. It does honour to the American race, and classes them with the Romans among the great creative geniuses of the universe.

The silence is so complete that it is contagious. From the quay I watched several merchant ships pass through, but not one word was uttered by the crews. Later when I myself went through on a big American liner filled with tourists, the effect was lost, for the noise of the gramophones ruined the illusion.

It takes exactly fifteen minutes to pass through a lock, which is then refilled in a further eight minutes. In the whole trip across the isthmus, the locks account for an hour and a half. It seems to be a triumph of the automatic, and yet the operators will tell you that each passage must be worked out differently. The currents, and also the tide which is especially strong on the Pacific side, influences the way in which the locks fill and empty themselves, so that experience and intelligence are as vitally important as ever. I must admit that I marvelled at the precision of the entire manœuvre. I was allowed to go through on the bridge of a ship, alongside the pilot and the captain. It was a heavy Swedish cargo boat of 15,000 tons, carrying a load of 22,000 tons of ore. The boat was 544 feet long and 35 feet in draught. I assure you not a single false movement was made, and not once did the boat so much as graze the side of the lock.

Every time the locks are used the lake loses a certain amount of water, but although this is easily replenished by the rivers during the rainy season, it is not made up during the dry period. The loss by evaporation on the lake must also be considered. It has been computed that the total amount of water used up and lost in a year averages 292 million cubic feet. Of this 22 million go in evaporation, 41 million through the locks, 31 million in making the hydro-electric power which is required, and 198 in seepage through the Gatun Dam. In these conditions the number of times that the locks could be worked necessarily had to be limited in the past until a decision was reached about a reserve dam.

The Madden Dam was finally completed in 1935 at the very spot where the French engineers had decided to build one. It fulfils the triple task of accumulating a reserve of water for the dry season, of furnishing the electric energy required to work the lock gates, and of controlling the floods on the Chagres River. In 1938 Lake Gatun received some 139 million cubic feet of water as its normal supply from various streams. In addition it received 105 million from what had been accumulated in the reserve dam, and 48 million came from rainfall — in all a total of 292 million cubic feet, which corresponds exactly to the amount consumed that we analysed above.

The construction of the Madden Dam has considerably increased the amount of traffic that can be handled by the canal, and the question of replenishing the water in the lake can be considered as settled. Previously it was possible to assure a traffic of only from 30 to 40 million tons a year. This figure has now been increased to 70 or 80 million, which is three times the actual tonnage handled during the last few years. In 1938 there were 5524 passages through the canal, or an average of 15 a day, with a nett tonnage of 28 million; they could, however, have accommodated 17,000 ships during the year, or a daily average of 48.

One reservation must be made, and that is with regard to the length and the beam of the ships, for locks only 1000 feet in length naturally could not contain the largest transatlantic liners such as the *Normandie* or the *Queen Mary*. Also, as they are only 110 feet wide, they give the slenderest margin for the big aircraft carriers of the American Navy. To overcome these difficulties and also for military reasons which are easy to understand, the American Government has decided to embark upon the construction of a third series of locks longer and wider than the preceding ones. In principle their use will be reserved for the Naval forces. They will be placed some distance away from the existing locks, in order to reduce the risk of damage from bombardment which might succeed in bringing all navigation to a standstill. On August 9th, 1939, when he was on a voyage to the isthmus, the American Secretary of War officially announced that this important work would be commenced at once. He estimated that it would take six years to complete and would cost $277,000,000.

The limitations imposed by the capacity of the existing locks apply only to certain special categories of ships, and on the whole commercial shipping does not feel them at all. Therefore one may say that the canal's margin of capacity to-day is capable of supplying all requirements for some time to come.

CHAPTER X

THE UNITED STATES, PANAMA AND COLOMBIA

I

THE canal zone was placed under the authority of the President of the United States and the control of Congress by a law passed on August 12th, 1912. Out on the isthmus the canal is directed by a governor who is nominated for four years. The chief engineer is the second in command, and he becomes governor in his turn when the four years are up. Both are recruited from the Corps of Military Engineers, and they report to the Secretary of War, considered here as the President's delegate and not as the head of a ministerial department. Further contact is assured with the President, Congress, and the State Department (or Ministry of Foreign Affairs) by means of an office in Washington. This office sees to the recruiting of the white personnel, and also purchases materials, foodstuffs and so forth for the zone.

Although this regime is essentially political in its conception, it has worked well in practice, because it has managed to ward off political interference. This has not been easy, for in the beginning at the time of Wallace and Stevens interference was rife, and undoubtedly the politicians would regain all their lost ground if vigilance were ever relaxed. For the moment, however, the results are a credit to the constructive genius of the Americans, who are following Napoleon's maxim, and have learned how to treat technical problems in a technical way. It is an interesting lesson in government.

The zone is ten miles wide and contains 40,000 inhabitants, all depending more or less directly on the canal. At first the Americans thought they could colonize this territory and they drew up an immigration programme, but the idea had to be given up and this strip of land is considered now only as an adjunct to the interoceanic route crossing through it. It is not surprising, therefore, to find that everything in this area depends on the canal administration. No private property is admitted. The houses are allocated to the civil servants as temporary residents only. The hospitals, clubs and hotels, and even the shops and the famous 'commissariats' are all the property of the canal.

There has never been the slightest attempt to consult the local electorate in connection with the canal regulations; the regime is simply a benevolent autocracy, essentially non-political in both spirit and methods.

The composition of the staff has remained much the same as it was during the period of construction. The gold force is still drawn almost exclusively from the Americans, and especially, it seemed to me, from the Protestant States of the south and west — one might even say that semi-officially the canal is Protestant in character. In Balboa, the administrative capital of the zone, a whole suburb is filled with Protestant institutions. They have been brought in to exercise a moral and cultural influence. The silver force is made up almost entirely of Jamaican negroes, who, being English-speaking and Protestant, are readily adaptable to American customs.

We can easily measure the relative importance of the two sections by studying their composition. On June 1st, 1938, the gold force comprised some 3386 engineers, white-collar employees, foremen, and skilled workmen, 2944 being on the canal and 442 on the railway. On the same date the silver force had 10,413 workmen, of whom 7737 were on the canal and 2676 on the railway.

The headquarters is at Balboa in the vast Administrative Building overlooking the canalized banks of the Rio Grande. The governor is paid $10,000 a year, and the heads of the various departments $8000 to $8750. The average pay in the gold force works out at $3000 a year. As for the workmen, their wage is about 32 cents an hour, and the unskilled labourers get 22 cents.

Allowing of course for the differences in climate and surroundings, we can see that a certain amount of resemblance exists between Balboa and Ismailiya. In both cases we have the same colonial outlook, the same mode of living, the same comforts which are absolutely necessary in these exotic regions, and approximately the same standard of living. Both towns seem to have taken the British establishments in India as their model.

II

The Republic of Panama, of which the canal zone still forms part, is an independent state with a population of 467,000. In area it is 32,000 square miles, of which the canal zone accounts for only 552. It lies between Costa Rica on the north and Colombia on the south, and contains two large urban districts. Panama-Balboa, the political and administrative centre, has a total of 101,000 inhabitants of which 83,000 are in Panama and 18,000 in Balboa. By contrast Colón-Christobal, the other great town, is commercial; Colón has 44,000 inhabitants and Christobal 11,000.

The population of Panama was originally composed of Indian and Spanish elements. There was an aristocracy of white families in the capital, and up-country there were

Indians who often were little better than savages. When the canal was being constructed, a negro element was brought into the isthmus, and principally into the canal zone. A certain number of the yellow race were also attracted, also some Hindus and Philippinos, and a host of other nationalities that absolutely defy classification. This conglomeration, particularly owing to the presence of whites in the country, gives an impression of extraordinary diversity.

First we have the contrast between an almost savage *hinterland* and an urban life which is almost that of the United States. The political life of the Republic is genuinely South American in character, as it is positively vibrating with the din of factionism. And that is not all, for the canal, as one of the great highways of the world, seems to have attracted and then mingled every race under the sun, until it has produced the most picturesque international bazaar imaginable. Nowhere else is it so difficult to determine the racial origin of the people that one meets in the street.

Panama is a sovereign State. It possesses its own diplomatic corps and concludes its own treaties; it is a member of the League of Nations and also of the Pan-American Union. It is very anxious to reaffirm this independence, and people are everlastingly talking about it with nationalistic fervour. The Hay-Bunau-Varilla Treaty, however, which is the charter of its relations with the United States, has introduced certain important limitations. It specifies first of all that the independence of Panama is guaranteed by the American Government, which means that the latter will not tolerate any interference in the isthmus other than its own. Although it is never mentioned, a form of control does exist over Panama's foreign policy, which rather resembles that of a protectorate. After all, it is necessary that the true nature of the bond between the two countries should be clearly defined, for the idea of a canal zone is so essentially new that it has already created a distinct place for itself in international law. For example, in 1909 Mr. Bonaparte, the American Attorney-General, declared that it was not a territory, 'but a zone occupied and held by the United States for a special and particular reason'.

In the canal zone itself one can say that the United States possesses all the sovereign rights that it would have had if in fact it had been sovereign, and that this excludes Panama from also exercising these same rights. Therefore it is not a question of American sovereignty nor even of joint sovereignty, but so far as the Americans are concerned only of the 'equivalent of sovereignty'. Or as an Irishman or Norman peasant would say, 'The United States are sovereign without being it, even while they are being it'. And we can say the same of the sovereignty exercised by Panama. The rights conceded to the occupying Power are only as a function of the canal. This was expressly recognized in a letter written on October 18th, 1904, by President Theodore Roosevelt to Mr. Taft, then Secretary of State:

'We have never had the slightest intention of establishing an independent colony in the middle of the State of Panama, nor even of exercising more governmental functions than are necessary to permit us to construct, maintain, and properly administer the canal in accordance with the rights conceded to us by the Treaty. Above all we do not desire to interfere in any way in the affairs of the people of Panama.'

The right to interfere for the purpose of maintaining order was nevertheless stipulated not only for the canal zone, which goes without saying, but also for the two big cities and also for the adjacent territory. Article 136 of the Constitution of Panama explicitly confirms this right. The Americans have intervened on many occasions since 1903, but their activity has usually been short-lived. It has often been at the request of the Panama Government itself, who sometimes were anxious to have protection against dangerous political adversaries. For their part the American forces have been very reluctant to place themselves at the disposal of local party politics. Generally speaking they have remained quite indifferent provided the canal and its working were not affected. Order has easily been maintained, for the American police are numerous, and work in constant co-operation with the local police force. As I watched the people in the dance-halls of Colón, it seemed to me that every sailor on leave was shadowed by at least three police officers.

III

The right of the Americans to intervene to carry out sanitary measures is scarcely less important. This was laid down in Article 7 of the Treaty. The local authorities have to obey the instructions given by the American administration, and if necessary the latter can make sure that their orders are properly executed. The organization created for this purpose is highly complex. First of all there is the quarantine, in which American doctors are employed by the Republic of Panama. Then there is the Pan-American Sanitary Bureau, which corresponds to the United States Public Health Service. It supervises incoming ships, and is informed by radio of any diseases they may have on board. Finally there are the sanitary boards in both Panama and Colón, and the American dispensaries throughout the zone. The American and Panama doctors are on excellent terms, for both appreciate to the full the importance of the objects for which they are working.

The diseases they are fighting are three in number. First

there is yellow fever, which is relatively easy to combat, because the type of mosquito which carries it does not fly far. Then comes malaria, but it is much more difficult, because its carrier-mosquito can travel as far as thirty-five miles. Lastly we have the plague, which as we know is transmitted by rats.

The first big effort was directed against stagnant waters, as they are the breeding grounds of the mosquitoes. The French, not realizing that mosquitoes were pernicious, had allowed them to multiply. The Americans began by covering all pools with a film of oil, and later they did away with them as completely as possible. They paved the towns and covered over the brooks, establishing a system of drainage slopes, canals, ditches, and sewers. Also windows are protected everywhere by wire-netting, so that Balboa to-day looks like a gigantic meat-safe.

This meant a definite long-range policy, and it has been admirably conceived and applied. As soon as the police discover the tiniest puddle, no matter how small, they insist that it shall be dealt with immediately. For example, water might be found lying in some gutter, or in a flower-pot, or even in an old motor car tyre thrown away in a corner. Houses must be built to conform to certain rules, and only approved plans are authorized. Where a body of stagnant water cannot be suppressed, as for instance the Lake of Miraflores, then it is always kept covered with oil.

Mosquito hunts are organized with the same meticulous care. They are directed from a central laboratory which has at its disposal ten inspectors who are constantly going through the zone and the neighbouring country, collecting and destroying larvae. They spray oil over the surface of any isolated water, and warn the laboratory whenever they discover the types of mosquito that are dangerous. Paul

Morand has given us a description in his inimitable style of this marvellous sanitary activity.

'To-day yellow fever, which is raging at Dakar, has disappeared from Brazil, Panama, and Guatemala', he writes. 'That is because the Americans have enforced the laws. You have a pot full of water over there in your garden. It must be emptied. It will attract mosquitoes. The next morning when the sanitary inspector passes, the pot is still full. "That will be $20 fine and the next time you will get three months in prison," he warns you. In Colón the moment anyone sees a mosquito, he is supposed to announce it by telephone. A young man immediately rushes up, armed with a butterfly net. The mosquito is captured, and is sent at once through the proper channels to the laboratory, where they trace its place of origin. That lets loose the whole sanitary offensive, and men arrive on the spot with motor cars like firemen, wearing white overalls, masks and gloves.'

These zealous efforts are concentrated in the two urban districts and the canal zone, except for Lake Gatun which is too extensive. Already they have been crowned with magnificent, though not yet total, success. So far as yellow fever is concerned, victory has been complete for the disease has disappeared, but malaria has only been held in check. People are perfectly protected in the zone and in the two big towns, but malaria is always present in the back country, and probably will never be completely stamped out. Nevertheless the result, such as it is, can be considered as one of the finest accomplishments of our civilization.

Let us not misunderstand the true nature of this astonishing achievement, however. It has not been due to new medical discoveries alone, but to the spirit in which the task has been organized, to the Americans' professional zeal, and hardly less to the firm authority with which the rules have been enforced. Science alone could not have done it, and this immunity will not continue should political order, which is the symbol of the Americans' presence, ever cease to exist.

IV

The task of providing food and other supplies for the zone is greater than is realized at first thought. Experience has shown it to be a very thorny problem indeed. In the beginning the Americans were naturally inclined to consider the canal and its adjoining territory simply as part of their own country, and this without malice aforethought or any imperialistic designs whatsoever. They began by applying the Dingley Tariff which was then in force, the zone being considered as part of the customs area of the United States. Then the administration created canal zone stamps, as distinct from those issued by the Republic of Panama. Finally they set up the famous 'commissariats', which were meant to supply the canal employees with goods at cheap prices. The tradespeople of the Panama towns protested, for they had quite reasonably expected to play this part themselves. 'The zone is not an enclave', the Panama Government said, 'and we contest your right to issue stamps or admit duty free goods other than what is directly required for the canal itself. Your proposed policy will ruin our local trade.' To that the administration replied that, as it wished to keep its employees, it had to see that they were getting proper food and other supplies at reasonable prices.

The quarrel has lasted forty years, and it is still going on. After endless discussions they have now arrived at a basis of agreement: the 'commissariats' are tolerated, but they have not the right to sell to anyone except canal employees, and to them only in reasonable amounts. This is only a compromise and not a very practical one at that, for how can one decide what is 'a reasonable amount'? Should the 'commissariats' be allowed to sell luxury goods, and if so what are luxury goods? How can one be certain that people are buying only for their own needs? Or how is it possible to prevent contraband? Quite recently certain foreign diplomats have singularly abused their privileges in this respect.

Also it is impossible to supervise in detail the purchases of the 40,000 civilians who live in the zone, although in America they are fairly accustomed to this kind of control. One can understand how the local tradespeople continue to get heated over this official competition which robs them of valuable customers.

The dispute over the postage stamps has been settled by means of a compromise. The zone uses stamps issued by the postal authorities of the canal who are completely independent and separate from the postal administration of the U.S.A. In this way the very natural susceptibilities of the Republic of Panama are entirely respected.

As for the customs regime, the way it functions is most complex. No duties are levied on articles imported into the canal zone from the Republic of Panama, nor are there duties on goods intended for use by the canal administration or its personnel. On the other hand any goods brought into the zone which are destined for use by other people or commercial companies are subject to the Panama tariff. This solution is the outcome of a perfectly logical system, and although its application is complicated, the good faith of all the administrations concerned has made it easy to carry out. We can thus say that the postage stamp and the customs duties have ceased to be thorny problems, although the commissariats still remain a delicate question.

Meanwhile the Treaty of 1903 still is a very useful basis for the relations between the United States and Panama. It really works, and that is the highest compliment that can be paid to this little masterpiece of diplomacy. On several occasions modifications of this initial charter have been considered and the preliminaries have even been signed. In 1926 a treaty was rejected by the Panama Congress. In 1936 another was drafted and was ratified by Panama. It was finally ratified by the American Senate on July 27th, 1939. This treaty is an expression of the 'good neighbour policy' for it tries as far as possible to consider the legitimate susceptibilities of Panama.

It replaces the previous guarantee of independence by a general alliance between the two countries. Also the American Government renounces its right to intervene in so far as this right was not specified in the text of the 1903 treaty. A road between the two oceans is to be built. The canal administration agrees not to requisition ground in future until it has received the consent of the Panama Government, whereas under the former regime all they needed to do was to give notice of their intention to do so. Actually no important right formerly enjoyed by the United States Government has been abandoned, but one can understand nevertheless that the American Senate hesitated for a long time before giving its approval.

v

All outstanding questions having been cleared up with both the French Company and the Republic of Panama, there remained only to liquidate the quarrel with Colombia.

As one could well imagine, Colombia had protested in good and due form against Panama's secession and the way in which the Government at Washington had followed it up. The protest produced no effect, although it undoubtedly was to the interest of the United States not to let the quarrel drag on indefinitely. As far back as 1909 they proposed a reconciliation which was to include the payment of an indemnity, but the Colombian Congress at Bogotá was still full of bitterness, and would not accept it.

A second treaty was negotiated and signed in March 1914, on the initiative of President Wilson, who apparently had an uneasy conscience over the matter. The American Government agreed to give Colombia an indemnity of $25,000,000 and also conceded favourable treatment for Colombian troops when passing through the canal. The Americans also offered their good offices in the re-establishment of normal relations between Bogotá and Panama, and finally they expressed their 'sincere regrets' for what had happened in 1903. The Colombian Parliament gave its approval, but this time it was the American Senate who refused to ratify. 'Sincere regrets' — was that not a condemnation by a Democratic regime of the attitude taken ten years earlier by the Republican Theodore Roosevelt? The Republicans rose up against this formula, and not without reason, for they felt it discredited them. The war intervened, however, before ratification had taken place.

When the discussion was reopened in 1921, the same partisan objections reappeared. 'Why', said the Republicans in the Senate, 'should we speak of "sincere regrets"? Have we done anything wrong? And if we haven't done anything wrong, why should we pay an indemnity, for is that not equivalent to a confession?' By this time the Government was Republican once more, as Wilson was no longer in power. So they jettisoned the 'sincere regrets', although they agreed to give the $25,000,000, which Colombia in spite of everything was still quite pleased to receive.

The reconciliation between Bogotá and Panama was the logical consequence of this treaty. It included delimiting the frontier, a task that had remained incomplete for more than twenty years. We must realize that it was a very difficult matter. It was almost impossible to recruit a boundary commission, for its members risked their lives whenever they went into the Darien jungle. So matters had to wait until June 19th, 1938, before the boundary could be finally settled. The boundary now starts from the heights of Arpave on the Atlantic Coast, and reaches the Pacific Ocean at Cocalito and Punta Ardita.

By the sudden appendix operation of the Panama secession, Colombia lost the chance of playing an international role, as she certainly would have done if the interoceanic canal had crossed through her territory. On the other hand she gained real political independence, to which otherwise she could scarcely have aspired, and here comparison with Egypt is most illuminating. Once when it was suggested that the capital of Colombia should be transferred to the town of Panama, a very wise Colombian statesman is reported to have remarked, 'When I wish to strangle a chicken, I seize it by the neck'. Owing to the amputation of Panama, Colombia's centre of gravity has shifted; the country has ceased to belong to Central America, but instead forms part of the massif of South America. Since 1932 Colombia has been in possession of the Leticia quadrilateral, which gives it access to the Amazon River. This acquisition had a symbolic value, for it opened up the possibility of Colombia's playing an international role in South American politics in the future.

It is not likely that these advantages have escaped the attention of Colombian politicians, but it is difficult for them to admit it, even when reason tells them plainly that they should acquiesce. Nevertheless, by an attraction which resembles the universal law of gravitation, Colombia still looks towards the north, for the powerful and irresistible mass of the United States lies in that direction. This attraction has become doubly strong since the progress recently made in aerial communications, for it now takes only seven days to go to Europe, and thirty-six hours to New York. Proximity is the strongest argument. Therefore, although Colombia may prefer the Latin civilizations, she cannot disregard the United States, and even in spite of her instinctive antipathy for the Anglo-Saxons, she is influenced by a sentiment on Continental American solidarity. This solidarity tends to unite all American countries against Europe, and to keep alive the independent attitude which helped them break away from Spain a century ago.

CHAPTER XI

THE TRAFFIC THROUGH THE CANAL

I

BEFORE 1914 maritime communication between the Atlantic and Pacific coasts of North America was almost impracticable. One had to circumnavigate South America, either rounding the Horn or going through the Straits of Magellan. In the days of sailing ships when time was no object, people were willing to undertake this enormous detour, but it was out of the question once steamships came into use. Nor was Europe in a better position for communication with the western coast of the American continent. Under such conditions the economy in time effected by the opening of the Panama Canal was simply enormous, as is evident from a glance at the following simplified table:

Destination	Miles by Magellan	Miles by Panama	Percentage of Distance saved
	EMBARKING AT NEW YORK		
Vancouver	13,925	6,049	57 via Panama
San Francisco	13,135	5,262	60 ,,
Valparaiso	8,385	4,633	45 ,,
Hong Kong	16,579	11,539	30 ,,
Sydney	13,000	9,332	29 ,,
	EMBARKING AT LIVERPOOL		
San Francisco	13,502	7,836	42 ,,
Valparaiso	8,747	7,207	18 ,,

In each of these cases Panama is preferable to Magellan, but when we proceed farther west we come to a limit beyond

333

which it is more advantageous to adopt the third route via
Suez:

Destination	Miles by Panama	Miles by Suez	Percentage of Distance saved
	EMBARKING AT NEW YORK		
Yokohama	9,714	13,042	26 via Panama
Singapore	12,633	10,141	20 via Suez
Wellington	8,500	14,136	40 via Panama
Sydney	9,704	13,431	28 „
	EMBARKING AT LIVERPOOL		
Yokohama	12,272	11,113	10 via Suez
Singapore	15,193	8,211	46 „
Wellington	11,058	12,206	9 via Panama
Sydney	12,262	11,501	6 via Suez

We can thus outline on a map of the world a Suez zone
and a Panama zone, though their boundaries will be slightly
different according to whether one starts from New York
or from Liverpool. In the former instance the Panama zone
includes all the countries bordering on the Asiatic shore of
the Pacific right down to Hong Kong, Borneo and Western
Australia. In the case of Liverpool, however, though the
Panama zone still includes New Zealand and Kamchatka,
it does not embrace the Far East or Australia.

Thus we see that the two canals compete only on a very
narrow fringe of country. If one takes into account factors
other than mileage, for distance is not the only one to come
into play, then the two zones scarcely overlap at all.

II

In view of Article 3 in the Hay-Pauncefote Treaty, which
was referred to in Article 18 of the Hay-Bunau-Varilla
Treaty, the canal tolls at Panama have to be the same for
the ships of all nations, even including those of the United

States. There can be no possible doubt as to the interpretation of these texts. This, it seems, was the opinion of the Government at Washington itself when, in 1912, it submitted the Panama Canal Act to Congress. Nevertheless, since the Presidential elections of 1908, the public had been decidedly in favour of exempting American intercoastal shipping between the Atlantic and Pacific ports of the United States. All three parties, Republican, Democratic, and Progressive, included this proposal in their platforms, arguing that the country could do what it wished since it exercised sovereign rights over the canal which it had constructed. As for the Treaty, well so much the worse for it; it should never have been signed. During the debate in Congress on the Panama Canal Act, an amendment of this nature was adopted on August 24th, 1912. In spite of strong opposition from the railroads and diplomatic protests from Great Britain, this amendment was included in the law signed by President Taft.

According to the American Government, this exemption, about which so much fuss was being made, simply amounted to a subsidy given to their own shipping.

'Have we not the right,' they said, 'to give what subsidies we like? Is that not the prerogative of every sovereign state?'

'That may be so,' replied the English, 'but it violates not only the letter and the spirit of the Hay-Pauncefote Treaty, but it also is contrary to the evident intention of those who drew it up.'

There can be no doubt that this second view is correct, and that the argument of Senator Root seems decisive in this matter.

'We hold the canal', he said, 'practically in virtue of a mandate, and we have recognized in the clearest way possible the fact that we have undertaken the obligations of a mandatory Power. Therefore, in order to obtain the problematical advantages of favouring our own coastal trade, are we to deny obligations which the whole world considers that we have accepted? The good name of our country is surely worth more than this miserable profit.'

However, so long as the Republicans were in power, the Government resisted any compromise, and refused England's proposal to arbitrate at The Hague. But the tone changed completely with the advent of President Wilson in 1912-1913.

'We are too great a Power', he declared in his Message of March 5th, 1914, 'and as a nation we have too much sense of our own dignity to go back on the terms of an agreement. It is our duty to revoke the decisions which we recently have taken.'

On July 4th of the same year, he returned to the charge with the most generous enthusiasm.

'I maintain that it is sometimes patriotic to prefer the honour of the nation to its material interests. When I have made a promise, I try to keep it. No other rule is admissible for any country.'

Here we have the Wilson we knew in the war, and it is to the credit of the United States that his influence was strong enough to persuade Congress to abandon the legislation in question. It is not too much to say that this fine example of political honesty made a considerable impression on the world at large.

Since then the principle of equality of treatment has always been respected, although proposals to exempt coastal shipping recur with astonishing regularity. Between 1915 and 1936 no fewer than 26 of these Bills have been proposed by the House of Representatives, but all have been rejected by the Senate. On December 16th, 1937, Senator MacAdoo returned to the attack once more. Though he was President Wilson's son-in-law he also represented California, and it was in this latter capacity that he very skilfully proposed the exemption of coastal shipping of a certain type to be approved by the Government. He wished it to be done in such a way that the subsidy might appear to be of military significance. In truth the arguments for and against were purely economic, but they are interesting to analyse since they throw a clear light on certain strictly American reactions to the opening of the canal.

The canal has made maritime communication both cheap and easy between the Eastern States and about a dozen bordering on the Pacific coast, the latter including a group of others in the immediate *hinterland*. These all receive at low rates via Panama the raw materials, machines and spare parts which they need. In return they can ship under the best possible conditions to Europe and the Atlantic shores of the United States both their foodstuffs and their manufactured goods. Considerable industrial development is growing up on the Pacific coast partly as a result of these shipping facilities. What a magnificent expansion there would be if navigation between the two seaboards, which is already so helpful, could be completely exempt from tolls! Los Angeles, San Francisco, Portland, and Seattle, are all converted to this point of view, as one can well appreciate.

The opposite opinion is not maintained so much by railways as is generally believed, as by the Middle Western States, which are obviously at a disadvantage owing to the distance separating them from the sea. Competition from the industries on the seaboard would be even more serious if intercoastal shipping were allowed free passage through the isthmus. Since the beginning of the century, as we realize, the centre of gravity of American industry has shifted towards the middle of the continent. Thus we now have in America the only example of an industrial area of first magnitude which is located far from the ocean. This economic paradox is partly explained by the fact that American industry caters chiefly to the home market. The new trade by-pass which has developed between New York and Los Angeles through the Panama Canal, has naturally stimulated competition, and this is worrying the Middle West. Furthermore, it emphasizes the danger of having the most important industrial bloc in the whole world situated over 600 miles from the sea. For example, Chicago's feeling of vulnerability in comparison with New York, Baltimore, and Los Angeles, explains the nervous hostility aroused everywhere between the Alleghanies and the Rockies, by proposals such as those of Senator MacAdoo.

Still, as we have already said, the arguments in favour of exemption have never prevailed since 1912. The Middle Western States are politically strong; also the Government does not seem to be in any hurry to diminish its own revenue from the canal, for the money would have to be found elsewhere. Finally, the written texts which limit American freedom of action are absolutely clear. In this dispute we can see the traditional conflict in the United States between the desire to carry out international engagements, on the one hand, and on the other an attitude of continental independence, which is little embarrassed by respect for diplomatic undertakings. It would seem, however, that in this affair the spirit of international law has carried the day.

III

The Panama Canal Act of 1912 provided that tolls were to be based on nett tonnage, which was defined according to the 'Panama' standard, which is analogous to the 'Suez' standard. Loaded ships were to pay $1.25 per ton, and ships in ballast 72 cents. Warships, except American, were to pay 50 cents. Then in 1915, as a result of political pressure exerted by the shipowners, a new 'American' standard was permitted whenever it worked out to the advantage of the canal users. In point of fact it was equal to a tariff reduction of about 25 per cent.

However, since March 1st, 1938, a new regime has been in force based on the 'Panama' standard, which is the only one now permitted. It is further laid down that tolls on loaded ships shall neither exceed $1.00 per ton nor be less than 75 cents. In addition, passengers shall not pay more than $1.50, but if the administration wish it, they may pass through free. Since then the tolls have actually been reduced to 90 cents for loaded ships, 72 cents for those in ballast, and 50 cents for warships (American excepted), while all passengers go through free.

We must realize that fixing the tolls, so far as the United States is concerned, is less of an international than a domestic matter, and all the more thorny as it is mixed up with local politics. The shipowners naturally want as low a tariff as possible, indeed to their way of thinking American coastal trade should benefit from preferential exemption. The railroads of course, or at any rate the transcontinental railroads, are diametrically opposed to this. But quite apart from these general positions, there are geographic points of view as well.

The industrialist and the merchant on the Californian coast and also those on the Atlantic are on the side of the shipowners, whereas the manufacturing group in the Central States feel that the tolls have never been high enough. The canal administration wants them to be neither too high nor too low, for they are trying to make the enterprise 'pay' —

if it is possible in this particular case to say just what 'paying' means. As the international status of the business forbids favouring the American coastal trade by total exemption, and as the Government does not want to impose a high rate on it, so they see themselves forced to lower the scale generally. Thus in the end they are allowing international shipping to profit from what virtually amounts to a most-favoured-nation clause. That is one of the reasons, and by no means the least important, why transit across Panama is about 40 per cent cheaper than through Suez. We must also remember that the American canal has no shareholders to remunerate, nor capital to amortize.

IV

The Panama Canal was inaugurated in 1914, but in 1915 it was blocked by another landslide in the Culebra Cut, with the result that it was closed for seven months. After that the war lasted for over two years, but then everything favoured the rapid development of its traffic. The difficulties of navigation by sail in the Red Sea, which were proving such an obstacle at the time that the Suez Canal was first opened, had no counterpart here, and in any event sailing ships no longer count in the twentieth century. Furthermore, when the Suez Canal was opened in 1896, everything had to be created anew along the maritime routes to the East. Nothing was organized, there were no intermediate ports of call, no agencies, and almost no hotels, because for four centuries ships had all gone round the Cape of Good Hope. In the Isthmus of Panama and along the routes leading to it, there were no difficulties of this nature at all owing to the proximity of the United States. Thus it was easy enough to get started and to obtain the necessary equipment. The second interoceanic canal thus benefited from a double advantage. It was born half a century later than the first one, and it had

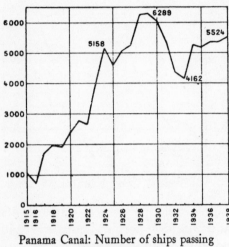

Panama Canal: Number of ships passing through the canal

the United States close at hand and ready to provide whatever was needed.

Maritime activity as distinct from the volume of trade is indicated in the two graphs on this page and the next, showing first the number of ships passing through the canal, and secondly the nett tonnage. Note that both reproduce more or less the same curves as those for Suez. The two canals experience the same vicissitudes during periods of world economic depression. Apart from the fact that at Panama the increase in traffic did not begin until 1922, both sets of graphs are similar. We find the same marked increase from 1922 to 1929, with the same hesitation in 1924. Then after 1929 we have the same sudden fall, continuing until 1933, and the same uncertain recovery from 1934 to 1938. After the nett tonnage at Panama had reached its record figure of 29,964,000 tons in 1929, it seemed to be stabilized for several years at about 28 million tons. In 1938 it was still 28,058,000 tons as compared with 34,418,000 at Suez.

Except that Suez suffered more during the Great War, we may say that the two canals obviously are affected by the same laws of expansion and contraction in the volume of shipping. The effects of course are modified by the differences in the continents they serve, and in the type of merchandise transported.

When we come to the movement of passengers on the other hand, there is absolutely no resemblance between the two canals. In 1938 the number of passengers who went through at Panama was 131,837, and

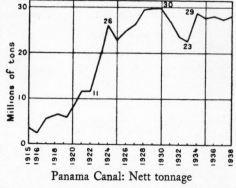

Panama Canal: Nett tonnage

100,226 in 1931, the first year for which statistics are given. In 1938 altogether 38,888 persons embarked and 41,086 disembarked on the isthmus. These figures are insignificant in comparison with the 697,800 souls carried through Suez, even if we deduct the 365,790 soldiers. The route to the East actually is a much more important line of passenger traffic, being the connecting link between the Orient and the Occident, whereas Panama does not lead anywhere in particular.

In any event it is not a migration route. The majority of the passengers are tourists, as is clearly shown by the fact that 47 per cent of the people who disembark and 51 per cent of those who embark hold first class tickets. There is nothing strange in this, however, if we look at a map, for where could the people go? So except for its military significance, we may say that the Panama Canal is not a passenger, but essentially a merchandise route.

CHAPTER XII

TRADE THROUGH THE CANAL

I

THE merchandise carried through the Panama Canal in 1938 amounted to 27,386,000 tons, which compares with its peak figure of 30,648,000 tons in 1929. For Suez the figures are

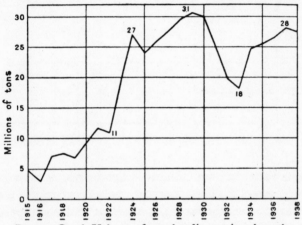

Panama Canal: Volume of merchandise passing through the canal

a little higher, 28,779,000 tons in 1938, and a record in 1929 of 34,516,000 tons. If we refer to the graph we again note a singular resemblance between the Suez and Panama curves, as both are very sensitive to fluctuations in international trade. We can therefore conclude that in spite of the present autarchic or self-sufficient regimes in so many countries, a certain degree of unity still does exist in the sphere of world economics even to-day.

It is important at Panama to study the two currents, just as it was at Suez. The traffic going from west to east, or from the Pacific towards the Atlantic, is heavier than that going in the other direction; it amounted to 68 per cent of the total in 1929, and 65 per cent in 1938. As in the case of the north bound traffic at Suez, it is principally composed of raw materials coming from young countries, and destined for lands that are more highly industrialized. On the contrary the westbound traffic distributes to less highly developed

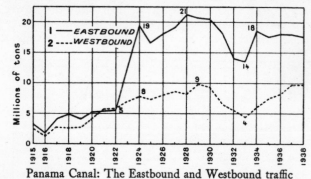

Panama Canal: The Eastbound and Westbound traffic

regions a variety of manufactured goods, which naturally are lighter in weight. This contrast is observed in the trade of countries all over the world, and is particularly apparent in the commercial balance of South America. It corresponds to a system of complementary exchange, which, though it is already breaking up, still exists between the industrialized parts of the world and countries which still depend on agriculture and mining.

Note also that the eastbound and westbound traffic curves were more or less the same up to 1922, because during its first years the canal traffic had not yet developed its true character. After that the eastbound traffic, so far as weight is concerned, decidedly took the lead. As its fluctuations are much more accentuated, it discloses the general design of the traffic current through Panama.

344

In 1938 out of a total traffic of 27,386,000 tons, the east-bound current accounted for 17,697,000 or 65 per cent. Divided into separate categories, it first comprised five groups of products, which alone made up 10,741,000 or 60 per cent of the total traffic proceeding in this direction:

1938	Tons	Percentage of Total
Oil	2,875,000	16
Timber	2,851,000	16
Minerals	2,127,000	12
Sugar	1,487,000	8
Nitrates	1,401,000	8
	10,741,000	60

Panama Canal: The proportion of the total traffic accounted for by the Eastbound current

Next we come to a secondary group of three products, which accounted for 2,394,000 tons or 14 per cent of this traffic:

1938	Tons	Percentage of Total
Tinned foods	991,000	6
Wheat	705,000	4
Metals	698,000	4
	2,394,000	14

If we compare this with the same traffic in 1924, when 19,134,000 tons, or 70 per cent of the year's total, passed eastwards through the canal, we find that the composition was similar, although the proportions were very different:

1924	Tons	Percentage of Total
Oil	9,671,000	50
Timber	1,824,000	9
Nitrates	1,745,000	9
Wheat	1,352,000	7
Metals	888,000	5
	15,480,000	80

The decline in oil seems alarming until we know the reason. The reduction in the Californian production coincided with the enormous increase not only in Venezuela but also in Texas and Oklahoma. The repercussions due to this displacement in the centre of gravity of the oil industry have been as great on the canal as on the internal American traffic between the two coasts, for after all this oil traffic is largely a form of domestic trade, and should be classified as local distribution rather than as international trade in the true sense. It is not surprising, therefore, to find that the tanker tonnage, which amounted to 40 per cent of the total traffic in 1924, had declined to 11.5 per cent in 1938. (At Suez the figure is 20 per cent.) Yet when we look back it actually was the oil traffic that was decisive in getting the canal under way.

There has also been a decline in nitrates and wheat, but timber and metals have shown marked progress, particularly certain metals from the Pacific coast destined for the Eastern States. The same applies to sugar, which did not appear among the first five products in 1924.

In a general way we can say that the traffic is made up of raw materials, for in 1938 they amounted to 80 per cent of this total. Besides those which we have just cited we should mention asphalt, phosphates, rubber, hides, wool and cotton. Among the foodstuffs, in addition to sugar and wheat are fish, fruit, hay, barley, beans, coffee, vegetable oils, copra, rice, soya beans, molasses and bananas. In this traffic 20 per cent consists of manufactures or partially converted products, among which are listed 1,855,000 tons of petrol (gasoline), 991,000 tons of tinned foods, and 234,000 tons of flour. These three headings alone make up 87 per cent of all the manufactures, and they are really only semi-manufactured. This confirms our earlier observation that the Pacific sends chiefly raw products to the Atlantic.

It is interesting to trace the exact origin and geographic destination of the trade between the two oceans. In the case of oil 55 per cent comes from the Pacific coast of North America, and 45 per cent from the Pacific coast of South America; 52 per cent of it goes to the United States and 48 per cent to Canada and Europe. When we come to timber, we find that 52 per cent is destined for the United States and 48 per cent for Europe and Canada, and it all comes from the Pacific coast of North America. All the minerals are absorbed by the United States, and they are entirely drawn from the Pacific coast of South America. Sugar comes from the Philippines, and goes to the United States. As for nitrates, they come from the western slopes of the South American continent, the United States taking

45 per cent and Europe 55 per cent. Wheat and other grains all come from American and Canadian ports and are shipped to Europe. The tinned foodstuffs can be classified almost entirely as part of the traffic between the two American seaboards.

The westbound traffic, which corresponds to the south-bound traffic at Suez, amounted to 9,689,000 tons in 1938, and over half was made up of five principal groups of products:

1938	Tons	Percentage of Total
Ores, metals, scrap iron, tin-plates	1,987,000	20
Metallurgical products	1,859,000	20
Oil and petrol	907,000	9
Machinery and railroad material	306,000	3
Motor cars and spare parts	300,000	3
	5,359,000	55

In 1924 the products were more or less the same as in 1938, although again the proportions were different:

1924	Tons	Percentage of Total
Metallurgical products	1,692,000	21
Oil and petrol	969,000	12
Machinery and railroad material	374,000	5
Cement	304,000	4
Motor cars and spare parts	110,000	1
	3,449,000	43

It is apparent that trade in this direction consists to a great extent of manufactured goods. They account for 57 per cent of the total, as compared with 27 per cent of raw materials; the remainder being made up of intermediary articles that are difficult to classify.

From this we may conclude that the older and more highly

industrialized countries such as the eastern American States and western Europe send their manufactures through the canal to supply countries that are younger economically, namely the western slopes of the American continents and the Far East. Exactly the same thing is taking place at Suez between Europe and Asia. This over-simplified analysis is really not sufficient, however, for there are many exceptions. California for example has become industrialized, and is now exporting a number of manufactured products to the Atlantic coast. Similarly Japan is intensely industrialized, and it imports through the Panama Canal cotton from Mississippi and also large quantities of scrap iron. The latter is merely a by-product in old-established metallurgical countries, but it is the equivalent of a raw material in new countries which are lacking in ore. Owing to those various factors, the westbound current here is less homogeneous than the opposite one.

No matter which current we examine, we find that the cargoes nearly always pass right through the canal without stopping. The merchandise transhipped there did not amount to more than 2,147,124 tons in 1938, out of a total traffic of 27,386,000 tons, or some 7.8 per cent. True, this is more than we found at Suez, but relatively it is unimportant. Panama is essentially a transit route uniting regions at long distances from one another. It also serves the permanent need of complementary trade between continents of different economic ages. This is the underlying basis of its traffic.

III

If we subdivide the ships going through the Panama Canal according to size, we find the following figures for 1938:

	Percentage of Total
Less than 4000 gross tonnage	15.8
From 4000 to 8000 „	66.7
Over 8000 „	17.5
	——
	100.0

Thus medium sized ships are the most numerous, actually those of from 4000 to 6000 tons, which alone account for 41.5 per cent of the total. The average size to-day is 5972 tons, whereas in 1930 it was 4862 tons; this difference reflects the steady increase in the size of cargo ships.

If we classify the ships according to their means of propulsion, however, we get quite an interesting comparison with Suez:

	Panama Percentage	Suez Percentage
Coal burners	27.3	40.9
Oil burners	32.8	27.8
Motor ships	39.9	31.3
	——	——
	100.0	100.0

Panama is thus much more of an oil route than Suez, no doubt because of its close proximity to the oil-producing regions, and also because Suez has always had an historic connection with coal and this still continues. Since 1925 coal burners have been dropping off rapidly at Panama, for in that year ships of this type still represented 33 per cent of the total; judging from the figures for the last two years, however, it would seem as if this decline has stopped. Sailing ships have practically disappeared. The most notable progress is in motor ships. It is very striking to find that the magnificent coal wharves at Christobal and Balboa are hardly used to-day.

The nationality of the 5524 boats which used the canal in

1938 may be subdivided as follows, taking account only of their number:

	Percentage of Total
United States	32
Great Britain	23
Norway	12
Germany	6
Japan	5
	78

France comes only tenth with a total of 1.9 per cent. Comparison with the year 1925 shows fairly important changes. If we study the figures showing the weight of goods transported, we see that the American share has decreased from 54.5 per cent to 36 per cent. At the same time England has gone down, but to a lesser degree from 24.6 per cent to 22.4 per cent. Germany on the other hand has progressed from 3.4 per cent to 6.9 per cent, Japan from 3.9 per cent to 5.5 per cent, and above all Norway from 3.5 per cent to 12.5 per cent.

The United States of course is the principal client, and yet in this respect the Panama Canal is less American than the Suez Canal is British, for there the Union Jack still flies over about half the total nett tonnage. Then if we examine the situation even more closely, we come to an important conclusion which considerably modifies the character of the Panama Canal from the point of view of its international economic relationships.

The American intercoastal trade between the Atlantic and the Pacific is entirely carried in American ships, and therefore it should not be regarded as international trade in any way. Most of this traffic is purely domestic, and as we have noted in connection with the oil trade, it should really be classed as a form of local distribution. It is very similar to the shipping activity on the Great Lakes on the Canadian border. Now in 1938 this intercoastal traffic amounted to 6,395,000 tons, out of a total of 27,386,000 tons or 23.3 per cent. Therefore, strictly international trade amounted to only the 20,991,000 tons left after subtracting the intercoastal trade.

When we analyse the latter figure of 20,991,000 tons, we find that the British share amounted to 6,417,000 tons or 30.5 per cent, whereas the American was only 3,498,000 or 16.6 per cent. This is the figure we get when we deduct the intercoastal traffic of 6,395,000 tons from the total 9,893,000 tons of merchandise carried under the American flag. From this angle the Panama Canal seems to be much more international, at any rate commercially, than it appeared to be at first sight. Even disregarding England's important role, we find that the Norwegian flag carried no less than 3,434,000 tons or 16.3 per cent of the strictly international traffic; in other words the Norwegian share was almost as great as that of the United States itself.

Although we naturally must not take this reasoning too literally, it does show that Europe is still carrying on a great international trade in contrast with the United States, whose interests are chiefly bound up with their own continent. Commercially the Americans are very active in the New World and the Pacific, but unlike Great Britain their influence is not universal. Whereas Britain thus plays an important role at Panama, the American share of the nett tonnage at Suez was only 1.1 per cent in 1938, and the highest figure it ever attained was 4.1 per cent in 1920. These conditions show emphatically that even after the crisis caused by the Great War, Europe is still a factor of first importance in world commerce. Nevertheless, when we examine the Panama

Canal from its political and military aspects, we reach an entirely different conclusion. We then see how much the Old Continent has lost in the last half century.

IV

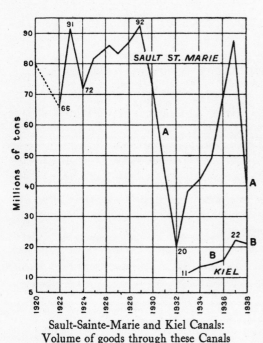

Sault-Sainte-Marie and Kiel Canals:
Volume of goods through these Canals

At Panama as at Suez, the local traffic is relatively unimportant, for it is only international trade that really counts, and the level of this trade depends on the rise and fall of the world's commercial tides. Hence the striking parallelism between the graphs showing the economic activity of the two canals. We can even extend this observation to the Kiel Canal, and the one at Sault Ste. Marie between Lake Superior and Lake Huron. These charts prove that at any given moment the economic temperature of the world is everywhere the same.

We have already shown that the number of ships passing through the Panama Canal, the nett tonnage, and the weight

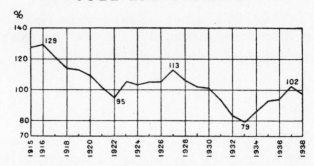

Panama Canal: The relationship between nett tonnage and the volume of goods. (The volume of goods is expressed as a percentage of the nett tonnage)

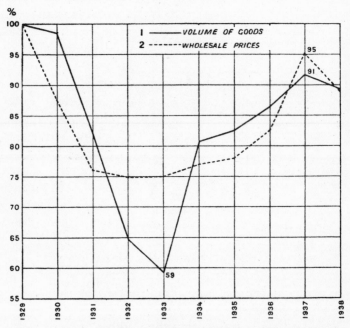

Panama Canal: Volume of goods and wholesale prices (expressed in sterling) in comparison with 1929 level.)

of merchandise, all vary in strict correlation to the general prosperity of the world. The percentage of the eastbound traffic as compared with the total merchandise also gives interesting indications. This percentage tends to sink at the end of each period of prosperity, when a slackening in business causes a diminution in the flow of raw materials towards the great industrial areas. This actually happened in 1919-1921 and again in 1929-1930. In the same way this percentage rises as soon as recovery sets in, as for example in 1923-1924.

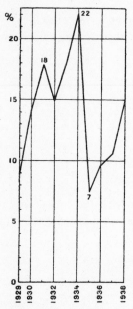

Panama Canal: Percentage of Westbound nett tonnage that went through in ballast

The relationship between the curves for nett tonnage and for the weight of cargoes is also instructive, just as it was at Suez. The weight curve passes the nett tonnage one so long as prosperity reigns, as for instance between 1924 and 1929, but the reverse takes place when business slackens or there is a depression, as between 1931 and 1938. Nevertheless these reactions are not immediately apparent, for the cargo arrives only after the order has been given, so there is bound to be a time-lag.

One can draw a similar lesson from the proportion of tonnage in ballast as compared with the total nett tonnage, as it rises rapidly during a depression and falls at the first sign of recovery. As was the case with the southbound current at Suez, we find that the westbound trade at Panama has its own special reactions. A sudden rise in the number of ships in ballast proceeding in this direction foretells recovery — or at least the hope of recovery — since the first preparation is to send empty ships towards distant sources of raw materials. Presently they will come back full, and so will help to get business going again.

From all these facts and figures we arrive at the conclusion that the activity of interoceanic canals is simply a function of general world activity.

CHAPTER XIII

THE PANAMA CANAL AND WORLD TRADE ROUTES

I

In the geography of the trade routes of the world, the zone served by the Panama Canal covers the North Atlantic and the whole of the Pacific Ocean. In this zone two channels of trade are of paramount importance, all the others being decidedly secondary in character. The first route joins the Pacific to the Atlantic coast of Central and North America. In 1938, 65.5 per cent of the total merchandise passing through the canal went along this route, while 31.4 per cent came along the second route which joins the same areas in the Pacific with the countries of Europe. The South American intercoastal trade through the canal is quite insignificant, for it amounts to only 1.3 per cent. Each of the above two important branches is made up of a whole sheaf of component trade routes, as is clearly shown in the tables given below:

I AMERICAN TRAFFIC BETWEEN THE ATLANTIC AND THE PACIFIC	*Per-centage*	*Per-centage*
1. With the Pacific coasts of North and South America		43.3
(*a*) With the Pacific coast of South America	12.8	
(*b*) Intercoastal between the Atlantic and the Pacific coasts of the United States	23.3	
2. With the Asiatic coast of the Pacific		18.3
3. With Australasia		3.9
		65.5

II EUROPEAN TRAFFIC WITH THE PACIFIC

	Per-centage	Per-centage
1. With the Pacific coasts of North and South America		26.9
(a) With the Pacific coast of South America	10.8	
(b) With the Pacific coast of the United States	8.8	
(c) With the Pacific Coast of Canada	6.6	
2. With Australasia		4.5
		31.4

The role which the Panama Canal fulfils as a connecting link distinctly emerges from these two tables. By far the greater part of the trade takes place with the western shores of the American continents. Note also that Europe does not rely on the canal to reach the Far East, although in trading with Australasia, particularly with New Zealand, she makes much more use of it than the United States does.

The countries which have benefited most from the opening of the canal are therefore those situated on the western coast of the Americas. In former years communication between them and Australasia or the Far East was easy enough, but direct relations with the Atlantic seaboard were practically out of the question. So a zone which formerly was far off and isolated has now been brought into the world circuit, and within reasonable distance of the principal economic centres. From the point of view of communications this has marked a decisive step towards world unity, and moreover, has occurred at a time when the current of political thought is flowing strongly away from any ideas of unity and internationalism.

A sketch map of the commercial routes using the Panama Canal is rather like a double fan. The handle of one fan starts at the point where the English Channel meets the Atlantic, and crossing the ocean to Panama it then spreads out into three main lines: one going to the west coast of North America, one to the west coast of South America, and the third to Australasia. Typical voyages on this fan are Liverpool to San Francisco, Liverpool to Valparaiso, and Liverpool to Wellington. The second fan is centred on the east coast of the United States; the typical voyages here are four in number: New York to San Francisco, New York to Valparaiso, New York to Yokohama or Shanghai, and lastly New York to Wellington or Sydney. In most of these cases the commerce is between countries economically young and others more highly developed, so in this respect Panama resembles Suez. Yet there is one difference, for the Panama traffic has two termini on the northern side, namely the United States and Europe, whereas for Suez, Europe is the sole objective on the west. As this fact is significant, we shall deal with it more fully later on.

In the preceding chapters we have distinguished between two currents passing through the canal, one westbound and the other eastbound. Let us now try to give precise details of the journeys of which they are composed.

WESTBOUND CURRENT

	Per-centage	Per-centage
I *Origins*		
1. From the Atlantic coast of the Americas		82.4
(*a*) From North and Central America	79.2	
(*b*) From South America	3.2	
	82.4	
2. From Europe		17.2
3. From other parts		0.4
		100.0

II *Destinations*

1. Towards the Pacific coast of the
   Americas   49.5
   - (*a*) Towards North and Central
     America   37.5
   - (*b*) Towards South America   12.0

           49.5

2. Towards the Pacific coast of the Far
   East   36.5
   - (*a*) Towards Japan   29.6
   - (*b*) Towards China   4.3
   - (*c*) Towards other Countries   2.6

           36.5

3. Towards Australasia   14.0
   - (*a*) Towards New Zealand   7.2
   - (*b*) Towards Australia   6.4
   - (*c*) Towards other Countries   .4

           14.0

           100.0

Generally speaking this traffic is made up of manufactured goods and we thus see that it is the United States which plays the leading role as the furnisher. Europe no doubt has important markets in the Far East, but she reaches them via Suez, and further we must remember that for her the Panama zone stops abruptly after Japan and New Zealand. There is a marked fall in percentages when we reach China or Australia, for we are now entering the areas where the competition of the Suez and Cape of Good Hope routes is making itself felt effectively.

EASTBOUND CURRENT

	Per-centage	Per-centage
I *Origins*		
1. From the Pacific coast of the Americas		84.5
(*a*) From North and Central America	52.9	
(*b*) From South America	31.6	
	84.5	
2. From the Pacific coast of the Far East		9.9
(*a*) From the Philippines	6.3	
(*b*) From Japan	2.2	
(*c*) From China, etc.	1.4	
	9.9	
3. From Australasia		5.6
		100.0
II *Destinations*		
1. Towards North and Central America		58.2
(*a*) Towards the United States	49.7	
(*b*) Towards Canada	2.3	
(*c*) Towards Central America	6.2	
	58.2	
2. Towards Europe		40.2
(*a*) Towards Great Britain	21.1	
(*b*) Towards Continental Europe	19.1	
	40.2	
3. Towards South America		0.4
4. Towards Asia and Africa		1.2
		100.0

The eastbound current is used to bring foodstuffs and raw materials to the industrialized countries. Since the Pacific coast of the American continent is in the front rank as one of the chief sources of supply, the merchandise traffic which passes through Panama towards the Atlantic is very important. Although Europe occupies quite a secondary place as an exporter in the westbound current, she absorbs a large proportion of the products which are coming eastwards, and accordingly her trade balance with these territories is always heavily in deficit.

Very different is the position of the United States, for though it buys more than it sells on the Pacific coast of the Americas, it sells to Australia and Japan much more than it buys from them.

After thus studying the traffic as it flows in both directions we are forced to classify the routes which emerge from Panama towards the Atlantic as among the most important trade highways in the world. The chart showing the position of British ships throughout the world in 1937 illustrated this point clearly. On this map one can trace three lines of navigation starting from the New World and directed towards the entrance of the English Channel. One comes from the Argentine and Brazil, the second from New York, and the third started at the Panama Canal, and in a general way from the Caribbean Sea and the Gulf of Mexico.

During a war these routes become of great strategic importance, particularly if the Mediterranean highway were not available. With its vast resources of raw materials and foodstuffs the continent of South America appears essentially as one of those world reservoirs to which the Powers controlling the seas turn in times of crisis. They will seek tin, copper and cotton from the Pacific slope, and oil, coffee, sugar and timber from the Caribbean zone. All these products are needed by the belligerents in western Europe, and they are being fetched via the maritime route joining Panama with the Old World. Previously this part of the planet was isolated more or less completely, but it is now mixed up in all the great economic intrigues, as well as in international politics. Whether this is good or bad for it, I hesitate to say, so for the moment we shall merely state that international currents now wash these shores.

The canal's activity does not consist entirely of through transit. Out of a total traffic of 27,386,000 tons, transhipment amounted in 1938 to 2,147,000 tons or 7.8 per cent; this figure is considerably higher than at Suez, where we found that it scarcely reached 5 per cent. Nine-tenths of these transhipment operations take place at Christobal-Colón, and are carried out by the railway administration which there owns the admirably equipped wharves. As a result quite a nice trade has sprung up with boats belonging to the great steamship lines, which collect and deliver cargoes in the smaller ports of Central and South America, and sometimes even as far afield as Tahiti.

Articles manufactured in Europe or the United States are thus spread over the local markets by these 'feeders', as these subsidiary ships are called. They are usually of shallow draught so that they can enter all manner of harbours. In the same way tropical products from both shores of the Americas, from the South Seas and even from the Far East — coffee, cotton, cocoa, rice, silk, etc. — are picked up from the local centres and brought to the isthmus to be reshipped thence to the great markets of the West. Thus Panama is becoming one of the most important transhipment points in the world, partly because the canal is now a nodal point for the maritime routes of the world, and partly because Central America is becoming actively engaged in trade and commerce. Ferdinand de Lesseps believed that an entrepôt would develop in this way at Ismailiya, but as matters turned out there was not enough economic activity in the eastern Mediterranean to support it. In this connection the Caribbean zone and the Republic of Panama offer better resources.

I I

The advent of the Panama Canal has profoundly modified the design of the world trade routes, and the aeroplane is now altering them almost as much again, especially passenger itineraries. So the map of human relationships changes under our very eyes.

When the canal was opened at the time that the Great War broke out, it made possible a certain number of voyages which had been impracticable up till then, at any rate not without transhipments. First of all it allowed ships to go from New York to Los Angeles or San Francisco without making the interminably long detour around Cape Horn, and it also put the western coast of South America within reasonable distance of New York. Thus in one day the whole of this part of South America which normally looks out across the Pacific was suddenly brought close to the great centres of Western civilization — London, Paris, and above all New York. The Chileans and the Peruvians who had always felt so remote now realized that they could get to the United States or to Europe quite quickly. The same thing had happened in India when de Lesseps had united the waters of the Red Sea and the Mediterranean.

When a traveller from the Pacific coast of South America arrives in Panama he has a choice of two main ways of going to Europe. He can continue direct by boat, or he can go to New York and there embark again on one of the great transatlantic liners bound for Southampton or Havre. The

364

recent development of an admirable system of aviation through the New World has caused this second itinerary to be used more and more, in competition with the direct route.

An intricate network of air lines now unites North and South America, using a certain number of basic routes which will likely remain unchanged for some time to come. A first line starts from New York and goes to Miami at the southernmost point of Florida, and then, via the Antilles and northern Brazil, reaches Rio de Janeiro and Buenos Aires. A second line also starts from New York, but at Miami it branches off to go via Cuba and Jamaica to Panama, or else to Barranquilla. The third line also leaves New York, but it goes overland by Mexico, and down Central America to Panama. A fourth departs from Los Angeles and meets the third line in Mexico. From Panama or Barranquilla we can fly on towards Ecuador, Peru, Bolivia or Chile, travelling down the west coast of the South American continent.

The economy in time is enormous. To give a single example: when I was in Panama I found that it would take me about eight days to get to New York by sea, unless I had the luck to find a specially fast ship. Now in an aeroplane I left Colón at seven o'clock in the morning, and arrived at Miami between four and five in the afternoon of the same day. Had I wished to continue by air I could have been in New York the next day at dawn. There was one disadvantage, however, and that was a serious one, the question of baggage. If I took more than 40 lb. with me, the charge would have been prohibitive.

These new facilities have brought with them the most far-reaching consequences. First of all, as Central and South America have become so near to the United States, the latter exerts an attraction that is becoming irresistible. Whether the American Government is imperialistic or not, the result is the same. All these regions will logically fall under American influence, with a corresponding weakening in their political ties with Europe.

No less important is the way that passengers destined for Europe are now altering their itineraries. If you are in a hurry, it is tempting to leave the ship at Panama and fly to New York, where a *Normandie* or a *Queen Mary* will soon deposit you at Southampton or Havre. It is all like a dream. If one makes exact connections the trip should not take more than six or seven days, instead of the two weeks required to go all the way by boat. Even with its excellent service, the Compagnie Générale Trans-Atlantique takes quite that time from Colón to Havre.

Speed of course is not the only factor which influences people to take this route. South American business men now find that they always have plenty to do in New York. They may have to buy or sell securities, or perhaps have a talk with their bankers, negotiate a loan, visit their publishers, or even, for all one knows, they may go there to prepare a revolution the way Dr. Amador did when he arranged the secession of Panama in October 1903! As for their wives, of course they feel that they should wait until they get to Paris to buy their frocks, and yet they can do that almost as well in New York, for Fifth Avenue is just as full of temptation these days as the rue de la Paix.

As a result of all this coming and going, New York is gradually taking her place as the capital city not only of America but of the whole world. It is not a question of having an international warehouse crammed with goods the way they have in London, for American genius decidedly does not lie in that direction. What is being created at the mouth of the Hudson River is a turntable of routes leading in and out from all directions. It is a great meeting place for travellers, and consequently it is simultaneously becoming an extraordinarily interesting clearing house of ideas. There are few capitals in the world which are truly international, but New York to-day is the most important of them all. For this reason it can imperiously attract many of the great routes of the world, and bend them into its orbit. Now the Panama Canal has certainly been one of the factors which has contributed to this concentration.

III

Passage through the Panama Canal is obligatory for a certain number of the routes which it serves, but naturally it has its competitors. Here we must study not only the question of distance, but also the kind of commodities transported, the influence of the tolls, refuelling facilities, and eventually even political and military considerations.

Suez, as we have already seen, is not a rival except in a comparatively narrow zone in the Far East. Each of the two canals has its own geographic domain, and far from injuring each other they have been mutually helpful in creating trade which increases the general level of prosperity. Experience has proved that neither can prosper at the expense of the other, and that their activity fluctuates in harmony with world economic conditions, which in fact shows that both live in the same atmosphere.

Also the rivalry existing between the American transcontinental railways and the canal has been greatly exaggerated, for each has developed its own special functions. The transport from one coast to the other of heavy goods which are not urgent can obviously be done satisfactorily via

Panama, so this type of transcontinental traffic has naturally been lost to the railways. On the other hand they continue their own type of service, which finds its way into various channels. Instead of being diminished by the competition of the canal many of their activities have actually been stimulated. For example, one effect has been the remarkable development in California. In so far as passengers are concerned, Panama has deprived the railways of only a certain type of tourist clientele, for people anxious to get to San Francisco or Los Angeles quickly will always take either a train or an aeroplane.

The aeroplane will eventually be a more dangerous rival to the canal than the railway, for in America it is becoming the normal means of communication, not only for those in a hurry, but also for the average traveller. It is already duplicating, and it may in time even supplant, the transcontinental express. No doubt it will steal part of the passenger traffic destined for South America which would otherwise go through the canal, and yet, in spite of all these factors, the airways have also helped to increase the activity on the isthmus. So Panama is gradually becoming a union station as it were, serving sea, earth, and sky all at the same time — a sort of merry-go-round of communications!

Is it worth while discussing competition from the Horn or from the Straits of Magellan? Hardly! The voyage is so long and far afield that it has scarcely been used since sailing ships disappeared from the high seas — if we could count on peace for ever we should not mention it at all. Nevertheless it is there as an alternative route to Panama, just as the Cape is to Suez. One cannot however describe it as entirely obsolete and deserted, for if the canal were to be put out of action, either by accident or design, the United States would be interested in it, just as she was during her war with Spain.

The British at any rate have never ruled it out of their system of interoceanic communications, for they still keep up their establishment on the Falkland Islands. Though they leave the control of the Caribbean Sea to the Americans, they have never relinquished anything east of Trinidad; Port-of-Spain in Trinidad is thus an important point in a diagram of maritime influence. May I recall here that earlier, in connection with the Cape, I observed that routes which are long but safe have by no means lost their value? Circumstances may arise when the problem will not be how to get there quickly, but how to get there at all.

Thus while the air is creating certain new itineraries, political insecurity is rejuvenating others, which in the nineteenth century seemed to have gone for good. Except for these two reservations, we may say that the routes which have come into being owing to the Suez and Panama Canals are now basic, and have etched themselves permanently into the plan of world communications.

CHAPTER XIV

THE CANAL AND ITS MILITARY DEFENCE

I

IRRESPECTIVE of the great economic value of the canal, it is safe to say that it was not for commercial reasons that the United States was persuaded to embark on it. To-day and yesterday, the dominant idea has been political, or, to be more specific, military. From the moment that it entered the minds of the American Government officials that inter-oceanic communications were necessary to assure the complete unity of their country, they were naturally determined that the canal should be protected, not as an international highway but as a strictly American undertaking. Accordingly the American State obtained through the Hay-Pauncefote and the Hay-Bunau-Varilla treaties, either explicitly or by means of significant omissions, the right to employ armed forces and to establish fortifications and naval bases in the Isthmus of Panama.

The military aspect of the isthmus is most impressive to visitors. 'Everything at Panama is run by soldiers', writes M. Georges Edgar Bonnet, in his book *Le Canal de Panama*, 'and everything seems to be done chiefly for military reasons.' But after all it was these preoccupations that brought the United States here in the first place. The whole of the canal zone is military; there are forts everywhere, fortified islands, and powerful batteries. Along the canal one meets settlements which exist solely as camps and garrisons. Actually a garrison of ten or twelve thousand men used to be kept here permanently, and to-day it has been increased to 25,000.

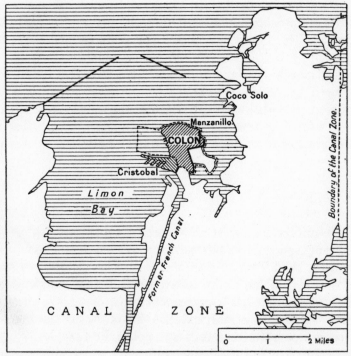

Colón and Cristobal

Between a third and a quarter of the total population are soldiers. It is for these troops just as much as for the benefit of its own staff, that the canal administration maintains the roads, houses, transports, hospitals, schools and clubs. The naval and aerial activity is intense. A naval squadron is located permanently at Balboa, and at Christobal there is a submarine depot and also a hydroplane station. The entire American fleet assembles every year at Panama, and it is here that it carries out its most important manœuvres.

In spite of the international engagements inscribed in the treaty, its military character makes the whole enterprise

371

anything but international. Theodore Roosevelt, the creator of the regime, openly boasted of it long before the canal was finished. 'It is only in this way (by military methods)', he wrote in 1910, 'that the United States can efficiently guarantee the neutrality of the canal, and be certain that it will not be used by others against her. Our naval power will be doubled, provided we do not commit the folly of looking for international guarantees, or of letting any other nations interfere in this exclusively American enterprise.'

II

The protection of the canal can be considered from two different aspects: first, tactical or local defence, and secondly, strategic or distant protection. The local defence of the isthmus is confided to the Army, which here is independent and supreme. It has a permanent force of 25,000 men, a figure which considerably exceeds that of the normal British forces at Suez. Its main task is to police the zone, and see to the security of the lock gates and other vulnerable points. Each group of gates possesses its own anti-aircraft defence. Trouble is not apprehended solely from outside, moreover, for there is serious danger of sabotage being committed on the spot, which means that vigilance can never be relaxed.

The defence of the surrounding territory is the duty of the Navy, and of the Naval Aviation Corps, both of which have their headquarters at Colón. The naval and submarine base is in the suburb of Coco Solo, and the aerodrome at Manzanillo. Powerful heavy artillery has been set up along the coast and on the little islands fringing the shore; in this way they can enfilade the entrance to the canal from both sides. The four islands lying out in front of Balboa are part of the Fort

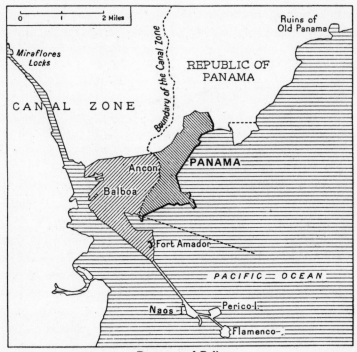

Panama and Balboa

Amador defence group, and they are joined to the mainland by a dyke with a railway line and a macadamized road running along it. The forts on the first and the last of these islands can be reached by a subterranean passage. The two big islands out in the Pacific rely on air defence rather than on artillery. Both Panama and Colón are equipped as naval bases but not of the largest class, and although there is a dry dock at Balboa its resources are not sufficient to carry out major repairs. In the American Navy the accepted theory is that the fleet should be able to maintain itself once it has quitted its own territorial waters.

The underlying principle of the strategic or distant de-

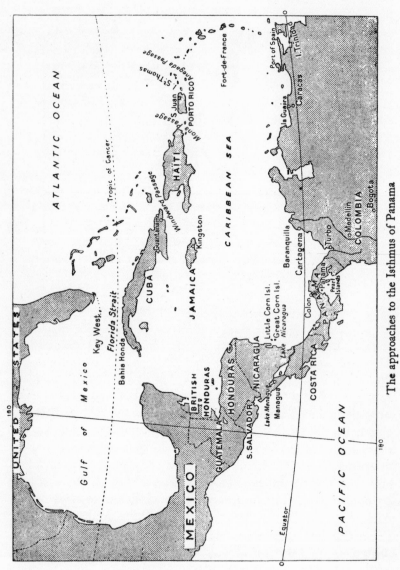

The approaches to the Isthmus of Panama

374

fence of the isthmus is that the United States should always
be warned of the approach of the enemy, and should be
able to prevent him from getting anywhere near the canal.
This is the duty of the Navy, to be carried out either by the
fleet, or by squadrons of long-range bombing planes.

As one approaches Colón, four main routes lead from the
Atlantic into the Caribbean, and each one is guarded by an
American naval base. Key West watches over the Straits of
Florida and so does the base near the westerly end of Cuba,
where the Bahia Honda station is situated. Use of the latter
is granted to the United States by the Republic of Cuba.
The base at Guantanamo, conceded under the same con-
ditions, similarly guards the Windward Passage between
Cuba and Haiti. The Mona Passage between Santo
Domingo and Porto Rico is protected by the naval base at
San Juan de Porto Rico on American territory. This base
is more and more becoming the main centre responsible for
protecting the approaches to Panama past the Antilles.
Finally the Anegada Passage between the Leeward Islands
and St. Thomas is in its turn supervised by the base at St.
Thomas, which has been an American possession ever since
the Virgin Islands were bought from Denmark by the United
States.

We might also enumerate various passages through the
Lesser Antilles which are presided over by the French base
at Fort-de-France on Martinique, and the British base at
Port-of-Spain, Trinidad. Though the equipment of these two
fine harbours is only mediocre, they are not without con-
siderable geographic and strategic importance. So the
American Government is content to see them in the hands of
Powers which it considers friendly. Within the Caribbean
Sea the United States possesses several other naval stations
which either have been thoroughly developed or are capable

of being equipped. In the latter category for example is Little Corn Island off the coast of Nicaragua.

Thus in the event of a war in which the United States was involved, the American fleet could establish itself in any harbour that it wished to occupy in these waters without meeting any resistance.

The only European military station is at Kingston in the British colony of Jamaica, but Great Britain certainly would do nothing here that was not agreed to by the United States. Ever since the Spanish-American War, Great Britain has given up all thought of naval domination in this zone, for in the Caribbean Sea there is no room for other control over and above that of the United States.

Approaching Panama on the Pacific side, the maritime routes first of all come from Mexico, California, and British Colombia on the north, and secondly from the coast of South America on the south. Then we have two coming across the Pacific Ocean, one from Hawaii and the Far East, and another from Australasia which touches at Fiji or Tahiti. The outstanding American naval bases on the Pacific slope of the North American continent are San Diego, San Pedro, San Francisco, Seattle, and Sitka in Alaska. Out in the ocean is Pearl City in the Hawaiian Islands.

At Cavite in the Philippines and Pango Pango at Samoa are secondary stations, but both are poorly equipped. There is an aviation base at Dutch Harbour in the Aleutian Islands, but it does not seem destined for major developments as the atmospheric conditions are so bad in these parts. However, as we found in the Caribbean Sea, the United States in case of a war in which it was involved no doubt would arrange to have access on the Pacific coast to such other harbours as it might require.

The strategic doctrine of the American fleet is that it must

376

rely almost entirely on its own resources, and be able to operate far from its principal bases, and above all be ready to pass from one ocean to the other. Accordingly it has built cruisers of great cruising range. This also accounts for the enormous importance attached to the possibility of passing unhampered across the Isthmus of Panama. Although the Pacific is considered the main field of operations, the best equipped dockyards for serious large scale repairs are on the Atlantic side at Hampton Road and Norfolk. Nevertheless, any Atlantic fleet that they do create would be only of secondary importance.

In these conditions the Panama Canal constitutes the key piece of the whole system of American security. Its maintenance is therefore primarily a question of strength, but it is also necessary to adopt a line of policy with regard to the various independent states in the vicinity of the isthmus. Up to 1932 the prevailing policy was first the 'Big Stick' of President Theodore Roosevelt, and then the 'Dollar Diplomacy' of President Coolidge. Both resorted to financial, political, and military pressure, which was very thinly veiled. Outstanding examples of this policy were the complete annexation of Porto Rico and the semi-annexation of the canal zone, the Cuban Protectorate under the regime of the Platt Amendment, and in the case of Nicaragua, Haiti and Santo Domingo, financial protectorates coupled with military occupation.

This phase is now over. It has been succeeded by the 'Good Neighbour' policy of President Franklin D. Roosevelt, which is based on systematic friendliness, good humour, courteous dealing, and the everlastingly repeated affirmation of solidarity between all the States of the New World. Under this regime the Platt Amendment has been abrogated, the military occupation of various countries has ceased, the 1936 treaty with Panama has been completed, and the American Government has tried to make friends everywhere. There is no proof as yet that this method will turn out to be really effective, and in certain cases it may still be necessary to take a strong line once more.

In any event the Monroe Doctrine still remains unchanged. No more to-day than yesterday will the United States permit a European Power to obtain a military or political foothold on the American continent, or even on the routes leading to Panama. Far from diminishing, this traditional attitude is growing stronger at present. The zone of approach to the New World in which the American Government feels itself interested, has recently been so greatly increased that it now extends not only to the Azores but as far as Dakar, Gibraltar, and the western shores of Europe.

For several years the United States has tried to draw together the various countries of Latin America and persuade them to adopt a common programme aimed at defending the integrity of the American continent. In October 1939, after the European war had broken out, the Pan-American Conference was held at Panama and at it was voted a resolution of great importance, though it is true its practical consequences are still far from complete. This declaration advocated the creation of a security zone around the American continent, which was to be patrolled by the warships and aeroplanes of the interested states. In this way they hoped to protect American shipping from any aggressive acts committed by warships of belligerent powers. In the Atlantic this zone was to start at the frontier between Canada and the United States, and was to extend 300 miles out from the coasts of the United States and Central America. Along the South American coast it was to extend 300 miles outside of Brazil and 100 miles outside of the Argentine. It is true that this is only a recommendation; yet it corresponds to a quasi-revolutionary innovation in international law. However, be that as it may, the tendency must be noted, for it expresses the wish of the American countries to protect the approaches of their continent as much as possible from European belligerents and in particular from Germany. Henceforth this will undoubtedly be an essential principle in the foreign policy of the United States, though of course it may cause many ulterior developments which it is impossible at present to foresee.

The free use of the canal by the United States depends therefore on a general policy, with which the Government is determined to succeed. Nevertheless, no matter what happens, the local defence of the canal is a very delicate matter, and one repeatedly asks oneself just how dangerously vulnerable the works on the isthmus really are. In spite of every precaution the lock gates are bound to be in danger, but even more vital are the mechanical installations, and above all there is the Gatun Dam. To breach the dam would be fatal, for then the whole of the artificial lake would empty itself, and so render the isthmus impassable for many months.

The danger is not so much a question of air raids from long-range bombers, as the possibility of a surprise attack made with the connivance of some neighbouring state on the isthmus. The Central and South American coasts are so vast, great stretches being deserted and almost unexplored, that it would be quite feasible, even without the slightest complicity of a local government, for the enemy to establish secret bases from which an effective attack might be launched. Hostile efforts doubtless would not long remain unobserved, but a single surprise attack might be sufficient to cause irreparable damage. An even greater cause for anxiety is the possibility of local intrigue being fostered by spies and secret agents who had insinuated themselves among the canal employees, or had arrived in the crew of some ship passing through the canal.

In such matters we may be magnifying the dangers. It would be ridiculous to regard every barber in Colón or Panama as a Japanese colonel in disguise, ready to blow up the locks at Gatun or Pedro Miguel. Still, it is necessary to be on one's guard, and the extent of the danger entirely justifies the precautions already taken, though at first sight some of them do appear to be excessive, and due to a bad attack of nerves. One must admit, however, that no amount of supervision, no matter how thorough, can ever amount to absolute security.

This brings us back to the problem of guarantees of another kind. Several alternatives have been considered. One, for example, is the building of a second canal in Nicaragua. This has always remained a favourite safeguard in the minds of the public. In 1939 Congress voted a credit of $200,000 to send a commission of eight engineers to the Isthmus of Nicaragua, where they were to examine on the spot the feasibility of canalizing the San Juan River, in order to make it navigable for vessels of shallow draught. However it should be noted that the idea of constructing in this area a real maritime canal capable of replacing Panama seems to have been finally abandoned. There is also no longer any suggestion of transforming the Panama Canal itself into a sea-level canal. Though such a task is not technically impossible, the business would be terribly costly. The solution that has now been adopted, as we have already seen, is the construction of a third series of locks, located at a sufficient distance from the others to minimize the risks of bombardment or sabotage.

If none of these various ideas seem to give adequate protection, then there always remains a final alternative, to which many appear to be turning at present, namely the construction of two fleets, one for each ocean ... But is that not an admission of defeat? True, the fleet could always go round by Cape Horn, but when would it arrive? The obvious reply, of course, is that the S.S. *Oregon* used this route and did arrive in time to win the battle of San Diego de Cuba.

I I I

The regime responsible for the Panama Canal does not even try to keep up the appearance of internationalism. The only international agreement that it has carried out effectively is equality of treatment. Perhaps one might also say that, according to the Hay-Pauncefote Treaty, the Government of the United States is in the isthmus as a mandatory Power. In reality they are there for their own ends, and they look after their affairs by themselves. At Suez the international character of the canal has been better preserved, and yet in both cases we come to the same conclusion, that each canal is controlled by its principal user, or to be more exact by its principal political user. When London wishes to communicate with Bombay she needs Suez, and when New York wishes to communicate with San Francisco she needs Panama. Neither Egypt nor the Republic of Panama can do anything about it, nor would Colombia be any more successful in resisting. This policy of world routes seems to be based on a natural law, and it is doubtful whether in 1968, when the concession granted to Ferdinand de Lesseps terminates, the Cairo Government will succeed in evading the consequenses of this natural law, no matter what its sovereign rights may be.

Truly we have wandered far from the beautiful humanitarian dream which the great de Lesseps inherited from St. Simon and his followers. Nevertheless, we must consider the practical results, and they are more than enough, for international commerce does use both the interoceanic canals under conditions of complete Liberty and Equality.

GENERAL CONCLUSIONS

I

THE chart of world economic routes that has resulted from the double network of maritime communications converging in the Suez and Panama Canals, faithfully reflects the general equilibrium of the world. On it, at any given moment in history, one can easily read the hierarchy, or order of precedence of the varous continents.

If we turn back to the end of the nineteenth century, it is the very unity of the tableau that is most significant. All itineraries then were directed towards north-western Europe which was still the unchallenged centre of an immense spider-web covering the whole globe. The Suez Canal was the vital artery, not only of the British Empire as it is customary to say, but also of that powerful industrial concentration which, since the invention of the steam engine, had made Europe the specialized workshop of the world. Under this regime, whose glories many of us can still remember, the whole world obeyed a centralized higher command imposed by the White Race. Here it sat, enthroned in the heart of the Western world. From the west and centre of Europe it inspired the organization and development of every part of the globe. At that time the Isthmus of Panama had not yet been cut through. The United States, that young giant, though already marvellously active and rich, was still entirely preoccupied with the conquest of its own great West, which it naively believed to be limitless. Beyond the borders of Europe the dependencies of the White Race continued to gravitate deferentially around the old homestead. It is hardly too much to say that the three terms, European, White Race and Western Civilization were still almost synonymous.

The twentieth century brought this majestic unity to a close. The dislocation in the system produced by the Great War reminds me of the dismemberment of the Roman Empire, as it approached its fall. In the same way we see independent centres arising in North America and in the Far East. While the Yellow Race is revolting in Asia, the United States, in accordance with an elementary principle in economic gravity, has become a new international centre of attraction. It is like a phenomenon in astronomy. The non-European sections of the White Race are everywhere breaking away from their old guardian, rebelling as soon as they reach maturity. Like Sleeping Beauties, the tropical races have been awakened from their long slumber, and in their turn they are demanding independence.

In the past, international traffic, working under the aegis of the Suez Canal, acknowledged one head only, and that was Europe. To-day, since the opening of the Panama Canal, it has become bicephalic. In future there will be two termini: first, the Old Continent which will still pursue its age-old function of providing a bridge-head, or central world distributing point; and secondly, the north-eastern districts of the United States which will range themselves more and more with the highly industrialized and economically developed parts of the world.

From the point of view of world equilibrium, Western Civilization is now dyarchic in form; it has become an economic empire with two capitals. This trend is as heavy with consequences as when Rome and Byzantium in ancient times became the twin heads of the Roman Empire.

The first consequence is that the Pacific is creating a centre of its own, with direct relationships between its members. The Old Continent instinctively regards this short circuit as a form of lese-majesty. The second consequence, which is merely another aspect of the first, is that Europe, being now more or less isolated from these new constellations, is no longer the uncontested centre of gravity that she used to be. Thus the world is separating into two distinct domains. One of these domains has the Suez Canal as its axis, and is mainly expressed in the trade carried on between Europe and Asia; the other, with the Panama as its axis, is expressed in the trade between the Atlantic and the Pacific.

Europe no longer maintains her former supremacy on the western coasts of the New World, but perhaps she is not as moribund as her successors seem to think, in their anxiety to see her decently buried. In point of fact, although the United States does not contribute to the economic activity of the Suez Canal, the Old Continent plays an important part at Panama. The United States has not as yet taken over from Europe the economic direction of the world, and Europe has still not ceded her place to America. The most we can say is that the Americans have set up a rival shop opposite the old trading establishment. Strong in her colonial traditions, Europe maintains unimpaired her financial and commercial genius, whereas America does not seem to have inherited any outstanding ability along these lines. So, in spite of everything, Europe still carries on her international trade, and although she no longer possesses a monopoly it is her spirit of initiative that even now directs the world just as it has done for the past four centuries.

The war in which we are now engaged hardly modifies or invalidates the above conclusions. It is of course always possible that as a result of the struggle, the Old World will be so completely exhausted that it will no longer be able to continue its world-wide functions. Yet it is equally possible that the peace which will eventually emerge may be such that Europe will once more find a genuine state of equilibrium.

Then, like a blade tempered in the flames, she will all the more easily grasp control once more, for the individual superiority of her sons will alone be sufficient to justify her reassuming this position. You will note that in spite of present differences I certainly do not abandon the habit of referring to Europe in the singular, and of regarding her civilization as a unit.

Instead of considering Europe and North America as rivals opposed to each other, it would be more accurate perhaps to classify them together under the one simple heading of Western Civilization. This brings us back to a simplified picture of the world, with a great centre of industrial production on the one hand, and on the other immense reservoirs of raw materials. In spite of the pitiless way in which nationalism is subdividing us into water-tight compartments, there still exists considerable collaboration between the economically young continents and those more highly developed. As this view is corroborated by the commercial statistics of both the Suez and Panama Canals, we may conclude that even to-day a minimum of complementary trade will remain as part of the logic of things, and that this will still be true to-morrow, no matter what to-morrow may bring forth.

II

Viewed from this angle we see that since the Renaissance the economic exploitation of the world has been almost entirely a European phenomenon. To-day, however, it has broadened into a Western phenomenon, for in spite of a certain amount of resistance the White Race always leads the way. The two interoceanic canals are the symbols and instruments of this conquest. It was the West and the West only that created them both, and that directs their functions now that they have become absolutely essential to the normal life of our civilization.

These two great international services work so well and so smoothly that we have almost lost sight of the conditions necessary for their maintenance. We do not sufficiently appreciate that a Western personnel — European at Suez and American at Panama — administers them according to rules laid down in Paris, London and Washington, and in conformity with political systems inspired by the White Race. The impulse undoubtedly comes from the White Race, and it is certainly they who furnish the executives, the engineers, and in a general way the whole of these two competent organizations. Perhaps we are too prone to forget this.

Many candidates are now rising up to complain against the administration of those who constructed these canals. 'We have learned now to use your tools', they say, 'and we shall be able to use them in the future. Therefore we are your equals. Why should we not take into our own hands these services which you have created, more especially as they are situated in our territories?' Yet how are we to know whether those who make these claims — and they are legion — possess the ability required to maintain the intricate mechanism on which, in the last analysis, rests the whole of our present civilization?

The superiority which the West has hitherto demonstrated is much more complex than those who hope to succeed it imagine. Copyists can, no doubt, acquire some of the necessary qualities, but others will elude them no matter how attentive they may be. It is not difficult to learn technique, and many of these competitors boast with reason that they know how to use European machines just as well as the inventors do. But then, to make a machine go is not very difficult. What counts is first to have invented it, and then to be able to perfect it, renew it, and adapt it to changing conditions. This creative genius has so far remained the sole prerogative of the White Race, and even of a limited section of that race. It is the first essential, if our civilization is to maintain its high material level. China, India, South America, and above all Japan, have splendid industries, which sometimes compete successfully with our own, but if left to themselves would they know how to renew them? How long would they survive if they were cut off hermetically for a long period from further technical aid?

Yet the qualities in Western administration that cannot be imitated do not really reside in technique, nor even in invention. After having visited several continents, I have come to the conclusion that the particular genius of the West — that is to say of Europe and North America — is its sense of large-scale administration. Our people can conceive, organize, and conduct great enterprises, exceeding in scope particular or even national interests. The majority of the non-European races, indeed many Europeans themselves, have not yet shown that they possess this executive ability. Such administrative technique requires a variety of qualities which may be based on something more deep-seated than we imagine. An instinct for order, a sense of proportion, the capacity to look ahead, the ability to take a broad general view, all these things require serious culture.

In the conduct of business these qualities are the very ones of which the public is least aware. They depend as much on moral standards as on technical skill. Consider, for example, the mistaken views held by many workmen about the importance of the function of management. This genius, this administrative capacity in the highest sense of the word, is an offshoot of genuine civilization, and decline would come rapidly if we tried to do without it.

Let us not deceive ourselves, entire sections of the world are now beginning to escape the control exerted by the West. Everywhere in the Near East, for example, I have seen local candidates impatient to supplant Europeans, and seize the posts which the latter still fill. They brandish their diplomas, and seem to think that once they take over, the machine will continue to work automatically, and all they have to do is to sit in the driver's seat. Doubtless that is true enough so far as daily routine and current business is concerned, but when it comes to maintaining material civilization at the high level to which we have brought it, then it is a horse of another colour, as the saying goes. The grandeur of the work accomplished by the West in the nineteenth and twentieth centuries may perhaps only be appreciated on the day when, like the Empire of Alexander the Great, it begins to sub-divide itself into separate sovereignties.

III

For these reasons, the problem of the interoceanic canals is neither local nor even national, but international in the fullest sense of the word. One might be inclined to think that the Suez Canal is just an Egyptian matter and that the Panama Canal concerns only the Republics of Panama and Colombia. Actually both questions rest on quite another plane. We regard the overland route across Syria to Baghdad and India in the same way, and also the complex organization of airways leading to Asia, or even the network of airlines between North and South America. Neither

Europe on the one hand, nor the United States on the other can disinterest itself in these problems, no matter what may be the opposition of local interests. Being of world-wide importance they cannot be submitted to nationalistic solutions, particularly if there is any question as to how these great international services are to be allowed to function.

The administration of the Suez Canal by the Universal Company, and of the Panama Canal by the United States Government in conformity with the Hay-Pauncefote Treaty have always respected the rights of international commerce. Should they in future be placed on any other footing, it would mean that world problems are no longer being solved in the general interests in accordance with the inspiration derived from the great traditions of ancient Rome, but that instead there was occurring a world-wide disintegration which might prove fatal to our civilization.

INDEX

INDEX

INDEX

INDEX

Financial disaster of Panama Canal, 258
Fish, Hamilton, U.S. Secretary of State, 228
Flamenco Island, 313
Florida, Straits of, 375
Flory, 273
Fontanes, 274, 276, 278
Forster, E. N., *Road to India*, 32
Fortifications on Isthmus of Panama, 370
Fort-de-France, 376
Fountains of Moses, 55
Fourrier, 55
France, cynical atmosphere, 239, 240, 241, 262
France, as Power of the future, 50
France, Republican Government, 240
Franco-Prussian War, 78
Frankenberg, Colonel von, 90
Freetown, 189
French invaders, 35
French Minister at Bogotá, 225
Freycinet, de, 83, 265
Frontier of Panama Republic, 331
Fuad, King, 94, 95

GAILLARD CUT, 210, 306, 312
Gambetta, 240, 241, 242, 271
Gamboa, 254, 255, 311, 312, 313, 314
Gantheaume, Admiral, 55
Garabit viaduct, 252
Garages on Suez Canal, 112
Garella, Napoleon, 224
Garfield, U.S. President, 228
Gatun Dam, 306, 311, 312, 316, 379
Gatun, Lake, 308, 311, 316, 326
Gatun locks, 381
Geneffa, 24, 25, 107
Genoa ruined, 54
Geographical Congress of Antwerp, 230
Geographical Congress of Paris, 230
Geographical Congress, Panama Canal estimates, 244, 256
Germain, Crédit Lyonnais, 263, 269
Germano-Turkish Army, 35
Germany, *drang nach osten* policy, 87, 162, 163
Germany, exploitation by land, 163
Germany, pre-war policy in south-eastern Europe, 14, 16
Gibraltar, 378
Gladstone, 67
Globe, the, 72
Gobineau, 177
Goethals, Lieut.-Colonel, 301, 302, 306
Goethe, 223
Goirand, 268, 269
Gold Force, 303, 320, 321
Gold mining rush of '49, 226
Good Neighbour policy, 377
Gordon, General, 36
Gorgas, 302
Granada, New, 224, 225
Grant, President of U.S., 229, 248
Granville, Lord, 84
Greater Britain, Dilke, 151
Greek Empire, 43
Greek invaders, 35
Grévy, President of France, 240
Grey, Sir Edward, 193
Guantanamo, naval base, 375
Guatemala, 209
Guatemala, yellow fever, 326
Guizot, 224

HADRAMUT, 43
Hague, arbitration at the, 336
Haifa, 23, 173, 190
Haiti, 208, 375, 377
Halévy, Daniel, *République des Ducs*, 240
Hamlet, 242
Hampton Road dockyard, 377
Hanna, Senator Mark, 288
Harvey, P. H., 193
Havre hostile to Suez Canal, 120
Hay, U.S. Secretary of State, 290, 292, 296
Hay-Bunau-Varilla Treaty, 296, 302, 322, 334, 370
Hay-Herran Treaty, 291, 292, 293
Hay-Pauncefote Treaty, 289, 334, 370, 381, 390
Hayes, President of U.S., 228
Hedjas Railway, 87
Heliopolis aerodrome, 34
Hellenistic East, 48
Heraclius, 39
Hercules, Pillars of, 32
Hérédia, 221
Heredia, Pedro de, 219
Herodotus, 24, 26, 28, 40
Herran, Columbian Minister Plenipotentiary, 291, 292
Herrick, Myron, 287
Hertz, Cornélius, 230, 278, 280
Hindus, 322
Holland as Power of the future, 50
Homs, 23, 47
Honduras, 209, 219
Honduras, Gulf of, 208
Honfleur, 308
Hong Kong in Panama zone, 334
Horn, *Oregon* rounds Cape, 285
Huertas, General, 295
Humbold, 222
Hussein Kamel, Sultan, 89

INDIA, 47, 389
India, fares to, 16!
India, route via Suez, 17, 21, 23, 26, 44
India threatened, 87
India, trade with Ancient Egypt, 42
Indian Ocean, 22, 28, 53
Indo-China, re-routing of traffic, 168
Industry, shifting of American centre of gravity, 338
Insecurity of Mediterranean, 166, 167
Insurance, marine, 105, 120, 167, 168
Intercoastal traffic through Panama Canal, 351, 352, 357
International trade temperature chart, 140
Invaders of Egypt, 35
Irak Petroleum Company, 172, 173
Irkutsk, 160
Irrigation of the Nile, 28
Ismail, Khedive, 36, 37, 73, 75, 78, 80, 84, 99, 292
Ismailiya, 107, 194, 321
Ismailiya as entrepôt centre? 109, 151, 153, 194, 363
Ismid, 191
Ispahan, 47
Isthme de Suez, Charles-Roux, 71
Isthmian Canal Commission, 254
Italian menace, 35
Italy, effect of British blockade, 189
Italy, increased traffic through Suez, 136

394

INDEX

Italy, no prestige in the Orient, 96
Italy, percentage of Suez Canal traffic, 197

JACQUIER, 252
Jamaica, 376
Jamaican negroes, 303, 304, 320
Japan, 388
Jerusalem, 32
Jordan Valley, 23
Jullien, Raymond, *Le Trafic du Canal de Suez*, 154
Justice, French Minister of, 273
Justinian, 39

KABRET, 24
Kabul, 47
Kamchatka, 334
Kashmir, 43, 47
Kelel, 46
Kellogg Pact, 85
Kermanshah, microbe source, 178
Key West, naval base, 375
Khartum, 26, 27, 28
Kiel Canal (graph), 353
Kingston, Jamaica, 376
Kirkuk Oil Field, 172, 173
Kitchener, 36
Klein, Mateo, 226
Konia, 47
Koptos, 42
Kosseir, 42
Koweit, 87
Kress, Colonel von, 90

LABOUR PARTY, 95
Lagos, 189
Lamartine, 60
Landslides, 307, 340
Laplace, 55
Laros, 190
League of Nations, 322
League of Nations, sanitary information centre, 179
Lebanon, 23, 43
Leeward Islands, 375
Leibnitz, project for Suez Canal, 52
Le Père, J. M., 55, 58, 100, 108
Le Père's memorandum, 55, 56, 63
Lépinay, Godin de, 266, 300
Lesseps, Charles de, 260, 262, 269, 273, 275, 276, 277, 278, 279, 281, 282
Lesseps, Ferdinand de, 10, 23, 37, 40, 53, 59, 61
  Abandoned by Parliament, 268
  Accepts chairmanship of Panama Canal Company, 238
  Accused of fraud, 274
  Appeals to the public, 265, 269
  Begins work at Suez, 65, 67
  Belief in omens, 62
  Calls in technical experts, 66
  Canal concession granted, 65
  Commander of Legion of Honour, 72
  Condemned to imprisonment, 276
  At Constantinople, 67
  Compared with Vasco da Gama and Magellan, 158
  Completes Suez Canal, 100
  Creator of a new world route, 75, 76
  English campaign, 67
  Estimates Suez Canal traffic, 126, 127
  Formal announcement of canal plan, 64

Lesseps, Ferdinand de (*contd.*)
  French Company, inception of, 230
  Friendship with Mohammed Said, 62
  Great Frenchman still, 283
  Lecture tour in 1879, 245
  Marries Mlle de Bragard, 75
  Marries Mlle Delamalle, 62
  Optimistic character, 258, 259, 260
  Organizes Panama Canal Company, 244
  Organizes Suez Canal Company, 68
  Persuaded to use locks, 267
  President of Society of Commercial Geography, 230
  President of Suez Canal Company, 71
  Presides over Paris International Geographical Congress, 232
  Protests against British control of Suez Canal zone, 84
  Receives English on board of Suez Canal Company, 82
  Refuses help from Rothschild, 70
  At Rome, 269
  A sportsman, 61
  Statue of, at Port Said, 106, 194
  A stroke, 270
  Suez Canal plan accepted, 64
  Terms with England, comes to, 84
  Tours Europe, 71
  At Tuileries, 67
  Visits Belgium, England and Holland, 247
  Visits Panama in 1879, 245, 246, 247
  Visits Panama in 1886, 264
  Visits United States, 247
  Welcomed by Mohammed Said, 63
Lesseps, Mathieu de, 61
Leticia, quadrilateral, 331
Leucos Limen, 42
Leurs Figures, Barrès, 274
Levasseur, 230
Lévy-Crémieux Syndicate, 248, 281
Liberalism, nineteenth century, 60
Libre Parole, La, 273, 274, 277
Libyan Desert, 97
Limes, 46, 48
Limon, Bay of, 219, 311
Linant Bey, 24, 66
Lisbon, 50
Liverpool, 334
Llanos Lowlands, 212
Lombardy, 27
Lorient, 52
Los Angeles and the Panama Canal tolls, 337
Loubet, President of France, 273
Louis XIV, 52
Louis XV, 53
Louis XVI, 53
Lucian, 40

MACADOO, SENATOR, 336
Madagascar, 189
Madden Dam, 311, 316, 317
Madrid, de Lesseps in consular service, 61
Magdalena River, 212, 213, 216
Magellan, explorer, 10, 75, 219
Magellan, route, 12
Magellan, Straits of, 368, 369
Mahmoud Canal, 30
Maillet, Benoist de, 53
Malaria, 325
Mallet, Sir Claude Coventry, 25
Mamelukes, 51

395

INDEX

INDEX

397

INDEX

INDEX